Two Modern American Tragedies

SCRIBNER
RESEARCH
ANTHOLOGIES

Martin Steinmann, Jr., GENERAL EDITOR

JOHN D. HURRELL
University of Minnesota

Two Modern American Tragedies:

REVIEWS AND CRITICISM OF *DEATH OF A SALESMAN* AND

A STREETCAR NAMED DESIRE

SCRIBNER
RESEARCH
ANTHOLOGIES

CHARLES SCRIBNER'S SONS   New York

Acknowledgments

"The Tragic Fallacy." From *The Modern Temper* by Joseph Wood Krutch, copyright, 1929, by Harcourt, Brace and Company, Inc.; renewed, 1957, by Joseph Wood Krutch. Reprinted by permission of the publishers.

"Tragic Perspectives," by John Gassner, reprinted by permission of the editor of *The Tulane Drama Review* and of the author.

"Tragedy and the American Climate of Opinion," by Orrin E. Klapp, reprinted by permission of the editor of *Centennial Review* and of the author.

"Tragedy and the Common Man," by Arthur Miller. Copyright © New York *Times*, 1949. Reprinted by permission of the author.

"On Social Plays," Introduction to *A View from the Bridge* by Arthur Miller. Copyright 1955 by Arthur Miller. Reprinted by permission of The Viking Press, Inc.

"The Timeless World of a Play," Introduction to *The Rose Tattoo* by Tennessee Williams. Copyright 1950 by Tennessee Williams. Revised and Published Version Copyright 1951 by Tennessee Williams. Reprinted by permission of New Directions.

Review by Brooks Atkinson of *Death of a Salesman,* reprinted by permission of *The New York Times.*

Review by George Jean Nathan of *Death of a Salesman.* Reprinted from *The Theatre Book of the Year 1948-1949* by George Jean Nathan, by permission of Alfred A. Knopf, Inc. Copyright 1949 by George Jean Nathan.

Review by Eleanor Clark of *Death of a Salesman.* Reprinted by permission of the author and of the editors of *Partisan Review.*

Review by Harold Clurman of *Death of a Salesman,* from *Lies Like Truth.* Copyright © Harold Clurman 1958. Reprinted by permission of The Macmillan Company, New York.

"Arthur Miller's *Collected Plays,*" by William J. Newman. Reprinted by permission of the editors of *The Twentieth Century.*

"Our Colossal Dad." Reprinted by permission of The Times Publishing Company Limited. All Rights Reserved. (C).

"A Matter of Hopelessness in *Death of a Salesman.*" Reprinted by permission of The *Tulane Drama Review,* the National Association of Educational Broadcasters, and Phillip Gelb, producer of the radio series *Ideas and the Theatre.*

"Confusion and Tragedy: The Failure of Miller's *Salesman,*" by Richard J. Foster. Published by permission of the author.

Review by George Jean Nathan of *A Streetcar Named Desire.* Reprinted from *The Theatre Book of the Year 1947-1948* by George Jean Nathan, by permission of Alfred A. Knopf, Inc.. Copyright 1948 by George Jean Nathan.

Review by Harold Clurman of *A Streetcar Named Desire,* from *Lies Like Truth.* Copyright © Harold Clurman 1958. Reprinted by permission of The Macmillan Company, New York.

"The Dilemma of Tennessee Williams," by Harry Taylor. Reprinted by permission of the editor of *Mainstream.*

Preface

Each Scribner Research Anthology is a collection of written sources upon a single historical, literary, or scientific topic—the Hungarian Revolt, Shakespeare's *Julius Caesar,* or extrasensory perception, for example. In addition to these sources, it contains (1) "Guide to Research," an account of the rationale and the methods of research and of research-paper writing, (2) an introduction to the topic of the anthology, (3) suggested topics for controlled research, and (4) suggested sources and topics for library research.

Each anthology is designed to serve two purposes. First, each gives the student access to important sources—texts, documents, letters, diaries, essays, for instance—on a given topic. Some of these sources are otherwise available in only a few libraries, some (manuscripts and historical documents) in only one. In any case, the collection as a whole is not otherwise available in one volume. Second, each anthology gives the student either all his sources for a controlled-research paper or some of them for a library-research paper. Each anthology can be valuable either for readings in courses in history, literature, science, or humanities or as the basis for a research paper in these or in other courses.

A controlled-research paper—a paper in which the student's search for sources is limited to, and in certain ways controlled by, those sources contained in one anthology—is not so noble an undertaking as a library-research paper. But it is often more successful—more rewarding for the student and easier for his instructor to teach effectively and judge fairly. Its advantages for both student and instructor are often considerable.

For the student, it sometimes provides sources unavailable in his school library. And it enables him to learn a good deal about research (selection, interpretation, and evaluation of sources; quotation and paraphrase; and documentation) without prior instruction in use of the library (and, incidentally, without overtaxing the facilities and the resources of his library and without loss of, or damage to, sources either irreplaceable or difficult and expensive to replace).

For the instructor, it permits focus of class discussion upon a limited set of topics. It enables him to track down the student's sources conveniently. And—perhaps the greatest advantage of all—it enables him to judge both conveniently and exactly how well the student has selected, interpreted, and evaluated his sources and how well he has quoted and paraphrased them.

In many schools, a controlled-research paper is either a preliminary to or a part of a library-research paper. A library-research paper is probably the most difficult paper that the student can be assigned to write. The problems that confront him are not simply those common to any paper—organization, paragraphing, and transitions, for instance—and those (already mentioned) common to all research papers. He has, in addition, the problem of using the library well—of, for example, using the card catalogue, periodical indexes, and other reference works. But, if the instructor assigns a controlled-research paper as a preliminary to or, as it were, an early part of a library-research paper, the student need not come to grips with all these problems at once.

Each Scribner Research Anthology is compiled according to the following editorial principles. Each source that is not anonymous is prefaced by a biographical note on its author. At the foot of the same page is a bibliographical note. Each source is reprinted exactly as it appears in the original except for (1) some typographical peculiarities, (2) explanatory notes, given in brackets, and (3) omissions, indicated by ellipses (". . ."). And, finally, for each source that has pagination in the original, page numbers are given in brackets within the source itself—thus: "**[320/321]**," where everything before the slash (and after the preceding slash, if any) is from page 320, and everything after the slash (and before the next slash, if any) is from page 321. For a source hitherto unpublished, no page numbers are given; and the student who uses it should cite the page numbers of the Scribner Research Anthology. Footnotes to a source are given as in the original. Where the original pagination of a footnote is not evident, its page number precedes it in brackets.

MARTIN STEINMANN, JR.

Bingham Bay
Lake Gogebic
August, 1960

Guide to Research

THE IDEA OF RESEARCH

Research is the organized, disciplined search for truth; the aim of all research is to discover the truth about something. That thing may be a historical object like the Stonehenge monuments or a historical event like the Hungarian Revolt or the Battle of Waterloo. It may be a work of literature like Shakespeare's *Julius Caesar* or Miller's *Death of a Salesman*. It may be a recurring event like the motions of the planets or the circulation of the blood. Or it may be an experimentally repeatable phenomenon like behavior of rats in a maze or perception apparently unaccounted for by the five senses. Archeology, history, literary criticism and scholarship, astronomy, physiology, and psychology—these are some of the many divisions of research. Indeed, all the sciences—physical, biological, and social—and all other scholarly disciplines share this organized, disciplined search for truth.

The search for truth has often been confused with such aims as confirming prejudice, instilling patriotism, and praising friends and blaming enemies. The attempt to prove the preconceived conclusion *that* one college is superior to another, for example, is not research (though the attempt to discover *whether* one college is so superior is). Research is hostile to prejudice.

General Methods of Research. The best general method of research is first-hand observation. But this method is not always possible and, when it is possible, not always practical.

The best method to begin discovering the truth about something is to observe that thing and the circumstances surrounding it. To discover the truth about *Julius Caesar* or *Death of a Salesman*, get the play and read it, or go to the theatre and watch a performance. To discover the

truth about the planets, observe them through your telescope. To discover the truth about the intelligence of rats, build a maze and run some rats through it.

This first-hand observation is not always possible, however. To discover the truth about the Battle of Waterloo, you can't observe the battle. The best that you or anyone else can do is to observe other persons' observations, the recorded observations of eye-witnesses: diaries, letters, and memoirs, for instance, of soldiers and generals who were in the battle. With more recent historical events—for example, the Hungarian Revolt—you are better off. You can watch films and listen to tape recordings. You may be able to interview people who were there. But these observations are still second-hand; and, on the whole, history can be observed only at second-hand. The sole exception is history that you have been part of. You may have fought in the Hungarian Revolt—though, if you did, you may be prejudiced.

Even when first-hand observation is possible, it is not always practical. You may have a copy of or tickets to *Julius Caesar* or *Death of a Salesman* but not know enough about the principles of dramatic criticism to interpret the play unaided. You may have a telescope but not know how to use it or, if you do, not know what to make of what you observe through it. You may have some rats but not know how to build a maze or, if you do, not know enough about animal psychology to run your rats through it properly. The best that *you* can do under these circumstances is to supplement whatever first-hand observations you can make with observations of the first-hand observations of other people better-trained or better-equipped than you. Read *Julius Caesar* or *Death of a Salesman* and also critics' interpretations of the play. Observe the planets, if you can, and read treatises on astronomy. Do what you can with your rats, and read reports of experiments with rats. After all, no one can master the special methods and come by the special equipment of all scholarly disciplines. Indeed, few people can do this with more than one discipline, and then not before they're thirty. But all people who want a liberal education should try to discover as much of the truth about as many scholarly disciplines as their abilities and their circumstances permit. Indeed, the achievement of this is what is meant by "a liberal education."

Primary and Secondary Sources. As the foregoing account of the general methods of research suggests, there is, ultimately, only one source of the truth about something—the thing, the event, or the phenomenon itself: the Stonehenge monuments, the Hungarian Revolt, or the Battle of Waterloo; the text of *Julius Caesar* or *Death of a Salesman;* the motions of the planets or the circulation of blood; extrasensory perceptions or rats running in a maze. Such a source is a *primary* source. And, in historical research, where the thing itself (the Hungarian Revolt or the Battle of Waterloo) cannot be observed at first hand, a report of an eyewitness or a film or a tape recording is also counted as a *primary* source. But any other second-hand source (an interpretation of *Julius Caesar* or *Death of a Salesman,* a treatise on astronomy, a report of an experiment with rats) is a *secondary* source.

A primary source is, of course, better. But, if a primary source is unavailable to you (if it is a book, perhaps your school library does not have it) or if you are not trained or equipped to use it (you don't know how to run rats through a maze or you have no telescope), then a secondary source must do. In any case, except for the most mature scientists and scholars, a good secondary source is useful and often indispensable.

It is worth noticing that being primary or being secondary is not an intrinsic char-

acteristic of the source itself. It is, rather, a relationship that either exists or does not exist betweeen a given source and a given topic of research. Consequently, a given source may be primary in relation to one given topic but secondary in relation to another. Two examples may serve to make this important point clear. Edward Gibbon's *The Decline and Fall of the Roman Empire* (1776-1788) is a secondary source in relation to the topic of the Roman Empire but a primary source in relation to that of eighteenth-century English prose style or that of eighteenth-century historiography. Samuel Taylor Coleridge's *Lectures on Shakespeare* (1811-1812) is a secondary source in relation to the topic of Shakespeare's plays but a primary source in relation to that of nineteenth-century principles of dramatic criticism or that of Shakespeare's reputation.

It is worth noticing also that a given source may be primary or secondary in relationship to more than one topic. James Joyce's novel *A Portrait of the Artist as a Young Man* is a primary source in relation not only to the topic of the structure of *A Portrait of the Artist as a Young Man* (and dozens of other topics on the novel itself) but also to the topic of use of the stream-of-consciousness technique in twentieth-century fiction.

THE RESEARCH PAPER

A research paper is a paper giving the results of research, the methods by which they were reached, and the sources, primary or secondary, which were used. A research paper attempts to tell the truth about a topic, and also tells how and where this truth was discovered. As we have seen, the sources of a research paper may be either written sources (literary texts and historical documents, for example) or sources of other kinds (experiments, for example). Since a research paper written in school is almost always based upon written (printed) sources, we shall here discuss only that kind. A research paper based upon written sources may be either a library-research paper or a controlled-research paper. A library-research paper is a research paper for which your search for sources is limited to those sources contained in the libraries available to you; a controlled-research paper, to those sources contained in one anthology —to those contained in this volume, for example. Here we shall emphasize the latter kind.

Finding Your Topic. The first step in writing a research paper based upon written sources, whether a library-research or a controlled-research paper, is finding a topic. We say "finding a topic" rather than "choosing a topic" because the process is more like finding a job than choosing a sandwich from a menu. Unless your instructor assigns you a topic, which he may do, you must look for one; and the one you find may not be just what you want but the best one that you can find. But, if you look long and carefully, you may find a topic that so well suits your interests, your capacities, and the time and the space at your disposal that your paper will almost surely be a success.

Finding a topic is the most important single step in writing a research paper, and the things that you should have in mind when looking for a topic are (1) your interests, (2) your capacities, and (3) the time and the space at your disposal. If you are interested in a topic, if you know something about the special methods of research that the topic requires, and if your topic is narrow enough to require no more time than you have for research and no greater development than you can give it in a paper of the length assigned you, then the paper that results will probably be satisfactory. For example, the topic of figures of speech in *Julius Caesar* may interest you greatly. But, if it does, you must ask yourself whether you know enough about figures of speech to do research on them and, if you do, whether this topic is narrow enough. Even the topic of metaphors in the play would be too broad for most

papers; metaphors in Brutus' soliloquies might be about right. In any case, before you take a topic for a paper, you should do some reading on that topic; otherwise, you won't know whether it is interesting, within your ability to handle, and within the scope of your assigned paper.

Once you think that you've found a topic, take great care in phrasing it. The best phrasing is a question or a series of closely related questions. Better than "The character of Brutus" is "To what extent is Brutus motivated by self-interest and to what extent by the public interest?" The latter is not only more narrow and more precise; it provides you with a criterion of relevance in selecting your sources. At the end of this volume, you will find a list of suggested topics, intended to call your attention to topics that might not occur to you. But these topics are suggestive rather than definitive or precise.

Finding Your Sources. Finding sources for a library-research paper and finding ones for a controlled-research paper, though different in several respects, are alike in certain others. Finding sources in the library requires knowledge of how to use the card catalogue, periodical indexes, special bibliographies, reserve shelves, and encyclopedias. Finding sources in this volume or a similar one does not. But, in either case, you must have a clear idea of what you are looking for; and you must be prepared to put up with a high ratio of looking to finding. In other words, you must have not only criteria of relevance but also a willingness to do a good deal of skimming and a good deal more of careful reading, some of it fruitless.

The basic criterion of relevance you provide by careful phrasing of your topic, a problem discussed in the preceding section. The other criteria you provide by making a preliminary or tentative outline —perhaps in the form of subtopics, perhaps in the form of questions. Such an outline is not to be used for your paper. The outline for your paper will probably be quite different and, in any event, cannot be made until after you find your sources and take your notes. This preliminary outline guides your research and, as we shall see, provides you with the subtopic headings necessary for your note-cards (see "Taking Notes," page *xi*).

Making Your Working Bibliography. Once you have found a promising source ("promising" because, though it seems to be relevant, it may turn out not to be) you want to make some record of it so that, once you have completed your search for sources, you can turn back to it, read it, and, if it turns out to be relevant, take notes on it. This record of promising sources is your *working* bibliography. It is so called for two reasons: first, because you work with it as you proceed with your research and the writing of your paper, adding promising sources to it and discarding irrelevant ones; and, second, because this designation distinguishes it from your final bibliography, which appears at the very end of your research paper and contains only sources actually used in the paper. For a controlled-research paper, your working bibliography may be nothing more elaborate than a series of check marks in the table of contents of your research anthology or a list of page numbers. For a library-research paper, however, you need something quite different.

A working bibliography for a library-research paper is a collection of three-by-five cards each representing a promising source and each containing full information about that source. Once you have completed your research, written your paper, and discarded all promising but (as they turned out) irrelevant sources, this bibliography is identical with your final bibliography. Having a separate card for each source enables you to add and to discard sources easily and to sort and arrange them easily in any order you please. Eventually, when this bibliography becomes identical with your final bibliography, you will arrange sources alphabetically by authors' last names. Having full information about each source on its card enables you

to turn back to it easily—to locate it in the library without first looking it up again. You find this information in the card catalogue, periodical indexes, or other bibliographical aids; or, when browsing through the shelves or the stacks of the library and coming upon a promising source, you find it in or on the source itself—for example, on the spine and the title page of a book.

If the source is a *book,* you should put the following information on the three-by-five working-bibliography card:
(1) the library call number,
(2) the author's (or authors') full name (or names), last name first for the first author,
(3) the title of the book,
(4) the name of the city of publication,
(5) the name of the publisher (*not* the printer), and
(6) the year of publication (often found on the other side of the title page).
See the example of such a card on the opposite page (note the punctuation carefully).

If the source is a *periodical article,* you should put the following information on the three-by-five working-bibliography card:
(1) the author's (or authors') full name (or names),
(2) the title of the article,
(3) the name of the periodical,
(4) the volume number,
(5) the week, the month, or the season of publication, together with the year, and
(6) the page numbers covered by the article.
See the example of such a card on the opposite page (note the punctuation carefully).

These two forms take care of the two standard cases. For special cases—such things as books with editors or translators as well as authors, books published in several editions or in several volumes, and daily newspapers—see any good handbook of composition.

860.3
J23

Jones, John A., and William C.
Brown. <u>A History of
Serbia</u>. New York: The
Rowland Press, Inc., 1934.

WORKING-BIBLIOGRAPHY CARD FOR A BOOK

Smith, Harold B. "Fishing
in Serbian Waters." <u>Journal
of Balkan Sports</u>, <u>VII</u>
(May, 1936), 26-32.

WORKING-BIBLIOGRAPHY CARD FOR A PERIODICAL ARTICLE

Taking Your Notes. Once you have found sources, entered them in your working bibliography, read them, and found them relevant, taking notes requires your exactly following a standard procedure if your notes are going to be useful to you when you come to write your paper. An extra five minutes given to taking a note correctly can save you a half hour in writing your paper. Here is the standard procedure:

(1) Take all notes on four-by-six cards. Never use notebooks, loose sheets of paper, or backs of old envelopes.

(2) Limit each note to information on a single subtopic of your preliminary outline *and* from a single source. It follows from this that you may have many cards on the same subtopic and many cards from the same source but that you may never have one card on more than one subtopic or from more than one source.

(3) On each card, in addition to the note itself, put

(a) the appropriate subtopic heading in the upper left-hand corner.

(b) the name of the source (usually the author's last name will do) in the upper right-hand corner, and

(c) the page number (or numbers) of that part (or those parts) of the source that you have used in taking your note. If you have used more than one page, indicate your page numbers in such a way that, when you come to write your paper, you can tell what page each part of the note comes from, for you may not use the whole note.

(If you follow these first three rules, you will be able, when you come to outline and to organize your paper, to sort your notes in any way you please (by subtopic, for example) and to arrange them in any order you please. Such flexibility is impossible if you take your notes in a notebook. If you follow the third rule, you will also be able to document your paper—write footnotes, for example—without again referring to the sources themselves.)

(4) In taking the note itself, paraphrase or quote your source or do both; but do only one at a time, and use quotation very sparingly.

Paraphrase and quotation require special care. Anything between paraphrase and quotation is not acceptable to good writers: you either paraphrase or quote, but do nothing in between. To paraphrase a source (or part of a source) is to reproduce it in words and word orders substantially different from the original. When you paraphrase well, you keep the sense of the original but change the language,

retaining some key words, of course, but otherwise using your own words and your own sentence patterns. To quote a source (or part of a source) is to reproduce it exactly. When you quote well, you keep both the sense and the language of the original, retaining its punctuation, its capitalization, its type face (roman or italic), and its spelling (indeed, even its misspelling).

Omissions and additions require special care. If, when quoting, you wish to omit some of the original, you may do so only if the omission does not change the sense of the original (never leave out a "not," for example!) *and* if it is indicated by ellipses (three spaced periods: ". . ."). If you wish to add something to the original, you may do so only if the addition does not change the sense of the original (never add a "not"!) *and* it is indicated by square brackets. The most usual additions are explanations ("They [i.e., the people of Paris] were alarmed") and disclaimers of errors in the original, indicated by the Latin *"sic,"* meaning "thus" ("Colombis [sic] discovered America in 1592 [sic]"). You must, of course, carry these ellipses and square brackets from your note-cards to your paper. And, if you type your paper, brackets may be a problem, for most typewriter keyboards do not include them. If your keyboard does not, you may do one of two things—either use the slash ("/") and underlining ("__" and "——") in such a way as to produce a bracket ("⌐" and "⌐") or draw brackets in with a pen. In any event, don't substitute parentheses for brackets.

In your paper, quotations no longer than three or four lines are to be enclosed within a set of quotation marks and run into your text; longer ones are to be set off from the text, without quotation marks, by indention from the left-hand margin and, especially in typewritten copy, by single-spacing. But never use either of these devices unless the language is exactly that of the original.

Your usual treatment of a source should be paraphrase; use quotation only if the

Fly - fishing   Smith
   Smith says that fly-fishing is a method of fishing used chiefly by wealthy Serbians and foreign tourists, that the flies used are generally imported from Scotland, and that "Serbian trout are so snobbish that they won't glance [27/28] at a domestic fly."
   [Query: How reliable is the information in this rather facetious article?]

NOTE-CARD

language of the original is striking (strikingly good or strikingly bad), if it is the very topic of your research (as in a paper on Shakespeare's style), or if it is so complex (as it might be in a legal document) that you don't want to risk paraphrasing it.

Let us look at the sample note-card on the opposite page. The topic of research is methods of fishing in Serbia; the subtopic that the note deals with is fly-fishing in Serbia; the source is Harold B. Smith's article "Fishing in Serbian Waters," from the *Journal of Balkan Sports* (see the second of the two working-bibliography cards on page *xi*).

Note the subtopic heading ("Fly-fishing") in the upper left-hand corner; the name of the source, abbreviated to the author's last name ("Smith"), in the upper right-hand corner; the page numbers ("[27/28]"), indicating that everything, both paraphrase and quotation, up

through the word "glance" is from page 27 and that everything after that word is from page 28; the sparing and appropriate use of quotation; and the bracketed query, to remind the note-taker that he must use this source with caution.

Writing Your Paper. Many of the problems of writing a research paper based upon written sources—organization, the outline, the thesis paragraph, topic sentences, transitions, and the like—are problems of expository writing generally. Here we shall discuss only those problems peculiar to such a paper. Two of these problems —paraphrase and quotation—we discussed in the preceding section. Two others remain: reaching conclusions and avoiding the scissors-and-paste organization.

When you come to make the outline for your paper and to write your paper, you will have before you three things: (1) your *preliminary* outline, containing ordered subtopics of your topic; (2) your working bibliography; and (3) your note-cards. These are the *immediate* results of your research; they are not the *final* results. They are only the raw material out of which you must fashion your paper. At best, they are an intermediate stage between finding your topic and making your final outline. The preliminary outline will not do for the final outline. The working bibliography will almost certainly require further pruning. And the note-cards will require sorting, evaluation, organization, pruning, and exercise of logic and common sense. All this needs to be done, preferably before you make your final outline and begin to write your paper, though almost inevitably some of it will remain to bedevil you while you are writing it. To put the matter in another way, you are, with these things before you, a Sherlock Holmes who has gathered all his clues but who has reached no conclusions from them, who has not come to the end of his search for truth. You must discard irrelevant clues, ones that have no bearing on the questions that you want answered. You must arbitrate the claims of conflicting or contradictory clues. You must decide which one of several probable conclusions is the most probable.

Once you have reached your conclusions, you must organize your paper and set forth this organization in your final outline. Organization and the outline are, of course, problems common to all expository writing. But a problem peculiar to the research paper is avoiding the scissors-and-paste organization—avoiding a paper that looks as though you had cut paraphrases and quotations out of your note-cards, pasted them in columns on paper, and connected them only with such phrases as "Jones says" and "On the other hand, Brown says." Such an organization is the result of a failure to reach conclusions (with the consequence that there is nothing but "Jones says" to put in between paraphrases and quotations); or it is a failure to see the necessity of giving the conclusions reached *and* the reasoning by

which they were reached (with the consequence that, though there is something to put between paraphrases and quotations, nothing is put there, and the reader is left to write the paper for himself).

Documenting Your Paper. To document your paper is to give the source of each paraphrase and quotation that it contains, so that your reader can, if he wishes to, check each of your sources and judge for himself what use you have made of it. To give the source is usually to give (1) either the information that you have about that source in your working bibliography (except that the name of the publisher of a book is usually not given) or the information that accompanies each source in a research anthology *and* (2) the information about page numbers that you have in your notes. This information you may give either formally or informally, as your instructor decides.

Formal documentation is given in footnotes. For a full discussion of footnotes, see any good handbook (one cheap and widely accepted one is *The MLA Style Sheet*). The form of footnotes is similar to, but not identical with, the form of bibliographical entries. With these three sample footnotes, compare the two sample working-bibliography cards on page *xi*:

[1] John A. Jones and William C. Brown, *A History of Serbia* (New York, 1934), p. 211.
[2] Harold B. Smith, "Fishing in Serbian Waters," *Journal of Balkan Sports*, VII (May, 1936), 27.
[3] Smith, pp. 27-28.

Informal documentation is given in the text of the paper, usually parenthetically, as in this example:

Fly-fishing in Serbia is chiefly a sport of wealthy Serbians and foreign tourists (Harold B. Smith, "Fishing in Serbian Waters," *Journal of Balkan Sports*, VII [May, 1936], 27), though in some mountain districts it is popular among the peasants (John A. Jones and William C. Brown. *A History of Serbia* [New York, 1934], p. 211). The flies used are generally imported from Scotland; indeed, Smith facetiously adds, "Serbian trout are so snobbish that they won't glance at a domestic fly" (pp. 27-28).

As this example suggests, however, informal documentation can be an annoying distraction. It probably works out best in papers that use only a few sources. In such papers, there are few occasions for long first-references to sources: for example, "(Harold B. Smith, "Fishing in Serbian Waters," *Journal of Balkan Sports,* VII [May, 1936], 27)." But there are many occasions for short succeeding-references: for example, "(Smith, pp. 27-28)" or "(pp. 27-28)." Occasionally, informal documentation may be profitably combined with formal, as in a paper about Shakespeare's *Julius Caesar.* In such a paper, references to the play might well be given informally —for example, "(III.ii.2-7)"—but references to critics formally.

How many footnotes (or parenthetical documentations) do you need in your paper? The answer is, of course, that you need as many footnotes as you have paraphrases or quotations of sources, unless you group several paraphrases or quotations *from the same page or consecutive pages of a given source* in such a way that one footnote will do for all. One way to do this grouping—almost the only way— is to introduce the group with such a sentence as "Smith's views on fly-fishing are quite different from Brown's" and to conclude it with the raised numeral referring to the footnote. Your reader will understand that everything between the introductory sentence and the numeral comes from the page or the successive pages of the source indicated in the footnote.

Making Your Final Bibliography. Your paper concludes with your final bibliography, which is simply a list of all the sources—and only those sources—that you actually paraphrase or quote in your paper. In other words, every source that you give in a footnote (or a parenthetical documentation) you include in your final bibliography; and you include no other sources (inclusion of others results in what is unfavorably known as "a padded bibliography"). The form for entries in your final bibliography is identical with that for ones in your working bibliography, given above. You should list these sources alphabetically by authors' last names or, if a source is anonymous, by the first word of its title, but not by "a," "an," or "the." For example:

BIBLIOGRAPHY

Jones, John A., and William C. Brown. *A History of Serbia.* New York: The Rowland Press, Inc., 1934.

"Serbian Pastimes." *Sports Gazette,* XCI (October 26, 1952), 18-19, 38, 40-42.

Smith, Harold B. "Fishing in Serbian Waters." *Journal of Balkan Sports,* VII (May, 1936), 26-32.

MARTIN STEINMANN, JR.

Contents

Introduction

There are few critics who would not agree that the most interesting and most important contemporary American playwrights are Arthur Miller and Tennessee Williams. Both have been rewarded, not only with money and popularity, but with serious—though not always entirely favorable—consideration by academic critics long accustomed to regarding the offerings of Broadway as too much of a compromise of art with profits to be of any lasting significance. To many readers and theatre-goers, these two dramatists have proved that there is no longer any doubt that the American theatre has come of age. It is no longer imitative of Europe; it has absorbed foreign traditions and, in the work of these two authors at least, gone on to create a drama that in its subjects, themes, characters, and language is distinctively, but not parochially, American.

Nor does the reputation of these two dramatists depend merely on a single play. Williams is a more prolific writer than Miller, but each of them has built up a body of work that marks him as having a style and a thematic preoccupation of his own. This does not imply that they have simply found a successful dramatic formula and exploited it, as many others have done. It means that with each new play they write they add something to the artistic statement that is the world of their plays as a whole. This creation of a body of work, with each item contained in it reinforcing and illuminating the others, the production of what French critics call an *œuvre,* is one of the principal signs of artistic stature. In the American theatre, before the arrival of Williams and Miller, it had been achieved only by Eugene O'Neill and, perhaps, Maxwell Anderson.

From the work of each of these two dramatists, however, one play stands out not only as the most representative but also as his greatest artistic achievement to date. *Death of a Salesman* is, without doubt, unmatched in Miller's work; not a few critics consider it unequalled in the American drama, and Miller himself thinks of it as his finest work. In the case of Williams, the choice is less obvious or certain. *The Glass Menagerie,* for instance, is a little less strident than *A Streetcar Named Desire,* and Williams makes greater artistic claims than most critics would be willing to admit for his *Camino Real.* But the greatest praise, foreign as well as American, has gone to *A Streetcar Named Desire* as his most ambitious play. It is certainly quite representative of his themes, his style, and his dramatic form. Thus, by comparing the two plays, *Death of a Salesman* and *A Streetcar Named Desire,* the student can fairly arrive at a critical estimate of the differences between these writers' contributions to the modern American theatre.

These differences are striking, as the reviews and critical essays in this anthology make clear. It is not without significance that Arthur Miller, after writing *Death of a Salesman,* made a modern adaptation of Henrik Ibsen's *An Enemy of the People,* one of the Norwegian's more overtly "social" plays; neither, perhaps, is it purely accidental that Williams' plays, setting aside his frankness in dealing with psychological and sexual themes, frequently bring Chekhov to mind. For it is here that we may see two dramatic movements, beginning around the turn of the present century, that have had a profound influence on modern playwriting.

The Ibsen tradition, broadly speaking, is that of prose realism. Derived ultimately from the "bourgeois" drama of the eighteenth century, it is more or less directly social and political in orientation. This is not to say that it is blatantly didactic or that it does not concern itself with the more subtle and personal aspects of human relationships. It simply focuses on man in his social and political context. To this tradition Miller clearly belongs: his comments on the Greek drama in his essay "On Social Plays," reprinted here, show the extent to which he regards the dramatist as "committed," and the concern in his plays with moral questions (as in *All My Sons*) and socio-political matters (*The Crucible*) is evidence of his attempts to found his art on themes centering round what he has called "the right way of living."

Tennessee Williams, on the other hand, while still placing his characters in a recognizable social framework, is more interested in the effects of family and social environment on the individual. Like Chekhov he is the observer of frustrated lives, the recorder of the constant clash of new societies with old, of the utilitarian with the beautiful. His plays, like those of Chekhov, have social and political *meaning*, but this meaning is most frequently brought home to us indirectly—by symbolism, for instance, or by the suggestion, never insisted upon but always present, that the sexual frustrations and maladjustments that are so large a part of his subject matter are symptomatic of the *malaise* of the South, in which most of the plays are set. Putting the matter simply, Miller's plays reach out from the individual to society as a whole, while Williams' move in from society to the individual—though it would be unwise to apply this distinction too rigidly. And the Chekhov tradition is essentially a poetic tradition, even though Chekhov's plays—and those of Williams—are written in prose. Williams is a writer whose language is always sensuous, evocative, rhythmic, full of symbolic allusions, pitched at a higher intensity than normal speech. It is a "poetry" which finds its origins, like the "poetry" of the Irish dramatist J. M. Synge, in a sharply observed reality. It is, of course, at the other extreme from what has been called—with no derisive intent—the "mundane" style and artistic vision of Arthur Miller.

A further point of comparison is that each of these dramatists, in a different way, attempts an answer to the frequently raised question "Does modern society, and modern thought about the nature of man and his universe, allow us to interpret human life in tragic terms?" They have answered it by writing plays which they claim—and in this they have the support of many critics—to be tragic in form and vision. In addition Miller, in his essay "Tragedy and the Common Man," has tried to establish a theoretical basis for his work. Here again, the two writers move in different directions. Miller's conception of tragedy is closer to that of the Greeks and of Ibsen, based on problems of personal and social morality, hinging on choices wrongly made, and with a pervasive, sometimes quite explicit, tone of criticism of society as it is presently constituted in America. Williams' conception of tragedy—which we have largely to deduce from his plays, since he is apparently reluctant to indulge in critical explanations of the themes of his work—seems to approach that of Chekhov and of Strindberg. The forces of social and natural environment bear down on his tragic heroines, but his main interest is the tragedy of the individual *in* society. Hence, criticism of *Death of a Salesman* most often utilizes the language of sociology, while writers on *A Streetcar Named Desire* usually phrase their observations in the terminology—and often, regrettably, the jargon—of psychology. There are, of course, notable exceptions to this: the two approaches are not mutually exclusive.

The foregoing comments have indicated the scope of this anthology and suggested some of the ways in which it may be used. Part One contains discussions of the problem of tragedy in the modern world and includes one of the major critical pronouncements on this topic, by Joseph Wood Krutch. Mr. Krutch not only suggests that is is exceedingly difficult, if not impossible, to write a tragedy in the context of the modern world; he also doubts whether we can bring to the tragedies of the past a more than intellectual appreciation. To this radical point of view John Gassner, in his "Tragic Perspectives," has some pertinent answers. The meaning of "tragedy" or "tragic experience" to the average American student, and the nature of his response to it, are examined by Orrin E. Klapp. Part Two contains statements by the dramatists on their art. Part Three contains critical essays on the playwrights and reviews of the plays, as they appeared on the stage and later in published texts. The concentration here is on *Death of a Salesman* and *A Streetcar Named Desire,* although some of the essays deal with Miller's and Williams' work as a whole and thus consider these two plays in a broader context.

Rather more discussion of *Death of a Salesman* appears than of *A Streetcar Named Desire.* This reflects the proportion of critical interest evoked by the two plays. There is, however, sufficient material for the volume to be used for the following broad types of controlled-research project: assessment of either or both of the plays in relation to the problems of modern tragedy; comparison of the plays from various critical viewpoints; comparison of the critical approaches represented here. More specific suggestions for research topics, and for further research in the library, will be found at the end of the volume. The instructor will, of course, be able to add to these.

PART ONE

TRAGEDY IN THE MODERN WORLD

The Tragic Fallacy*

JOSEPH WOOD KRUTCH (1893-   ), American dramatic and literary critic, has been Brander Matthews Professor of Dramatic Literature at Columbia University (1943-1952) and drama critic of the *Nation* (1924-1932 and 1937-1950). His best-known books on the drama are *Comedy and Conscience after the Restoration* (1924), *The American Drama Since 1918* (1939, revised edition 1958), and *"Modernism" in Modern Drama* (1953). An excerpt from the last-named book appears in Part Three of the present volume. *The Modern Temper* is principally a study of the impact of science, Freudianism, Darwinism, and rationalism on twentieth-century man's religious, philosophical, and cultural traditions. Chapter V, "The Tragic Fallacy," is the only part of the book to deal specifically with the drama, but it is probably the most influential and provocative statement of the problems surrounding the writing and appreciation of tragedy in the modern age. Mr. Krutch has revised some of his opinions about the "modern temper" in *The Measure of Man* (1954).

Through the legacy of their art the great ages have transmitted to us a dim image of their glorious vitality. When we turn the pages of a Sophoclean or a Shakespearean tragedy we participate faintly in the experience which created it and we sometimes presumptuously say that we "understand" the spirit of these works. But the truth is that we see them, even at best and in the moments when our souls expand most nearly to their dimensions, through a glass darkly.

It is so much easier to appreciate than to create that an age too feeble to reach the heights achieved by the members of a preceding one can still see those heights towering above its impotence, and so it is that, when we perceive a Sophocles or a Shakespeare soaring in an air which we can never hope to breathe, we say that we can "appreciate" them. But what we mean is that we are just able to wonder, and we can never hope to participate in the glorious vision of human life out of which they were created—not even to the extent of those humbler persons for whom [115/116] they were written; for while to us the triumphant voices come from far away and tell of a heroic world which no longer exists, to them they spoke of immediate realities and revealed the inner meaning of events amidst which they still lived.

When the life has entirely gone out of a work of art come down to us from the past, when we read it without any emotional comprehension whatsoever and can no longer even imagine why the people for whom it was intended found it absorbing and satisfying, then, of course, it has ceased to be a work of art at all and has dwindled into one of those deceptive "documents" from which we get a false sense of comprehending through the intellect things which cannot be comprehended at all except by means of a kinship of feeling. And though all works from a past age have begun in this way to fade there are some, like the great Greek or Elizabethan tragedies, which are still halfway between

---

*Joseph Wood Krutch, "The Tragic Fallacy," *The Modern Temper* (New York: Harcourt, Brace and Company, Inc., 1929), pp. 115-143.

the work of art and the document. They
no longer can have for us the immediacy
which they had for those to whom they
originally belonged, but they have not
yet eluded us entirely. We no longer live
in the world which they represent, but
we can half imagine it and we can measure
the distance which we have moved away.
We write no tragedies today, but we can
still talk [116/117] about the tragic spirit
of which we would, perhaps, have no conception were it not for the works in question.

An age which could really "appreciate"
Shakespeare or Sophocles would have
something comparable to put beside them
—something like them, not necessarily in
form, or spirit, but at least in magnitude
—some vision of life which would be, however different, equally ample and passionate. But when we move to put a modern masterpiece beside them, when we
seek to compare them with, let us say, a
Ghosts or a *Weavers,* we shrink as from
the impulse to commit some folly and we
feel as though we were about to superim-
pose Bowling Green upon the Great Prai-
ries in order to ascertain which is the larger. The question, we see, is not primarily
one of art but of the two worlds which
two minds inhabited. No increased powers of expression, no greater gift for
words, could have transformed Ibsen into
Shakespeare. The materials out of which
the latter created his works—his conception of human dignity, his sense of the
importance of human passions, his vision
of the amplitude of human life—simply
did not and could not exist for Ibsen, as
they did not and could not exist for his
contemporaries. God and Man and Nature had all somehow dwindled in the
course of [117/118] the intervening centuries, not because the realistic creed of
modern art led us to seek out mean people, but because this meanness of human
life was somehow thrust upon us by the
operation of that same process which led
to the development of realistic theories of
art by which our vision could be justified.

Hence, though we still apply, sometimes, the adjective "tragic" to one or another of those modern works of literature
which describe human misery and which
end more sadly even than they begin, the
term is a misnomer since it is obvious
that the works in question have nothing
in common with the classical examples of
the genre and produce in the reader a
sense of depression which is the exact opposite of that elation generated when the
spirit of a Shakespeare rises joyously superior to the outward calamities which
he recounts and celebrates the greatness
of the human spirit whose travail he describes. Tragedies, in that only sense of
the word which has any distinctive meaning, are no longer written in either the
dramatic or any other form and the fact
is not to be accounted for in any merely
literary terms. It is not the result of any
fashion in literature or of any deliberation
to write about human nature or character
under different aspects, any more than it
is of either any greater sensitiveness of
feeling which would [118/119] make us
shrink from the contemplation of the suffering of Medea or Othello or of any greater optimism which would make us more
likely to see life in more cheerful terms.
It is, on the contrary, the result of one of
those enfeeblements of the human spirit
not unlike that described in the previous
chapter of this essay, and a further illustration of that gradual weakening of
man's confidence in his ability to impose
upon the phenomenon of life an interpretation acceptable to his desires which is
the subject of the whole of the present discussion.

To explain that fact and to make clear
how the creation of classical tragedy did
consist in the successful effort to impose
such a satisfactory interpretation will require, perhaps, the special section which
follows, although the truth of the fact that
it does impose such an interpretation
must be evident to any one who has ever
risen from the reading of *Oedipus* or *Lear*
with that feeling of exultation which
comes when we have been able, by rare
good fortune, to enter into its spirit as
completely as it is possible for us of a remoter and emotionally enfeebled age to

enter it. Meanwhile one anticipatory remark may be ventured. If the plays and the novels of today deal with littler people and less mighty emotions it is not because we have become interested in commonplace [119/120] souls and their unglamorous adventures but because we have come, willy-nilly, to see the soul of man as commonplace and its emotions as mean.

II

Tragedy, said Aristotle, is the "imitation of noble actions," and though it is some twenty-five hundred years since the dictum was uttered there is only one respect in which we are inclined to modify it. To us "imitation" seems a rather naïve word to apply to that process by which observation is turned into art, and we seek one which would define or at least imply the nature of that interposition of the personality of the artist between the object and the beholder which constitutes his function and by means of which he transmits a modified version, rather than a mere imitation, of the thing which he has contemplated.

In the search for this word the estheticians of romanticism invented the term "expression" to describe the artistic purpose to which apparent imitation was subservient. Psychologists, on the other hand, feeling that the artistic process was primarily one by which reality is modified in such a way as to render it more acceptable to the desires of the artist, employed various terms in the effort to describe that distortion which the wish may produce in vision. And [120/121] though many of the newer critics reject both romanticism and psychology, even they insist upon the fundamental fact that in art we are concerned, not with mere imitation, but with the imposition of some form upon the material which it would not have if it were merely copied as a camera copies.

Tragedy is not, then, as Aristotle said, the *imitation* of noble actions, for, indeed, no one knows what a *noble* action is or whether or not such a thing as nobility exists in nature apart from the mind of man. Certainly the action of Achilles in dragging the dead body of Hector around the walls of Troy and under the eyes of Andromache, who had begged to be allowed to give it decent burial, is not to us a noble action, though it was such to Homer, who made it the subject of a noble passage in a noble poem. Certainly, too, the same action might conceivably be made the subject of a tragedy and the subject of a farce, depending upon the way in which it was treated; so that to say that tragedy is the *imitation* of a *noble* action is to be guilty of assuming, first, that art and photography are the same, and, second, that there may be something inherently noble in an act as distinguished from the motives which prompted it or from the point of view from which it is regarded. [121/122]

And yet, nevertheless, the idea of nobility is inseparable from the idea of tragedy, which cannot exist without it. If tragedy is not the imitation or even the modified representation of noble actions it is certainly a representation of actions *considered* as noble, and herein lies its essential nature, since no man can conceive it unless he is capable of believing in the greatness and importance of man. Its action is usually, if not always, calamitous, because it is only in calamity that the human spirit has the opportunity to reveal itself triumphant over the outward universe which fails to conquer it; but this calamity in tragedy is only a means to an end and the essential thing which distinguishes real tragedy from those distressing modern works sometimes called by its name is the fact that it is in the former alone that the artist has found himself capable of considering and of making us consider that his people and his actions have that amplitude and importance which make them noble. Tragedy arises then when, as in Periclean Greece or Elizabethan England, a people fully aware of the calamities of life is nevertheless serenely confident of the greatness of man,

Cartharsis - letting go of the emotions

whose mighty passions and supreme fortitude are revealed when one of these calamities overtakes him.

To those who mistakenly think of it as something [122/123] gloomy or depressing, who are incapable of recognizing the elation which its celebration of human greatness inspires, and who, therefore, confuse it with things merely miserable or pathetic, it must be a paradox that the happiest, most vigorous, and most confident ages which the world has ever known—the Periclean and the Elizabethan—should be exactly those which created and which most relished the mightiest tragedies; but the paradox is, of course, resolved by the fact that tragedy is essentially an expression, not of despair, but of the triumph over despair and of confidence in the value of human life. If Shakespeare himself ever had that "dark period" which his critics and biographers have imagined for him, it was at least no darkness like that bleak and arid despair which sometimes settles over modern spirits. In the midst of it he created both the elemental grandeur of Othello and the pensive majesty of Hamlet and, holding them up to his contemporaries, he said in the words of his own Miranda, "Oh, rare new world that hath *such* creatures in it."

All works of art which deserve their name have a happy end. This is indeed the thing which constitutes them art and through which they perform their function. Whatever the character of the events, fortunate or unfortunate, which they recount, they so [123/124] mold or arrange or interpret them that we accept gladly the conclusion which they reach and would not have it otherwise. They may conduct us into the realm of pure fancy where wish and fact are identical and the world is remade exactly after the fashion of the heart's desire or they may yield some greater or less allegiance to fact; but they must always reconcile us in one way or another to the representation which they make and the distinctions between the genres are simply the distinctions between the means by which this reconciliation is effected.

Comedy laughs the minor mishaps of its characters away; drama solves all the difficulties which it allows to arise; and melodrama, separating good from evil by simple lines, distributes its rewards and punishments in accordance with the principles of a naïve justice which satisfies the simple souls of its audience, which are neither philosophical enough to question its primitive ethics nor critical enough to object to the way in which its neat events violate the laws of probability. Tragedy, the greatest and the most difficult of the arts, can adopt none of these methods; and yet it must reach its own happy end in its own way. Though its conclusions must be, by its premise, outwardly calamitous, though it must speak to those who know that the good man is cut off and that the [124/125] fairest things are the first to perish, yet it must leave them, as *Othello* does, content that this is so. We must be and we are glad that Juliet dies and glad that Lear is turned out into the storm.

Milton set out, he said, to justify the ways of God to man, and his phrase, if it be interpreted broadly enough, may be taken as describing the function of all art, which must, in some way or other, make the life which it seems to represent satisfactory to those who see its reflection in the magic mirror, and it must gratify or at least reconcile the desires of the beholder, not necessarily, as the naïver exponents of Freudian psychology maintain, by gratifying individual and often eccentric wishes, but at least by satisfying the universally human desire to find in the world some justice, some meaning, or, at the very least, some recognizable order. Hence it is that every real tragedy, however tremendous it may be, is an affirmation of faith in life, a declaration that even if God is not in his Heaven, then at least Man is in his world.

We accept gladly the outward defeats which it describes for the sake of the inward victories which it reveals. Juliet died, but not before she had shown how great and resplendent a thing love could be; Othello plunged the dagger into his own breast, but [125/126] not before he had revealed that greatness of soul which makes his death seem unimportant. Had he died in the instant when he struck the blow, had he perished still believing that the world was as completely black as he saw it before the innocence of Desdemona was revealed to him, then, for him at least, the world would have been merely damnable, but Shakespeare kept him alive long enough to allow him to learn his error and hence to die, not in despair, but in the full acceptance of the tragic reconciliation to life. Perhaps it would be pleasanter if men could believe what the child is taught—that the good are happy and that things turn out as they should— but it is far more important to be able to believe, as Shakespeare did, that however much things in the outward world may go awry, man has, nevertheless, splendors of his own and that, in a word, Love and Honor and Glory are not words but realities.

Thus for the great ages tragedy is not an expression of despair but the means by which they saved themselves from it. It is a profession of faith, and a sort of religion; a way of looking at life by virtue of which it is robbed of its pain. The sturdy soul of the tragic author seizes upon suffering and uses it only as a means by which joy may be wrung out of existence, but it is not to be forgotten that he is en- [126/127] abled to do so only because of his belief in the greatness of human nature and because, though he has lost the child's faith in life, he has not lost his far more important faith in human nature. A tragic writer does not have to believe in God, but he must believe in man.

And if, then, the Tragic Spirit is in reality the product of a religious faith in which, sometimes at least, faith in the greatness of God is replaced by faith in the greatness of man, it serves, of course, to perform the function of religion, to make life tolerable for those who participate in its beneficent illusion. It purges the souls of those who might otherwise despair and it makes endurable the realization that the events of the outward world do not correspond with the desires of the heart, and thus, in its own particular way, it does what all religions do, for it gives a rationality, a meaning, and a justification to the universe. But if it has the strength it has also the weakness of all faiths, since it may—nay, it must—be ultimately lost as reality, encroaching further and further into the realm of imagination, leaves less and less room in which that imagination can build its refuge. [127/128]

III

It is, indeed, only at a certain stage in the development of the realistic intelligence of a people that the tragic faith can exist. A naïver people may have, as the ancient men of the north had, a body of legends which are essentially tragic, or it may have only (and need only) its happy and childlike mythology which arrives inevitably at its happy end, where the only ones who suffer "deserve" to do so and in which, therefore, life is represented as directly and easily acceptable. A too sophisticated society on the other hand—one which, like ours, has outgrown not merely the simple optimism of the child but also that vigorous, one might almost say adolescent, faith in the nobility of man which marks a Sophocles or a Shakespeare, has neither fairy tales to assure it that all is always right in the end nor tragedies to make it believe that it rises superior in soul to the outward calamities which befall it.

Distrusting its thought, despising its passions, realizing its impotent unimportance in the universe, it can tell itself no stories except those which make it still more acutely aware of its trivial miseries. When its heroes (sad misnomer for the pitiful creatures who people contemporary fiction) are struck [128/129] down it is not, like Oedipus, by the gods that they are struck but only, like Oswald Alving, by syphilis, for they know that the gods, even if they existed, would not trouble with them, and they cannot attribute to themselves in art an importance in which they do not believe. Their so-called tragedies do not and cannot end with one of those splendid calamities which in Shakespeare seem to reverberate through the universe, because they cannot believe that the universe trembles when their love is, like Romeo's, cut off or when the place where they (small as they are) have gathered up their trivial treasure is, like Othello's sanctuary, defiled. Instead, mean misery piles on mean misery, petty misfortune follows petty misfortune, and despair becomes intolerable because it is no longer even significant or important.

Ibsen once made one of his characters say that he did not read much because he found reading "irrelevant," and the adjective was brilliantly chosen because it held implications even beyond those of which Ibsen was consciously aware. What is it that made the classics irrelevant to him and to us? Is it not just exactly those to him impossible premises which make tragedy what it is, those assumptions that the soul of man is great, that the universe (together with whatever gods may be) concerns itself [129/130] with him and that he is, in a word, noble? Ibsen turned to village politics for exactly the same reason that his contemporaries and his successors have, each in his own way, sought out some aspect of the common man and his common life—because, that is to say, here was at least something small enough for him to be able to believe.

Bearing this fact in mind, let us compare a modern "tragedy" with one of the great works of a happy age, not in order to judge of their relative technical merits but in order to determine to what extent the former deserves its name by achieving a tragic solution capable of purging the soul or of reconciling the emotions to the life which it pictures. And in order to make the comparison as fruitful as possible let us choose *Hamlet* on the one hand and on the other a play like *Ghosts* which was not only written by perhaps the most powerful as well as the most typical of modern writers but which

is, in addition, the one of his works which seems most nearly to escape that triviality which cannot be entirely escaped by any one who feels, as all contemporary minds do, that man is relatively trivial.

In *Hamlet* a prince ("in understanding, how like a god!") has thrust upon him from the unseen world a duty to redress a wrong which concerns not merely [130/-131] him, his mother, and his uncle, but the moral order of the universe. Erasing all trivial fond records from his mind, abandoning at once both his studies and his romance because it has been his good fortune to be called upon to take part in an action of cosmic importance, he plunges (at first) not into action but into thought, weighing the claims which are made upon him and contemplating the grandiose complexities of the universe. And when the time comes at last for him to die he dies, not as a failure, but as a success. Not only has the universe regained the balance which had been upset by what *seemed* the monstrous crime of the guilty pair ("there is nothing either good nor ill but thinking makes it so"), but in the process by which that readjustment is made a mighty mind has been given the opportunity, first to contemplate the magnificent scheme of which it is a part, and then to demonstrate the greatness of its spirit by playing a role in the grand style which it called for. We do not need to despair in *such* a world if it has *such* creatures in it.

Turn now to *Ghosts*—look upon this picture and upon that. A young man has inherited syphilis from his father. Struck by a to him mysterious malady he returns to his northern village, learns the hopeless truth about himself, and persuades his mother to [131/132] poison him. The incidents prove, perhaps, that pastors should not endeavor to keep a husband and wife together unless they know what they are doing. But what a world is this in which a great writer can deduce nothing more than that from his greatest work and how are we to be purged or reconciled when we see it acted? Not only is the failure utter, but it is trivial and meaningless as well.

Yet the journey from Elsinore to Skien is precisely the journey which the human spirit has made, exchanging in the process princes for invalids and gods for disease. We say, as Ibsen would say, that the problems of Oswald Alving are more "relevant" to our life than the problems of Hamlet, that the play in which he appears is more "real" than the other more glamorous one, but it is exactly because we find it so that we are condemned. We can believe in Oswald but we cannot believe in Hamlet, and a light has gone out in the universe. Shakespeare justifies the ways of God to man, but in Ibsen there is no such happy end and with him tragedy, so called, has become merely an expression of our despair at finding that such justification is no longer possible.

Modern critics have sometimes been puzzled to account for the fact that the concern of ancient tragedy is almost exclusively with kings and courts. [132/133] They have been tempted to accuse even Aristotle of a certain naïveté in assuming (as he seems to assume) that the "nobility" of which he speaks as necessary to a tragedy implies a nobility of rank as well as of soul, and they have sometimes regretted that Shakespeare did not devote himself more than he did to the serious consideration of those common woes of the common man which subsequent writers have exploited with increasing pertinacity. Yet the tendency to lay the scene of a tragedy at the court of a king is not the result of any arbitrary convention but of the fact that the tragic writers believed easily in greatness just as we believe easily in meanness. To Shakespeare, robes and crowns and jewels are the garments most appropriate to man because they are the fitting outward manifestation of his inward majesty, but to us they seem absurd because the man who bears them has, in our estimation, so pitifully shrunk. We do not write about kings because we do not believe that any man is worthy to be one and we do not write about courts because hovels seem to us to be dwellings more appropriate to

the creatures who inhabit them. Any modern attempt to dress characters in robes ends only by making us aware of a comic incongruity and any modern attempt to furnish them with a language [133/134] resplendent like Shakespeare's ends only in bombast.

True tragedy capable of performing its function and of purging the soul by reconciling man to his woes can exist only by virtue of a certain pathetic fallacy far more inclusive than that to which the name is commonly given. The romantics, feeble descendants of the tragic writers to whom they are linked by their effort to see life and nature in grandiose terms, loved to imagine that the sea or the sky had a way of according itself with their moods, of storming when they stormed and smiling when they smiled. But the tragic spirit sustains itself by an assumption much more far-reaching and no more justified. Man as it sees him lives in a world which he may not dominate but which is always aware of him. Occupying the exact center of a universe which would have no meaning except for him and being so little below the angels that, if he believes in God, he has no hesitation in imagining Him formed as he is formed and crowned with a crown like that which he or one of his fellows wears, he assumes that each of his acts reverberates through the universe. His passions are important to him because he believes them important throughout all time and all space; the very fact that he can sin (no modern can) means that this universe is watching his acts; and though [134/135] he may perish, a God leans out from infinity to strike him down. And it is exactly because an Ibsen cannot think of man in any such terms as these that his persons have so shrunk and that his "tragedy" has lost that power which real tragedy always has of making that infinitely ambitious creature called man content to accept his misery if only he can be made to feel great enough and important enough. An Oswald is not a Hamlet chiefly because he has lost that tie with the natural and supernatural world which the latter had. No ghost will leave the other world to warn or encourage him, there is no virtue and no vice which he can possibly have which can be really important, and when he dies neither his death nor the manner of it will be, outside the circle of two or three people as unnecessary as himself, any more important than that of a rat behind the arras.

Perhaps we may dub the illusion upon which the tragic spirit is nourished the Tragic, as opposed to the Pathetic, Fallacy, but fallacy though it is, upon its existence depends not merely the writing of tragedy but the existence of that religious feeling of which tragedy is an expression and by means of which a people aware of the dissonances of life manages nevertheless to hear them as harmony. Without it neither man nor his passions can seem great enough [135/136] or important enough to justify the sufferings which they entail, and literature, expressing the mood of a people, begins to despair where once it had exulted. Like the belief in love and like most of the other mighty illusions by means of which human life has been given a value, the Tragic Fallacy depends ultimately upon the assumption which man so readily makes that something outside his own being, some "spirit not himself"—be it God, Nature, or that still vaguer thing called a Moral Order—joins him in the emphasis which he places upon this or that and confirms him in his feeling that his passions and his opinions are important. When his instinctive faith in that correspondence between the outer and the inner world fades, his grasp upon the faith that sustained him fades also, and Love or Tragedy or what not ceases to be the reality which it was because he is never strong enough in his own insignificant self to stand alone in a universe which snubs him with its indifference.

In both the modern and the ancient worlds tragedy was dead long before writers were aware of the fact. Seneca wrote his frigid melodramas under the impression that he was following in the footsteps of Sophocles, and Dryden probably thought that his *All for Love* was an improvement upon Shakespeare, [136/137] but in time we awoke to the fact that no amount of rhetorical bombast could conceal the fact that grandeur was not to be counterfeited when the belief in its possibility was dead, and turning from the hero to the common man, we inaugurated the era of realism. For us no choice remains except that between mere rhetoric and the frank consideration of our fellow men, who may be the highest of the anthropoids but who are certainly too far below the angels to imagine either that these angels can concern themselves with them or that they can catch any glimpse of even the soles of angelic feet. We can no longer tell tales of the fall of noble men because we do not believe that noble men exist. The best that we can achieve is pathos and the most that we can do is to feel sorry for ourselves. Man has put off his royal robes and it is only in sceptered pomp that tragedy can come sweeping by.

IV

Nietzsche was the last of the great philosophers to attempt a tragic justification of life. His central and famous dogma— "Life is good *because* it is painful"—sums up in a few words the desperate and almost meaningless paradox to which he was driven in his effort to reduce to rational terms the far more [137/138] imaginative conception which is everywhere present but everywhere unanalyzed in a Sophocles or a Shakespeare and by means of which they rise triumphant over the manifold miseries of life. But the very fact that Nietzsche could not even attempt to state in any except intellectual terms an attitude which is primarily unintellectual and to which, indeed, intellectual analysis is inevitably fatal, is proof of the distance which he had been carried (by the rationalizing tendencies of the human mind) from the possibility of the tragic solution which he sought; and the confused, half-insane violence of his work will reveal, by the contrast which it affords with the serenity of the tragic writers whom he admired, how great was his failure.

Fundamentally this failure was, moreover, conditioned by exactly the same thing which has conditioned the failure of all modern attempts to achieve what he attempted—by the fact, that is to say, that tragedy must have a hero if it is not to be merely an accusation against, instead of a justification of, the world in which it occurs. Tragedy is, as Aristotle said, an imitation of noble actions, and Nietzsche, for all his enthusiasm for the Greek tragic writers, was palsied by the universally modern incapacity to conceive man as noble. Out of this [138/139] dilemma, out of his need to find a hero who could give to life as he saw it the only possible justification, was born the idea of the Superman, but the Superman is, after all, only a hypothetical being, destined to become what man actually was in the eyes of the great tragic writers—a creature (as Hamlet said) "how infinite in capacities, in understanding how like a god." Thus Nietzsche lived half in the past through his literary enthusiasms and half in the future through his grandiose dreams, but for all his professed determination to justify existence he was no more able than the rest of us to find the present acceptable. Life, he said in effect, is not a Tragedy now but perhaps it will be when the Ape-man has been transformed into a hero (the Übermensch), and trying to find that sufficient, he went mad.

He failed, as all moderns must fail when they attempt, like him, to embrace the tragic spirit as a religious faith, because the resurgence of that faith is not an intellectual but a vital phenomenon, something not achieved by taking thought but born, on the contrary, out of an instinctive confidence in life which is nearer to the animal's unquestioning allegiance to the scheme of nature than it is to that critical intelligence characteristic of a fully developed humanism. And like other faiths it is not to be re-[139/140]captured merely by reaching an intellectual conviction that it would be desirable to do so.

Modern psychology has discovered (or at least strongly emphasized) the fact that under certain conditions desire produces belief, and having discovered also that the more primitive a given mentality the more completely are its opinions determined by its wishes, modern psychology has concluded that the best mind is that which most resists the tendency to believe a thing simply because it would be pleasant or advantageous to do so. But justified as this conclusion may be from the intellectual point of view, it fails to take into account the fact that in a universe as badly adapted as this one to human as distinguished from animal needs this ability to will a belief may bestow an enormous vital advantage as it did, for instance, in the case at present under discussion where it made possible for Shakespeare the compensations of a tragic faith completely inaccessible to Nietzsche. Pure intelligence, incapable of being influenced by desire and therefore also incapable of choosing one opinion rather than another simply because the one chosen is the more fruitful or beneficent, is doubtless a relatively perfect instrument for the pursuit of truth, but the question (likely, it would seem, to be answered in the nega-[140/141]tive) is simply whether or not the spirit of man can endure the literal and inhuman truth.

Certain ages and simple people have conceived of the action which passes upon the stage of the universe as of something in the nature of a Divine Comedy, as something, that is to say, which will reach its end with the words "and they lived happily ever after." Others, less naïve and therefore more aware of those maladjustments whose reality, at least so far as outward events are concerned, they could not escape, have imposed upon it another artistic form and called it a Divine Tragedy, accepting its catastrophe as we accept the catastrophe of an *Othello*, because of its grandeur. But a Tragedy, Divine or otherwise, must, it may again be repeated, have a hero, and from the universe as we see it both the Glory of God and the Glory of Man have departed. Our cosmos may be farcical or it may be pathetic but it has not the dignity of tragedy and we cannot accept it as such.

Yet our need for the consolations of tragedy has not passed with the passing of our ability to conceive it. Indeed, the dissonances which it was tragedy's function to resolve grow more insistent instead of diminishing. Our passions, our disappointments, and our sufferings remain important to us though important to nothing else and they thrust themselves upon [141/142] us with an urgency which makes it impossible for us to dismiss them as the mere trivialities which, so our intellects tell us, they are. And yet, in the absence of tragic faith or the possibility of achieving it, we have no way in which we may succeed in giving them the dignity which would not only render them tolerable but transform them as they were transformed by the great ages into joys. The death of tragedy is, like the death of love, one of those emotional fatalities as the result of which the human as distinguished from the natural world grows more and more a desert.

Poetry, said Santayana in his famous phrase, is "religion which is no longer believed," but it depends, nevertheless, upon its power to revive in us a sort of temporary or provisional credence and the nearer it can come to producing an illusion of belief the greater is its power as poetry. Once the Tragic Spirit was a living faith and out of it tragedies were written. Today these great expressions of a great faith have declined, not merely into poetry, but into a kind of poetry whose premises are so far from any we can really accept that we can only partially and dimly grasp its meaning.

We read but we do not write tragedies. The tragic solution of the problem of existence, the reconcilia- [142/143] tion to life by means of the tragic spirit is, that is to say, now only a fiction surviving in art. When that art itself has become, as it probably will, completely meaningless, when we have ceased not only to write but to *read* tragic works, then it will be lost and in all real senses forgotten, since the devolution from Religion to Art to Document will be complete.

Tragic Perspectives: A Sequence of Queries*

JOHN GASSNER (1903-   ), historian and critic of the drama and a member of the New York Drama Critics' Circle, is presently Sterling Professor of Playwriting and Dramatic Literature at Yale University. He has edited a number of anthologies of dramatic literature, the best-known being *A Treasury of the Theatre* (1935, revised edition 1960). Combining a wide scholarly knowledge of dramatic literature and theatrical history with a strong interest in contemporary plays and playwrights, John Gassner is one of our most authoritative critics, although he always refuses to be bound by theoretical conceptions or by tradition. Modern drama, for him, must always be seeking new forms, or combinations of old, to provide a significant reflection of its cultural background. This view he puts forcibly in *The Theatre in Our Times* (1954), and in *Form and Idea in Modern Theatre* (1956), as well as in the present essay.

I

"It is about time someone wrote a new *Poetics*," my friend said. He was thinking of Tragedy, of course, and he looked hopefully at me, or so my vanity led me to believe. And it occurred to me at once how easy it would be to join this enterprise of drafting new or modified "laws" for tragedy, and how difficult to extricate oneself from it. There hasn't been a generation since the fifteenth century that hasn't tried to rewrite Aristotle's text whether by interpretation or augmentation. Yet nothing absolute has ever been said on the subject that went perceptibly beyond the prejudices or ambitions of a period, a nation, a species of litterateur, or a class of play-goers and readers. The very effort to define the limits of tragedy appears to have introduced more confusion into criticism and playwriting than it has eradicated. Surely, tragedy is never quite the same thing from place to place, from one playwright's work to another. Even Sophocles, the ideal tragedian of most critics, did not conform to any "tragic blueprint."

Only the most superficial reading could fail to disclose glaring differences between *Ajax* and *Antigone*. In the former, for example, the hero's *hamartia* is a decisive factor whereas the heroine's in the latter is of small consequence, if any. (And from one point of view she can be said to have none, while from another point of view her *hamartia* is her chief glory, and idealists or romanticists right up to Anouilh cannot but endorse it whereas the "tragic flaw" was surely not intended for praise, least of all in the *Ajax*.) How different, too, is tragedy if the model we take is *Oedipus at Colonus* rather than either of the aforementioned plays. And are there not differences between tragic form if the protagonist is overthrown, as in *Oedipus the King*, or triumphant, as in *Electra*. How insecure would be the tragic status of the latter if it had to be validated as a tragedy solely by analysis rather than by our feelings. The temptation to generalize has been too strong to be resisted by reasonably active critics. But we have reached such fluidity in theory and practice that a "new" *Poetics* could have

*John Gassner, "Tragic Perspectives: A Sequence of Queries," *Tulane Drama Review*, II (May, 1958), 7-22.

only a tangential relevance. It has always been necessary to evaluate plays as separate entities, [7/8] and we surely have more reason now than ever before to examine individual works with a view to ascertaining their uniqueness rather than degree of conformity to *genre*.

II

If it is no longer customary to lay down dogmatic principles for tragedy, there is still a tendency to cherish some "ideal" of tragedy. *Oedipus the King* represents it in Aristotle's thought and can still do so in the opinion of contemporary critics. Carried to the point of idolatry, however, respect for "ideal tragedy" becomes inhibitory. It conduces to the notion that a single work or single conception of drama contains all the possibilities of tragic art. This conclusion, latent in every definition of ideal tragedy (the definitions imply an ideal), is made absurd by the facts. *Hamlet* includes elements of tragic experience and perception not contained in *Oedipus the King*, just as Sophocles' play includes tragic qualities absent in *Hamlet*. And *Phèdre* has a concentration of feeling lacking in the *Hippolytus*, just as Euripides' play has a dimension of idea absent in Racine's. This much will probably be granted, but literary warfare is sure to be declared whenever we look to modern drama on its altitudes or plateaus. We are in difficulties, for instance, whenever we suggest that treatments of destructive femininity, such as *Hedda Gabler* and *The Father*, have added tragic elements not contained in the *Phèdre* and the *Hippolytus*. I would not hesitate to make this claim myself, with the understanding, of course, that the addition of a new dramatic element or dimension does not necessarily make a late play superior to an early one. It is even possible to assert that an Oedipus play so far below Sophocles' masterpiece as Cocteau's *The Infernal Machine* has enriched the tragic action in at least one respect; I refer to the psychological element—the fatal attraction of

Jocasta and Oedipus for each other—that deepens the husband-son and wife-mother relationship in the Cocteau version.

Another danger latent in idealization of *one* type of tragedy is the danger of our regarding every other kind of play as a necessary descent from some isolated individual achievement (*Oedipus the King*, probably) or some golden age (the fifth century Attic period, no doubt), never recovered or recoverable. This viewpoint seems to me altogether too rigid and fatalistic for dramatic art. Consistently maintained, this view would leave too little room for the appearance of *Hamlet*, *Macbeth*, or *King Lear* and the emergence of an Elizabethan age of tragedy two thousand years after the death of Sophocles. It would make the writing of "true" tragedy conditional upon the recovery of esthetic and social norms that prevailed only once, centuries or millenia ago. It would predicate failure for all contemporary efforts to attain tragic art and forbid the mobility that is the life of the theatre. [8/9]

III

A major source of error may be our tendency to certify one work as *more* tragic than another, as if quantitative measures could possibly be as valid in art as they are in physical science. To formulate judgments on the drama on this basis is to create a false hierarchy of values. For playwrights to think in terms of making themselves tragical at all is to court academicism in the worst sense of the term. It would encourage epigonal tendencies rather than the spontaneously creative spirit of the theatre. Maxwell Anderson has especially favored the epigonal approach in most of his verse plays, but his popular success with *Elizabeth the Queen* or *Mary of Scotland* has had no effect on dramatic writing in our time. He had a number of predecessors in the nineteenth century theatre such as George Henry Boker and Stephen Phillips, but none of these succeeded in revitalizing tragedy by adopting Elizabethan and romantic modes of drama. To worry about how much more tragic one piece is than another can be utterly misleading. A question not only relevant but seminal would be not "how much *more* tragic" but "how *differently* tragic."

Common sense would suggest, of course, that we employ a theory of limits as an alternative to dogmatism. That is, we are to assume that some dramatic works are completely tragic whereas other works are only incompletely so. And from this view it is only a step to predicating gradations of tragedy until we reach a borderline between the tragic and the melodramatic. If this meant nothing more than that we rate some tragedies higher than others there would be no problem of definition. We would be saying nothing more than that we like one play better than another because its content, structure, or style impresses us more. But if we say that we like one play better than another because it is "more tragic," or that one play is less meritorious than another because it is less tragic, then we only compound our difficulties in arriving at judgment.

In the first place, we omit too many values by making tragicality a major criterion. Maxwell Anderson's verse play *Elizabeth the Queen* meets many long-accepted criteria for tragedy. The exalted lovers Elizabeth and Essex have all the nobility, all the "tragic stature," that has long been required of the protagonists of a tragedy, and their action has "magnitude" in almost any sense of the term. A well defined *hamartia* produces the downfall of Essex and the unhappiness of the Queen. The "reversal of fortune" in their case is the most tragic of possible reversals. It is caused, moreover, by their own strong will; *proairesis* is in good order here, for the chief characters make critical choices and are highly aware of the consequences of their decisions; their *dianoia* and *ethos* dominate the action. Neither their intellectual nor ethical bent can be considered revolting, and their conduct does not outrage our sensi- [9/10]

bilities even at the point of highest tension. The "tragic rhythm" of "purpose, passion, and perception," Kenneth Burke's well known formulation, determines the movement of the action quite satisfactorily, and when Essex dies he departs from life in a manner obviously calculated to elevate the public. The "dignity of man" is affirmed by his refusal to save his neck, and I would suppose that an audience affected by Essex and Elizabeth about as much as the public was moved (by "pity" and "fear"?) when Alfred Lunt and Lynn Fontanne played the leading roles in the successful Theatre Guild production of 1930, would experience a *katharsis*—if, after having written extensively on the subject, we really knew what *katharsis* is.

We have no difficulty in certifying *Elizabeth the Queen* as a tragedy, whereas the same cannot be said of Euripides' *Electra*, at which we have looked askance for a long time. It does not, however, follow that the latter is the inferior—that is, the less penetrating and stirring—play. In calling *Electra* a melodrama in his noteworthy book on Greek tragedy, Professor Kitto did not indeed deny that the play had an excellence of its own that was not to be slighted simply because he would not validate it as a "tragedy." And, to move on to our own times, *A Streetcar Named Desire* is not to be considered inferior to *Elizabeth the Queen*.

It is entirely conceivable that a play may be non-tragic and yet more absorbing than a work we can easily certify as a tragedy. Can there be any doubt about this matter when we compare, let us say, the *Paolo and Francesca* of Stephen Phillips or any of the poetic tragedies of our English romantic and Victorian poets with *The Cherry Orchard*, which its author called a "Comedy," or *Juno and the Paycock*, in which the admixture of comic and tragic elements can be disconcerting only to purists. Then there are, of course, all the modern plays from *Ghosts* to *Death of a Salesman* whose tragic status has been sharply questioned; how shall we account for their relative excellence and their patent superiority to many tragedies? If there are more obvious reflections than these I am sure they have not occurred to me, but they remain heretical; they cannot be countenanced by those for whom tragedy is an honorific term. It would seem that they cannot abide the thought that a tragedy may be inferior to a non-tragic work. For them, above all, there seems to be no such thing as a *bad* tragedy, even if the Elizabethan and Jacobean theatre abounded with exalted rubbish, as did the neo-classic theatres of France, England, and Germany after *Athalie*. The manner of reasoning is flagrantly circular; it amounts to saying that if the play is bad it cannot be a tragedy, and if it is a tragedy it cannot be bad.

Reasoning of this sort turns "tragedy" into a value rather than a *genre*. A rejected tragedy is then called a "melodrama." Even though it is apparent that the authors of such plays as *The Spanish [10/11] Tragedy* or *The Revenger's Tragedy* had only the genre of tragedy in mind, it becomes necessary to find a separate pigeonhole for them in order to preserve the ideal of Tragedy from debasement or criticism. But what if we should differ as to the excellence of a play, then one man's tragedy will become another man's melodrama. John Webster was dismissed by Bernard Shaw as a "Tussaud laureate." Those who agree with this judgment and use the term tragedy honorifically have no choice but to deny that Webster was a tragic poet. The honorific view of tragedy, moreover, is conducive to imitative and inflationary writing. Why should Maxwell Anderson be made to think that he has to fit *Winterset* to the pattern of *Hamlet?* His first "journalistic" treatment of the Sacco and Vanzetti case, *Gods of the Lightning*, had a truer ring and possessed more integrity in action and dialogue than a play in which a gangster speaks diluted Elizabethan verse and a mobster-melodrama, combined with a jettisoned exposé of social injustice, blossoms at the end into a rabbinical sermon on the tragic dignity of man. And the *reductio ad absurdum* materializes when, having come to the conclusion that the writing of a social drama is not a passport to immortality, the playwright tries to make doubly or trebly sure that his treatment will have the requisite tragic "nobility" and "universality" by combining the *Hamlet* theme with the *Romeo and Juliet* and the "mad Lear" motifs that have been traced in *Winterset*. It is indeed a tribute to Maxwell Anderson's abilities that the fragments coalesce as well as they do and produce a tolerably unified impression. But the danger is manifest in trying to write tragedy as the high art that assures "significance," if not indeed immortality, instead of simply writing a play. Tragedy should be the end-result of a writer's struggle with his matter rather than a collection of previously assembled attitudes, caveats, and aspirations to which the playwright endeavors to conform with a view to uplifting the theatre.

IV

What is the use of devising finely ground definitions of tragedy unless they can be serviceable to one's own time?

I cannot but agree that the current definitions can increase our understanding and appreciation of the work of other periods than our own. Even a vital theatre has to rely on classics as well as on more or less newly hatched writing. Do the definitions help? To some degree they do in elementary approaches to specific plays. But never so much as the study of the play as a *play* rather than as a *tragedy*. Besides, there is little that is new or penetrating to be said about the masterpieces of the past by confining ourselves to *genre* or giving it preference over other considerations. What we can say about Euripides' *Electra* after noting that it is not a tragedy is more important, because it deals with more essential aspects of [11/12] the play, than does the mere "proof" that the play is untragic. It may have been more valuable and necessary to have written an untragic *Electra* at a certain point in the Attic period than to have written a version that would conform to conventional requirements for Tragedy. (Conventional requirements of a later period, of course. There is no evidence of rules in Euripides' time that invalidated unheroic, "clinical," or even tragicomic plays as "tragedy.") For an art to remain vital and to give birth to viable offspring it is necessary for it to be constantly violated.

Genre is, so to speak, an *a posteriori* postulate. First come the specific works, then comes the classification; and the classification undergoes modification in accordance with modifications in the works we presume to classify. *Genre* is something we can usually determine meaningfully only after we have noted enough significant resemblance between works that at the same time also display significant variety. And *genre* tends to stagnate unless an individual genius of a later period violates it, as he fortunately does from time to time. There is no surer way to destroy a genre than to venerate it. (What a holocaust in the English theatre from the veneration of blank-verse tragedy, for example!) What have we accomplished, besides, in determining that T. S. Eliot's *The Family Reunion* is a tragedy? The question of its merit or success as a play still remains to be determined, as would also be the case if we classified *The Family Reunion* as a "divine comedy" or a symbolic comedy of salvation. As Eliot discerned, the essential question, from the viewpoint of literature, would concern the texture of the writing; and the prime problem, so far as the theatre is concerned, would involve not the tragic quality of the theme and the main character, but the degree to which they have been credibly and vividly activated as an effective "imitation of an action."

Another concession I am prepared to make is that the tragic measure is a handy one to have around. With it we can threaten to take the height and width of some plays that have been stretched artificially by sensation-mongering play-wrights and stage directors. With it we can take soundings, too, to ascertain whether there is any depth in a contemporary work presented to us with an air of profundity, whereas there is usually a false bottom to it. For such purposes as these, it is good to have a measure that does not shrink opportunistically to suit the marketplaces of art, ideas and ethics. Our concept of tragedy must not be cheapened to conform to cheapness in our feelings, ideas, and social values. But opportunism is not the sole alternative to dogmatism, and works of art are never wholly measurable. The negative value of tragic absolutism in detecting false coinage is greater than its positive value. Above all, our problem is how to maintain reasonable standards without atrophying dramatic art by preventing the theatre from responding to new knowledge, new awareness, and new issues. Yes, [12/13] new *issues,* too, since "the universal" has to be embodied in the concrete if it is to be perceived at all as something more than an abstraction of little use to the theatre. Timeless drama, in an absolute sense, is a romantic delusion; issueless drama is an academic illusion.

Ultimately, we shall come to realize, I believe, that, so far as tragedy is concerned, no standard interpretation of the *Poetics* and no "new" *Poetics* will have positive value for us unless it can give support and guidance to our century's major ventures in serious playwriting—"psychological drama" and "social drama." Psychological and social elements we have always had in the drama. But in their proponderance since about 1870 they have eventuated as more or less distinct types of plays, and these have usually been denied certification (sometimes justly) as tragedies even when their action has included the extreme suffering or death of the protagonist. With validation, moreover, may come the clarification, as well as the encouragement, that will translate "psychology" and "journalism" into universal tragic terms—and this not by means of rhetorical inflation of language after evisceration of the psychological or social content. Acceptance of new knowledge need not compel abdication from tragic eminence if new knowledge can be assimilated into old principle.

A review of Ernest Jones's third volume of *The Life and Work of Sigmund Freud* (by David Baken in the December 9, 1957 issue of The New Republic) opens as follows:

Freud once wrote that the world had experienced blows to its narcissism: the cosmological blow from Copernicus, the biological blow at the hands at [sic] Darwin, and the psychological blow from psychoanalysis. Each of these, from the vantage point of 1957, has had a paradoxical effect. In spite of the seeming abasement of man, each has, in its turn, increased man's power over the forces that govern him, and has thus served to enhance man's dignity.

Combined with the greater sense of reality and the greater courage demanded of men deprived of comforting ignorance, the increase in man's awareness can be viewed as a factor in making tragic art more, rather than less, possible. "Blows to narcissism" may be interpreted as incentives, rather than deterrents, to tragic art. The tragic art of past ages would have been pinchbeck indeed if it had subsisted on our narcissism rather than on men's sense of reality and readiness to face it. (The many respects in which Tragedy is our most realistic art, indeed, would fill a separate long essay.) We can face reality—or at least we should be able to face it—even with new knowledge undermining old egotism and security. When everything else fails us, it may be that our oldest support—to wit, our sense of tragedy—will continue to prop us up. [13/14]

V

Why indeed cannot "social drama" *be* tragedy?

It can be that (and what does this mean other than that the work can have an effect called tragic . . .) if the protagonist looms humanly large among his fellow-creatures of the play and if his values, however deplorable in their particular results, magnify rather than diminish him as human being. If the sympathies asserted by the author favoring the common man and emphasizing social causation do not cheapen life! And if the struggle involving the principal characters has in view issues whose references are not less personal than social.

Hebbel's *Maria Magdalena,* which meets these provisions, is virtually the *locus classicus* of "social tragedy"—a term preferable in many ways to "middle-class tragedy" even though the milieu is indubitably that of the provincial bourgeoisie. So long as the individual is not dwarfed by the social analysis or transformed into the puppet of social forces, "theme" is in little danger of being reduced to "thesis." So long as theme is not whittled down to thesis, there is little danger of the characters being reduced to puppets. The real impediments to the writing of social drama are want of talent and want of intelligence. Want of talent will result in the absence of life in the work, in abortive character-creation or even total absence of individualization. Want of intelligence will result in failure to surmount thesis. The playwright will be incapable of realizing the implications of the social situation and of letting his mind carry the initial social issue beyond its journalistic immediacy. The playwright will see case histories rather than humanity, problems rather than the human condition; he will be unable to see the forest for the trees.

He will, we may also say, fail to apprehend the *moral* nature of the issues, contenting himself *exclusively* with their political and social character or their news value. The tragic imagination is essentially a moral one, though by no means a moralizing one—unless, as in the *Agamemnon,* the moralizer employs dramatic agents and his moral is the dramatic action itself.

One reason why so spirited a social drama as John Wexley's Scottsboro case play about racial prejudice, *They Shall Not Die,* could not be tragedy is that the author seemed to be content with indignation instead of being willing to give scope to the moral imagination. Mr. Wexley expressed his sense of morality in attacking social injustice with vigor and clarity; beyond that he did not go and, considering the vogue of propaganda-drama in the nineteen-thirties, did not think it necessary to go. Indignation carries us only as far as condemnation, as a result of which we are enabled only to see the issue, the victim, and the culprit rather than human beings. Imagination begins where the clear-cut issue fades, where "Victim" and "Culprit" conclude their roles and begin to live, [14/15] ideally also acquiring some degree of insight as sentient and rational members of the human race.

The great limitation of our writers of ordinary social drama has been a limitation of the creative imagination, which is also a limitation of moral insight. Condemnation is especially limiting because it simplifies everything to the point of banality. The greatest of all moral tragedians was Aeschylus. But Aeschylus would have had little stature as a tragic poet if the *Agamemnon* had amounted to nothing more than a demonstration that it is wrong for a woman to murder her husband, or if the *raison d'etre* of *The Libation Bringers* had been simply to assure Greek audiences that it is a crime to kill one's mother. Too many modern social dramas have been focussed on the demonstration of the obvious, too much effort has been expended upon proving that which it requires no creative effort to prove. The moral imagination is a form of understanding, whereas indignation is judgment signed and sealed. Tragedy, with its largeness of spirit, is an estate possible to social drama whenever the moral imagination takes precedence over the indictments humanity invites at all times and never more so than during the travail of social and political transitions.

Even thesis drama is not unalterably antipodal to tragedy, as the Oresteian trilogy alone would suggest. But theme and thesis must then be fused in one imaginative conception, so that "myth" and "argument" become the same thing, as in the Oresteian trilogy or in *Hippolytus* and *The Bacchae*. (That is, if we can agree that these are thesis plays in which Aphrodite and Dionysus symbolize natural forces that wreak destruction when denied and thwarted.) The difficulty of perceiving tragic possibilities in thesis drama has been due largely to the fact that thesis is the prose of drama whereas tragedy is its poetry. The difficulty vanishes when the prose of argument is interfused with the poetry of feeling. Whenever that is the rare case, as it is in Tolstoy's peasant-drama *The Power of Darkness*, it should not be anomalous to actually speak of "thesis tragedy."

Another difficulty has been the tendency in thesis drama—indeed, generally in modern social drama—to present error and suffering as wholly eradicable by legislation or by a formal change in opinion, custom, or education, and as neither involving any fundamental change in human nature nor encountering human nature as an insuperable obstacle. Or, for that matter, encountering other impediments of a non-sociological character such as moral law, divine caprice, Tychê, or Fate in the universe.

Genuine tragedy has always been more realistic than melioristic drama—or, for that matter, than moralistic drama. Tragedy has extended recognition to a "built-in" capacity for disaster in man and his world, and tragedians have given evidence of knowing that [15/16] life has its "impossibilities" whereas reformers have ever been concerned, as they should be, with life's "possibilities." Tragedy may therefore be less *useful* than comedy, farce, and even melodrama. And the tragic sense of life might well be useless to humanity in periods of moral reformation, uplift, and reorganization, as in the period of the establishment of the Christian Church. Had there been any vogue of tragedy in St. Augustine's time, the great Bishop of Hippo would probably have had to regard it as subversive as Manicheism, unless he could have moralized tragedy and employed it to demonstrate "original sin." The author of the *Confessions* might well have done so, but original sin is, of course, precisely what modern progressive writers, scions of the 18th century Enlightenment, would have discounted before undertaking to produce thesis drama. Tragedy indeed may be the one luxury a society urgently in need of reformation cannot afford. Only perhaps to discover, after piling up blasted hopes, that tragedy is the one luxury it *can* afford!

VI

Realism? It is often maintained that the vogue of realism has destroyed tragic drama. But can we really place the onus on *realism of outlook,* which is the essence of the tragic sense of life? It is true that some contemporaries write about tragedy as though its outlook had to be almost desperately romantic. They give that impression when they refer to tragic art as idealistic, spiritual, elevating, or consolatory. Maxwell Anderson, for instance, sounded a familiar note in *The Essence of Tragedy* by declaring that the tragedian "must so arrange his story that it will prove to the audience that men pass through suffering purified, that, animal though we are, despicable though we are in many ways, there is in us all some divine, incalculable fire that urges us to be better than we are." And other writers, practicing critics such as Joseph Wood Krutch and John Mason Brown among them, have entertained more or less romantic interpretations, with the former going so far in *The Modern Temper* as to regard the tragic outlook as *ersatz*-belief for the religious faith that scientific thought has allegedly made untenable. Yet no one has seriously invalidated the hard realism of tragedy that connects life with suffering, crime with expiation, disequilibrium (in the individual and in society) with painfully arrived at restorations of equilibrium. Even the most romantically disposed writers would agree that nobody

escapes from the consequences of his conduct and that even the "innocent" may suffer (from the disorder of other individuals or the disorder of the world) in tragic drama.

"Realism" is held culpable, in the main, as the literary and theatrical movement that has given primacy to *verisimilitude, illusionism,* and *intellectualism* or *rationalism*. There is something to [16/17] this indictment, which is not of recent origin in fact; it was made as early as the last quarter of the fifth century B.C. and applied to Euripides. Yet the indictment is not really air-tight. *Verisimilitude* is not intrinsically anti-tragic. What did the Greek audiences get when they saw the blinded Oedipus or the Furies at the close of *The Libation Bringers* but verisimilitude? And consider the impact of Lear's dying line, "Pray you, undo this button." *Illusionism* is something even the Attic and Elizabethan, not to mention the French neo-classic and the Baroque, stages endeavored to effectuate in some respects. Illusionism, like verisimilitude, is a highly relativistic concept. Technical devices and a manner of acting that would strike us as anything but illusionistic today provided sufficient "illusion of reality" for their own times. Garrick's Shakespearian acting would undoubtedly impress us as exaggerated or "ham", whereas his contemporaries acclaimed it as the high-water mark of realistic performance. *Intellectualism* or *rationalism* is not inconsistent with passionateness or with a concern with the passions, as the example of Euripides and Racine would go far to prove. Did not Aristotle, who would have been the last person in Greece to overlook Euripides' intellectualism, call him the "most tragic" of the Greek poets.

What else has realism been blamed for? *Prose drama* and the so-called *fourth-wall convention*. But do these factors really destroy the possibility of writing tragedy? As for prose drama, the fact that it came into vogue long before Ibsen introduced genuine realism into the theatre is to be considered. To be considered, too, is the fact that the prevalence of verse drama has not assured the successful writing of tragedy in many periods. *Verse* may provide a certain degree of formalism that can dignify a dramatic composition and provide considerably more "esthetic distance" than colloquial prose can do. But tragedy needs a great deal more than "dignity" and "esthetic distance." Much formalistic drama has been patently untragic. Formalism may even militate against the art of tragedy by destroying the reality of the characters through whose agony and its consequences tragedy is produced. *Poetry* is another matter: Its absence is apt to be accompanied by lack of imaginativeness, universalization, and "reverberation" (the failure of the surface action to start vibrations below and above the surface), and without these qualities a play, however serious and catastrophic the action, will be untragic. But it is no secret that it has been possible to write poetic drama without composing dialogue in verse. And realism, far from discouraging poetic prose in the theatre has been favorable to its employment, as may be observed in plays by Chekhov, Synge, O'Casey, Maeterlinck, Andreyev, Masefield, Lorca, Obey, Giraudoux, Anouilh, Zuckmayer, and many others. For anyone familiar with their writings, the charge that realism, or "naturalism," destroyed poetic writings in [17/18] the theatre must seem a tiresome canard. Those who persist in making the charge draw up their indictment on insufficient evidence.

As for the "fourth-wall" convention of realism, it may have limited the articulateness of dramatic characters by virtually outlawing soliloquies. Hamlet without his soliloquies would certainly be that much less than Hamlet. But it does not follow that articulateness in the theatre depends upon the actor's addressing the audience directly. Too much blame has been attached to the fourth-wall convention that bans direct address.

As a matter of fact, a psychological wall between the drama's characters and the drama's audiences was bound to be established in almost any sort of theatre the moment the actors played a scene with each other. Nor has it mattered much whether the play has been staged in the open or in an enclosed theatre, within a box-set or on a platform stage, with scenery or without, and whether or not there were three other "walls." The moment the actors are "in scene" or, shall we say, "in action"—the moment they are truly interacting—they belong to themselves and not to the public, so that they are psychologically shut off from those who watch the performance. Actors indeed have had to especially stylize their performance, they have had to adopt a "sophisticated" attitude and break their concentration upon each other in order to speak to the audience. They used to violate their self-containedness and break through the psychological wall only by employing "asides," a crude device at best for tragedy.

In tragedy, the characters play "for keeps" rather than for the audience. With few exceptions, such as Iago's and Richard III's speeches, in which the effect is one of wit or comedy however sultry or diabolical, even the soliloquies are likely to establish a wall around the character. "To be or not to be" or "Tomorrow and tomorrow and tomorrow" and similar speeches were surely not intended to be plumped into the lap of the audience as a bouquet. The characters are perhaps never more isolated than when they give their soliloquies, and the isolation of the protagonist has contributed greatly to the power and significance of tragedy. Great tragedians such as Sophocles, Shakespeare, and Racine appear to have made a special effort to effect the "tragic isolation" of their protagonists. We may observe, for example, the lack of rapport between Antigone and the Chorus or between Hamlet and his mother. Isolation is also an integral factor in minor tragedies such as Schiller's *Maria Stuart* and *Wallensteins Tod*. But it is unnecessary to pursue this argument further when it is apparent that expressiveness can be achieved *without* soliloquy. If necessary, the protagonist can address himself even at great length to other characters, as Hickey does in a fifteen-minute harangue to his friends in *The Iceman Cometh.* This monologue, [18/19] and the actor delivers it without any need to address the audience, is the most memorable episode of O'Neill's play, which is never more genuinely tragic than at that point. Dialogue, of course, invariably allows expression of viewpoint or of inner stress at considerable length behind the "wall." Anouilh, who did not hesitate to reach across the proscenium arch and break the "picture-frame" in his *Antigone* with a Narrator who even lectures the audience on the subject of Tragedy, actually reached the peak of his effectiveness in the play with a behind-the-fourth-wall discussion between the heroine and Creon.

So much for regarding the "fourth wall" as an impediment to tragedy. There is no reason to fear that the protagonist's *état d'âme* will remain hidden behind that "wall." The really pertinent question is whether the playwright actually has an *état d'âme* to express or one that is interesting enough to be worth expressing.

That question is another matter, and much thought has been expended upon it. Joseph Wood Krutch's essay "The Tragic Fallacy," published in 1920 in *The Modern Temper,* expressed doubts as to the survival of the tragic spirit in the modern world, and it has not yet been possible to allay them entirely. Into the quicksands of that controversy, which would entail evaluations of the "modern soul," few of us can venture with any competence. I am sure *I* cannot. But I doubt that realism *per se* must destroy the "tragic spirit"; the realism of Tolstoy and Dostoevsky, surely the greatest literary realism of the past century, did not do so. Realism can be considered intrinsically anti-tragic only by identifying it narrowly with materialism and mechanism, an identification that literary realists have never really had to accept and that exponents of contemporary scientific philosophy have actually rejected. Besides, man is often a paradox; the less reason he has to think

well of himself the better he thinks of himself. Men did not consider themselves insignificant even when nineteenth-century mechanism and determinism found the widest theoretical acceptance.

The resilience of the human spirit tends to be underestimated whenever we assert that this or that outlook, this or that philosophy, is destroying man's "tragic sense of life." It is certainly true, moreover, that the tragic character has been a paradox in any case; with his noble and ignoble elements existing in delicate balance he could hardly be anything else. If a particular era, our own not the least, depletes the supply of tragic values available to a generation, the talented playwright's sympathy and insight can still supply restorative and redemptive elements. He may, of course, be under the influence of his times, but no creative writer is exclusively under that influence. He may be the child of his own age, but he is also the proud heir of past ages of humanism. The creation [19/20] of art is not a conditioned reflex. Tragedy especially must be thought of as a thing consciously *made*—made by the tragedian in collaboration with the whole human estate as well as with his age. And the tragic character, incidentally, is usually shown *making himself tragic* or, as in the case of Oedipus, making himself more tragic.

Still, in representing inner conflicts or in clashing with characters holding opposed values, the protagonist brings the common and ignoble elements of a society, as well as of human nature, into the tragic action. Every age, in brief, contributes its meanness as well as its nobility to the tragedies written in its time. The meanness and the gross values of our own age, I would conclude, cannot be regarded as an inexorable injunction against the existence of tragic art. The meanness and evil of modern times, on the contrary, *belong* to modern tragedy, just as the deplorable aspects of the Renaissance belonged to Elizabethan tragedy.

Without incorporating the unadmirable qualities of men and their times, indeed, tragic literature would be literature in a void. We tend to see the heroic element without the antiheroic in the old masterpieces. We ennoble the "tragic flaw" and play down that which is shameful about it or about the milieu that produced it. I like, therefore, Cedric Whitman's reference to "the self-slain greatness" of the tragic character and William McCollom's statement in his recent book, *Tragedy* (page 167), that "the hero's shame is the corollary of his genius." But the role of the "unnoble" element in drama has yet to be explored. We have to pick up the clue that Nietzsche left us in juxtaposing Dionysian and Apollonian aspects in *The Birth of Tragedy*.

The heroic element or the "genius" of the tragic character should, of course, also receive due weight. But we must come to understand it a little better than we usually do in the case of contemporary characters such as Willy Loman, the salesman-hero of *Death of a Salesman*. Arthur Miller has insisted upon the tragic worth of this greatly flawed character, and anybody familiar with the struggles of the little man and not too sheltered or snobbish to be capable of sympathy should know what heroism is required of the Willy Lomans of the world. Or if this appeal is too "common" for some members of the literary and academic world perhaps they will respond to the monitions of the poem by Goethe in which admission to the Moslem paradise of heroes is claimed on the grounds that it was heroic enough to be a human being. Willy Loman indeed makes himself a tragic hero of sorts by his abundant capacity for suffering in the present action; by his fine resentment of slights, by his battle for self-respect, and by his refusal to surrender all expectations of triumph for, and through, his son. Willy is passionately unwilling to resign himself to failure and the cheat of days. His very agony gives him tragic stature within the recog- [20/21] nizable world of middle-class realities, and it is surely true that the tragic hero is not tragic by status prior to his action in a play. Tragedy is no one's prerogative; it is, rather, *earned* damnation and redemption. The tragic hero *makes himself* tragic—by his struggle and suffering.

Moreover, he makes himself tragic *differently* in different societies. Even awareness on the hero's part, the "tragic awareness" upon which so much stress has been placed of late, is bound to be different in the case of different characters differently conditioned by the social situation. Miller would be justified in insisting that, within limits that are themselves valid dramatic factors in *Death of a Salesman*, Willy does arrive at self-realization—that is, at a degree of self-realization that can be convincingly Willy's. And I, for one, fail to perceive any virtue in recognitions that are conspicuously out of character and have been imposed upon the play from without—that is, from the author's philosophy of tragedy or from "literature," as in the case of *Winterset*.

The most convincing and, to my mind, also the most significant characters make themselves tragic in collaboration with their world. In tragedy, as William McCollom has rightly observed, there is both "self-determination" and "social determination." In various scenes set in the present and the past, Willy seeks the truth about himself and his situation. The search is his, for we must not ignore the fact that all the flashbacks and hallucinations in *Death of a Salesman* are in Willy's own anguished consciousness. Willy pursues the "truth" and struggles against it within his personal and social limits no less arduously and catastrophically than Oedipus. It is possible to say, then, that Miller's protagonist brings both personal and social meanness into his play, but that he also brings personal stature and heroism into it.

The one thing Miller could not do—that Miller's scrupulousness indeed would not have allowed him to do—is to give Willy *an interesting mind*. And it is chiefly this limitation, along with a limitation of language (because the character is an urban commoner while the author is rarely a poet), that has made me contemplate the use of such a term as "low tragedy," my intention being to distinguish modern democratic drama from the aristocratic "high tragedy" of earlier ages. Perhaps indeed the genius of our century resides precisely in "low tragedy," if we are to allow ourselves a generalization concerning the taste and aptitude of the age. For there is a difference in the degree of tragic exaltation and exhilaration, of tragic realization and liberation or catharsis, as well as a difference in tone such as appears when we contrast the relative informality of discourse by a Giraudoux or Cocteau with tragic dialogue by Marlowe, Shakespeare, and Racine. "Low tragedy" is the only term that seems sufficiently descriptive of *The Lower Depths* and *The Iceman Cometh, The Tragedy of Nan* and [21/22] *Desire Under the Elms, The Three Sisters* and *The House of Bernarda Alba, The Weavers* and *The Plough and the Stars, Drayman Henschel* and *Death of a Salesman, Rosmersholm* and *John Gabriel Borkman,* and even Giraudoux' *Electra* and Cocteau's *The Infernal Machine.*

If "low tragedy" were employed descriptively rather than pejoratively, it could become useful in calling attention to a modern type of tragedy different from the typical forms of classic and Elizabethan tragic writing. And surely the term does not have to be derogatory; powerful dramatic impressions have been created, for instance, by O'Casey's colloquial passionateness and O'Neill's prosaic masonry. When I use the terms "low comedy" and "high comedy" to describe the work of Plautus and Terence respectively, I certainly do not intend a slur on Plautine comedy. It is possible to describe differences without establishing hierarchies. And when I nevertheless, accept the superiority of *Hamlet* to, let us say, *Death of a Salesman,* it is not because I think of Shakespeare's tragedy as "more tragic," but because I consider it more expressive, and *more beautiful.*

Tragedy and the American Climate of Opinion*

ORRIN E. KLAPP is Professor of Sociology at San Diego State College. His professional interest prompts him, in this article, to consider tragedy in a specifically American context and from the point of view of a sociologist rather than of a literary critic.

America has always taken tragedy lightly. Too busy to stop the activity of their twenty-million-horse-power society, Americans ignore tragic motives that would have overshadowed the Middle Ages; and the world learns to regard assassination as a form of hysteria, and death as a neurosis, to be treated by a rest-cure. Three hideous political murders, that would have fattened the Eumenides with horror, have thrown scarcely a shadow on the White House.—HENRY ADAMS

I

It has sometimes been remarked that Americans have a kind of armor against tragic experience. Courage, optimism, realism, the Pollyanna spirit—what should it be called? "Somehow missing from this land of plenty," says Norbert Wiener, is an awareness that "the world is not a pleasant little nest made for our protection, but a vast and largely hostile environment, in which we can achieve great things only by defying the gods; and that this defiance inevitably brings its own punishment."[1] We have our share of troubles, to be sure, but without the conviction that trouble is permanent and necessary; rather, it is an exceptional phenomenon that we must be good sports to face when it comes and work hard to eliminate as soon as possible. A poll would easily show [396/397] that most Americans think of tragedy simply as fortuitous. Other typical attitudes support this general view: we should accentuate the positive and not dwell on the gloomy side, religion should make us happy,[2] stories should come out all right in the end. We are not, then (as Edith Hamilton said of the Greeks and Miguel Unamuno of the Spanish), a tragic people.

Probably this is why, though such plays are part of our cultural inheritance, they cannot be said to have much popular appeal. You could watch movies and television continuously for a month and not see a single example of tragedy, properly speaking.[3] One student of the mass mind, Leo Gurko, claims, however, that the success now and then of movies like *Hamlet* or Broadway plays like *A Streetcar Named Desire* is proof of a hunger for mature art in the general public.[4] I would like to believe it but would be more convinced by his argument if the evidence of demand were clearer in the popular media. How many movie stars may be called tragedians?

The lack of tragedy in America is the

[1]*The Human Use of Human Beings* (New York: Houghton Mifflin, 1954), pp. 183-184.
[2]Paul Hutchinson, for instance, deplores the "cult of reassurance" that has so largely taken the place of the tragic conception of Christianity, in "Have We a 'New' Religion?," *Life*, April 11, 1955, pp. 138ff. See also Reinhold Niebuhr, *Beyond Tragedy* (New York: Charles Scribner's Sons, 1955).
[3]American movies, say Martha Wolfenstein and Nathan Leites, are shallow emotionally, however many great lovers and gunmen stalk the stage. Love is easily transferred and does not commit one to tragic consequences; crises take the form of external, not inner, conflict, in which winning is all-important and suffering is "pointless and unnecessary,"—*Movies, A Psychological Study* (Glencoe, Illinois: Free Press, 1950), pp. 94-99, 295-301.
[4]Leo Gurko, *Heroes, Highbrows and the Popular Mind* (Indianapolis: Bobbs-Merrill, 1953), pp. 198, 302-304.

*Orrin E. Klapp, "Tragedy and the American Climate of Opinion," *Centennial Review of Arts and Sciences*, II (Fall, 1958), 396-413.

more curious when we consider that it is a *pleasure* we are missing. Those who may claim to understand it say that it is one of the keenest joys of the spirit to see a man plunge into a course of suffering from which he does not choose to escape. Edith Hamilton, indeed, states the paradox that "the greater the suffering, the more terrible the events, the more intense our pleasure." This joy has been described by Joseph Wood Krutch as an **[397/398]** *elation* based on confidence in the greatness of man, from having watched him pass through mighty passions with supreme fortitude; and by Shelley as an exalted *calm* in which there is neither censure nor hatred but only knowledge and self-respect. If calm and elation are the products of tragedy, then why does it not rank with tranquillizing pills as a commodity on the American market? The same needs that favored the vogue of "peace of mind" books should make it a popular art form. It should be on a par with westerns and musical comedies. It should sell soap on the radio theatre. It should play a prominent part in American religion. But it clearly does none of these things. The explanation must be that the needs served by tragedy are different from those served by comfort; that the words like joy, calm, and elation are perhaps inadequate to convey to our minds what tragic satisfaction consists of —that the difficulty is semantic and ultimately cultural. We simply do not have a culture in which tragedy makes much sense.

Two main questions, then, emerge. First, what difference does it make, after all, whether or not Americans understand tragedy? The other requires an explanation: what are the elements of culture, or, as Kurt Lewin calls it, social climate, that stand in the way of the proper appreciation of this kind of art and its hero?

II

As to whether it makes any difference, there is an impressive number of thinkers like C. E. M. Joad, Reinhold Niebuhr, Paul Hutchinson, and J. W. Krutch, to name a few, who are concerned about the moral implications of the lack of tragedy. They see an impoverishment of spirit inherent in the inability to see positive value in tragedy and its hero. Their concern, it need hardly be said, is not whether Americans will lose a pleasure, but whether they will sacrifice the hard-won maturity, wisdom, and religious understanding that seem **[398/399]** somehow connected with the fate of the tragic hero. There is a political issue, too, best shown in novels like Huxley's *Brave New World* and Orwell's *Nineteen Eighty-Four*; that is, what kind of relation of man-to-man and state-to-man is implicit in an attitude lacking the tragic sense. Since tragedy is at the same time a check on pride and a testimony of human dignity, we may be fearful that without this perspective, leaders may act with too much assurance that they are right and with too little respect for the individuals under them.

It is to the underlying cultural and semantic problem, however, that I wish to give most attention here—to find out more about how and why the tragic hero is *misunderstood* in America. At the center of the problem, it seems to me, is the fact that the average American does not get the happiness—the sense of triumph, affirmation, and understanding—that experts say he should out of this kind of experience. So we may judge that he misinterprets it. And by looking at American culture and studying the reactions of audiences we may hope to see what it is that stands in the way of adequate understanding. My thesis is that there are three main reasons: (1) a stock of cultural images (social types) that displace or inhibit tragic perception; (2) an unfavorable climate of opinion and belief; and (3) an actual shrinkage that has occurred in the stature of the heroes being presented, making it easier to fail to see them as having the dignity necessary to be tragic.

On the score of competing cultural images, let us first look at some of the conceptions, the popular types, that stand in the way of tragic understanding. Because of their partial resemblance to the tragic figure, they may easily be assigned to any man who gets himself into serious trouble, and thus prevent people from seeing him in what may be called a deeper way. And because they are themselves appealing, they are interesting enough to steal the show from the tragic hero. One of these competing types is the *victim*, the sufferer of a disaster or wrong. While he gets plenty of sympathy, he is [399/400] too innocent to be tragic: he lacks willful fault and inner conflict; he has not brought the trouble on himself; and so we feel only a melodramatic conflict between him and the villains or forces that have harmed him. The *soap opera heroine* suffers also, to be sure; but she also is melodramatic, rather like the victim, basically good, for whom in this case things work out well in the end. These features disqualify her as a tragic heroine. The *martyr,* too, suffers, but his is a willing and knowing sacrifice for a noble cause; he, too, is a melodramatic hero in conflict with villains; and on both counts he is too good, too "perfect," to be tragic. (On this reasoning, the death of Jesus is not a tragedy, strictly speaking,[5] nor is that of Joan of Arc, Nathan Hale, or any other noble soul who dies for a cause. They are simply too good in their crucial acts; they have not the flaws you find in an Othello, a Macbeth.) The *villain* suffers also; but he is not tragic because we are glad of what he gets, more or less; he is too bad to deserve much sympathy. When newspapers report that gangsters shoot one another, we are likely to say, not "tragic" but "so much the better." Yet many a man whom we write off as a villain might have been tragic if we had looked at him a little more closely. Still another figure competing with the tragic hero is the *daredevil,* who courts death and sometimes provides a morbid thrill at the curve of the racetrack. His smash-up is akin to disaster if it affects the audience, or to folly if the actor kills only himself. In the latter case, he is a fool, at a far pole from the tragic hero. Then there is the patho-

logical *case,* a person who comes to ruin because of sickness or insanity. However horrible such an end may be, [400/401] it has nothing of the essentially tragic, because, for one thing, it is not voluntary, and if we sympathize at all, it is as with a victim. Besides, if we see such a man as a crackpot or other kind of mental deviant, his abnormality works against tragic compassion; instead of sympathizing, more than likely we will be repelled. Finally, among all the other types competing with the tragic figure for popular interest and understanding must be mentioned the outright *fool,* who gets himself into absurd or disgraceful trouble; he suffers, to be sure, but usually receives more laughter than sympathy.[6]

With such a repertory of distracting types, it is small wonder that when a real tragic figure appears he is misunderstood. It is so easy to think of him in terms of these other types! How many times, for instance, has Hamlet been called a dreamer who couldn't make up his mind?—or psychoanalyzed to the point that he became a "case," and his tragic dignity disappeared into an Oedipus complex? Madame Bovary is strictly a tragic character, but many of us are tempted to classify her as either a very foolish or a very bad woman. Or, in the case of someone like Othello, we may lay all the blame on a villain who got him into trouble; we see him merely as a victim; and thus we deprive him of guilt and conflict. In other words, because we are used to thinking in terms like "villain," "fool," and other types with which our culture provides us, we easily miscast the tragic hero.

[5]"Jesus is, superficially considered, a tragic figure; yet not really so. Christianity is a religion which transcends tragedy. Tears, with death, are swallowed up in victory. The cross is not tragic but the resolution of tragedy. . . . Christianity's view of history is tragic insofar as it recognizes evil as an inevitable concomitant of even the highest spiritual enterprises. It is beyond tragedy inasfar as it does not regard evil as inherent in existence itself but as finally under the dominion of a good God."—Reinhold Niebuhr, *Beyond Tragedy* (New York: Charles Scribner's Sons, 1937, 1955), pp. 155, x-xi.
[6]Viewed in terms of his social status, he is a ridiculed figure. See my "The Fool as a Social Type," *American Journal of Sociology,* LV (1949), 157-162; also Enid Welsford's excellent study, *The Fool, His Social and Literary History* (London, 1935).

These misunderstandings may be of some help, however, in seeing, by contrast, what a tragic hero ought to be. He should be a complex figure, whose self-imposed punishment and conflict within challenge our compassion and understanding. He must (however foolish or wicked his course of action may superficially seem) keep his dignity and remain heroic. Any tendency to "write him off" as a fool, no-account, mental [401/402] case, etc., is a sign of failure of understanding; so, also, is it to simplify him in the opposite way, to a point where he is all good, others are to blame, and he has no inner conflict.

If such are the miscastings likely to happen because of competing types in American culture, let us look at actual responses of audiences to tragedies, both in real life (news) and in art. By asking people what they think about a character and his fate, it is possible to analyze the main perceptual images and decide whether he is being understood or misunderstood, and in what ways.

First, an interpretation by a group of college students of news-stories of real life "tragedies," as they might be called in ordinary parlance. Two of these appeared on the same day in a local paper: one of a deserted husband who ran amok and killed his children; the other of a jealous ex-husband who dogged the life of his divorced wife, finally entered her apartment, and shot her, then himself. I discussed them with the group on the day they were reported. The interpretations were on the surface different. There was consensus that killer #1 was a poor fellow driven out of his mind by his wife's meanness; #2 was simply a villain and no sympathy was shown him. The main reason for this difference seems to have been the way the news was reported. An interview in the papers had brought out #1's point of view, telling how his wife had wronged him, showing her, in other words, as the villain, him as the victim. There had been no such interview, however, with the dead #2: only the external features of the crime were reported; so he

remained a villain though his crime was somewhat less serious in terms of numbers of people injured. Did killer #1 become tragic, then, in escaping from the villain's part? On the contrary, *neither* of the interpretations could properly be called tragic. It was simply a case of locating the villain. I cite these cases to show how hard it is to develop—one might say manufacture—such a complex viewpoint toward reality without a favorable cul-[402/403]ture and suitable art form to, as it were, blow up the experience to bigger than life-size.[7] All of the elements of a classic tragedy—a *Hercules Distracted,* an *Othello*—were there, no doubt, if one could only see them. But under the perceptual conditions of American culture, it is so much easier to see the simpler types of villain, victim, fool, and so on. In case #1 (which came closer to being tragic), sympathy had merely shunted from the victims to the killer (as a sick man, who became another victim), and hatred and blame had transferred to his wife. The basic melodramatic pattern remained.

But, you may say, it is too much to expect of any audience that they will see in raw facts—especially such as can be gotten from news reports—the elements of tragedy well enough to get the right feeling. The important question is, what do they see in an ideal drama, where the meaning and impact have been heightened by an artist?

I have, in fact, also discussed classic tragedies with adult groups after a recent reading. My experience has been (and I

[7] As Lord Chesterfield said, "Tragedy must be bigger than life, or it would not affect us." Behind this is the assumption that tragedy is not something that people just naturally grasp, but is a complex perception made possible by a set of cultural conditions and an invention—a device, an art form, for improving our perception of reality by enlarging certain aspects of it. So it is a contrived thing, unlikely to happen without the help of an artist. Since it is an invention, we do not expect a people to have tragedy, however hard their lot, unless they have borrowed or inherited it. This seems to accord with the fact that the distribution of tragedy is limited: the outlook of primitive peoples, judging by their tales and myths, is generally melodramatic; some advanced civilizations, such as India, are without the tragic sense; there have been only two great centers of tragic development, ancient Greece and Elizabethan England, both in the Western tradition.

wonder how many teachers of literature will agree with me) that when people know it is a classic they are talking about, they make an effort to understand it according to the approved literary formulas, but, when the amenities are done, they usually get around to finding fault with the hero. There seems to be a need to blame him as a villain, or to escape involvement with him by calling him a fool, or to see him as a victim and put the blame on somebody else. This re- [403/404] action is entirely consistent, as I see it, with my remarks about the armor that Americans have against tragic experience.

To find out more about this, especially the ways in which they were interpreting the hero and the extent to which alienation from him might be felt, I made a thematic analysis of responses to tragedy, asking 134 college students to choose a play or story with which they were familiar from a list of twenty well-known ones,[8] ranging from Sophocles' *Oedipus* to modern ones by O'Neill, Dreiser, Anderson, Williams, and Miller. Twenty-five of the students had seen the J. Arthur Rank production of *Romeo and Juliet* within a week and chose this for interpretation.

Let us look first at the side which is favorable to the appreciation of tragedy. More than half said "a deeply significant and worthwhile experience" (61%); "symbolic of the experience of mankind" (53%). Somewhat less than half said "sympathize deeply with the hero" (43%); "a better-than-average person who displayed along with merits a serious fault or mistake" (44%). A third thought of the protagonist as "basically heroic" (30%); a fourth as "an admirable person" (25%). A fourth thought that the story had "a terrible but noble ending" (28%). Only a fifth thought the play demonstrated the "fortitude and dignity of the central character" (18%), and a sixth that it showed "the frailty of even strong or worthy people" (16%). These, of course, are not necessarily responses to tragedy as such, but they could be; they are [at] least oriented in that direction.

Much of this sympathy, however, is for that special kind [404/405] of misunderstanding of tragedy that we have designated as martyrdom, for over a fourth saw the hero as "a kind of martyr for a social cause or value" (28%), and more sympathy is for the helpless victim, as shown below.

Many showed signs of missing the point and substituting an inadequate conception; for instance: "could have avoided trouble if he had used more sense" (53%) seems to imply that he is a fool and that the ending should have been happy (i.e., would have been but for his bungling). So does: "he brought it all on himself through mistakes or weaknesses" (40%). Throwing reproach on the hero tends to alienate the audience from him; he has spoilt the story as they expected it to work out. They leave him, so to speak, to stew in his own juice.

Very few, however, condemned him as an outright villain (7%). About half, on the contrary, "pitied him" (52%), as a "victim, helpless and not to blame for most of what happened" (45%). Some said "people took advantage of him or got him into trouble" (16%), or that he was "a good person injured by bad persons" (13%). These remarks excuse him, no doubt. But do they not do so by weakening him?

About one out of five were simply alienated by the story. It was: "something that shouldn't have happened" (20%), a "gloomy and unpleasant story" (19%), "a pointless catastrophe" (12%); it "would have been better if it had ended more happily" (11%). Nineteen per cent were indifferent to or repelled by the hero.

As you see, many of these responses

---

[8]The heroes rated were: Willy Loman in *Death of a Salesman* by Arthur Miller, Blanche DuBois in *A Streetcar Named Desire* by Tennessee Williams, Romeo in *Romeo and Juliet*, Hamlet, Macbeth, Mio in *Winterset* by Sherwood Anderson, Emperor Jones in *Emperor Jones* by Eugene O'Neill, Clyde Griffiths in *An American Tragedy* by Theodore Dreiser, Captain Ahab in *Moby Dick* by Herman Melville, Mrs. Alving in *Ghosts* by Henrik Ibsen, Hedda Gabler in *Hedda Gabler* by Henrik Ibsen, Raskolnikov in *Crime and Punishment* by Dostoyevski, Brutus in *Julius Caesar* by Shakespeare, King Lear, Antigone in *Antigone* by Sophocles, Orestes in *Electra* by Sophocles, Medea in *Medea* by Euripedes, and Phaedra in *Phaedra* by Racine.

appear to fall short of a tragic interpretation. Those who are alienated or see the story as just something that shouldn't have happened fall into this category. So also do those who weaken the hero till he is only a victim or a fool, since they rob him of dignity and free will. Less than half would grant that he was a better-than-average person, showing that in the eyes of many the tragedy endowed the sufferer with no special stature—that [405/406] his manner of bearing misfortune was no better than that of anybody else. Those who melodramatized him as a martyr (about a third) generated sympathy at the expense of tragic insight, since, as we have seen, the martyr concept tends to exonerate a person for his trouble and throw the blame on villains.

More specifically, the main ways a tragic hero can be misinterpreted seem to be as: (1) a melodramatic good guy who for some inexplicable reason has failed, (2) a villain, (3) a fool, or (4) a passive and pathetic victim.

I feel this shows how in some ways we Americans have difficulty doing justice to the tragic character, especially to his complexity and dignity. Even if sympathetic, we are inclined to reduce him to a simpler or an inferior type (the martyr is simpler though not inferior). Sympathy (as for a victim or martyr) is no guarantee of tragic understanding; yet we may suspect that if it were not for the artist's working skillfully to build up sympathy, most tragedies would be villainies or follies of one kind or another.

Why does this reduction occur? Aside from the usual limitations of the human mind (such as ignorance and laziness), I think a theory of short-circuiting by cultural images is called for. That is, people respond to an event in terms of their stock of available images. They are likely to go to the image that is closest and easiest, among those which seem at all to fit the situation. We may grope for a name to call Medea, and fall back upon something like "villainess!" This amounts to a displacement of complex and delicate interpretations by simpler ideas. The ease of short-circuiting will depend on the prominence, range, and availability of character types in the culture; for example, whether art and drama have favored the building up of certain types more than others. The ratio of tragic to non-tragic stories in our culture should be expected to affect our ability to make such interpretations. Our interpretations should depend, also, on [406/407] current conditions, such as whether a "crisis" mentality exists. Crises apparently favor villains, and it is generally recognized that melodrama is the enemy of tragedy. So a culture that favors melodrama (with its happy endings) works against tragedy. Something like this might also be said for comedy. That is, though its "relief" function in tragedy is recognized, too much slapstick in popular media probably creates an atmosphere in which people find it hard to make serious interpretations—they are looking for the fool, not for dignity.

After all, so much is wrong with the tragic hero! To the superficial view he is plainly a failure. Willy Loman kills himself. What satisfaction are people supposed to get out of that? A tragic hero is asked to perform the paradoxical feat of lifting the human spirit while plunging it into the most appalling catastrophes. And this is to be symbolized by a character who is full of weakness and conflict (compared with a folk hero like Sigurd or some of the more primitive dragon-slayers). His very mistakes and flaws may alienate the audience to the point that they see him as a villain or fool. If he does not positively err, he may, like Hamlet with his hand suspended over the back of Claudius, be unable to deliver a fully satisfying blow. In any case, all that comes out of his downfall is a triumph obscurely implied.

Much depends, then, on a delicate set of conditions that would allow such a triumph to be perceived. Indeed, unless a culture were especially prepared to accept him, we might very well expect the tragic hero to be a total wash-out.

III

This brings our attention to the second main factor in American culture that makes it hard for the tragic hero to succeed: the climate of opinion, sometimes called the ethos. Some peoples seem to have an ethos that keeps them from seeing tragedy at all.[9] Ours is not so limiting as that, of course; but [407/408] it does contain unfavorable perspectives or beliefs, three in particular that we shall try to analyze with the help of experts.[10]

One is the optimistic presumption that keeps us from appreciating the extent to which things—God, fate, history, nature —are not on our side. A vivid awareness of evil, says O'Connor, is essential to the idea of tragedy. Nietzsche said the same: "Banish evil, and it will go hard with the writers of tragedy." Now our age has managed to a great extent to banish evil by considering it not in the scheme of things. Characteristically, A. J. Cronin says, "If we think correctly and courageously, there is no misfortune inherent in human existence that we cannot turn to our ultimate advantage." Such a view is no doubt "healthy," but it is purely a presumption that the world is set up so that man can exploit it. Things should come out all right, says the optimistic presumption; but *this* did not come out all right; therefore something is wrong with it. So optimism must arm its hero with Excalibur, give him a horseshoe in his glove to guarantee success. One of these symbolic horseshoes in American life is the idea of progress. Another is the scientific optimism inherited from the eighteenth century. Another is the invincible belief in romantic marriage in spite of one failure out of three or four. A people used to the aspirin of optimism ask, quite reasonably, why should we experience pain in our dramas any more than in our dentist chairs? The best use they can make of tragic pain is didactic: a lesson about how to do better next time. [408/409]

Optimism belongs, then, among the opiates that soften the awareness of evil and make life look like a set-up especially prepared for man. (Oddly, those who most often use the term "opiate," the Marxists, are themselves equally victims of this optimism, feeling that history is working out some kind of dialectic in favor of the society they want.) Other cultural opiates, not so prevalent in America, include: Puritanism, which tried to ostracize evil as the work of the Devil; fatalism, which takes all the responsibility for evil off man; other worldliness, which denies reality to material misfortunes; and the patriotic sentimentalization of death. It was the Romans, says Edith Hamilton, who thought it sweet to die for one's country; "the Greeks never said it was sweet to die for anything." Clearly, you can't have tragedy when such notions act as buffers to take the edge off the bitterest blows.

Equally unfavorable to the tragic hero is the naturalism which, developed as an artistic technique by European writers, has become an integral part of the American outlook. The American takes this view of things as normally as the medieval man did miracles and the Devil. Coming under a variety of names (mechanism, determinism, environmentalism, behaviorism, materialism, positivism, relativism, amoralism), it is essentially a picture of man submerged in an impersonal and subhuman nature. Naturalism is, of course, not just the realism of the naked eye but a scientific, largely materialistic and mechanical *interpretation* of human phenomena—a model. To be submerged in nature may mean such things as the following: all events have causes; the external causes of human acts are environment and heredity; morals are not metaphysical laws but natural parts of

[9]For example, the Zuni Indians, who have no place for struggle and extreme individualism, for heroes who, "fighting, fighting, fighting, die driven against the wall."— Ruth Benedict, *Patterns of Culture* (Penguin edition), p. 119. The Hindus lack tragedy because their ethos prevents them from seeing material misfortune as significant; nor is the individual important enough to them for tragedy to be meaningful.

[10]Especially Joseph Wood Krutch, *The Modern Temper* (New York, 1929). Besides Krutch's brilliant diagnosis, I have used others who have analyzed cultural conditions favorable and unfavorable to tragedy, notably William Van O'Connor, *Climates of Tragedy* (Baton Rouge, 1943), and Willard Farnham, *The Medieval Heritage of Elizabethan Tragedy* (Berkeley, 1936).

culture; man is not separated from other animals by a gulf, he is just the star performer in the zoo.

Such a view is bound to shape both the kinds of figures made by artists and the way they are interpreted. Stress on [409/410] meaningless mechanism, external causation, may reduce a tragic hero to a beetle crushed under a rock. Studs Lonigan on a morgue slab is in some sense a symbol of the avalanche of naturalism over tragedy. So also is Clyde Griffiths, who, as depicted by Dreiser, is a puppet of circumstances. A mass of documentation is piled up to prove how social forces—home, education, deprivations, snubs, and denatured American ideals—move him toward his crime and to this extent lessen his freedom and responsibility. The pile-up of environmental forces also dulls the perception of evil, which (as O'Connor has shown) is essential for feeling tragedy. If I may try to explain this, it is because the evil of anything depends on two things: how important is he who suffers and how much of the trouble is due to the will of man. Reduce man either as sufferer or willing agent and it is impossible to have evil. This may lend significance to Krutch's observation that "the idea of nobility is inseparable from the idea of tragedy," and that "no man can conceive it unless he is capable of believing in the greatness and importance of man." What it seems to add up to, then, is that making nature more makes man less.

Yet, for all its threat, naturalism need not be fatal to a hero if, amid the mass of circumstances that seem to overwhelm him, he is allowed some loophole for noble choice. Thus Willy Loman in *Death of a Salesman* is a victim only to the extent that spurious American values—in this case the good-fellow ideal of success—have collapsed for him. But this victimization is not the last word; it becomes an *opportunity,* as Miller himself explains, for that burst of heroic determination in defeat which is the essence of tragedy. So by this play Miller claims that sordid life, for all its relentless pressures, need

not be "below tragedy, as often asserted." The common man can take on such stature "to the extent of his willingness to throw all he has into the contest" to maintain his "chosen image" of what and who he is in the world.

A more serious blow to the hero's dignity and volition is [410/411] to psychologize him, especially to analyze his conflicts in terms of psychopathology to a point where he is neither normal nor in control of what he does. The clinical character of many modern tragedies (such as those by O'Neill and Williams) is too obvious to need emphasis. Let me say only this: when a man becomes a "case," he ceases to be human to some extent. The disease occupies the foreground and, as it were, plays the part. Other writers have described this morbid effect as "converting art into an alienist's notebook," or an "obsession with filth" that obscures dignity. A possible result is disintegration of tragedy into mere horror and sensation.

If naturalism hurts tragedy, there is another element of the American ethos that gives little less than a *coup de grace* to this kind of hero. It is the inability to make absolute commitments, called by David Riesman other-directedness (by moralists, opportunism). Anyone puzzled by the success of "brain-washing" on soldiers need not be so puzzled if he recognizes that many people today hold their beliefs conditionally, not absolutely. That is, their beliefs are inconsistent, come from all kinds of sources, and need to be upheld by agreement with others in the situation. Remove this condition of group support and there is no strong impulse to maintain them. Now a basic requirement of tragedy is to throw oneself completely into action, to "play the game through." Every great tragic figure has been true to his fault, so to speak. This is his tragic commitment. But the average American, while he may admire a martyr with a clear-cut cause of service, does not like to follow a course through to tragic consequences. He has too much common sense, for one thing. There is in him the spirit of the world, of compromise, of opportunism. He is proud of being flexible, able to start in a new direction when one line of action peters out. In other words, he is not obligated. "Die-hard" is his name for one who sticks too long to a cause. This is both a strength and a weakness. Putting it in terms of Riesman's character-types, a [411/412] tragic actor must be *inner*-directed; it is commitment to something within and private that makes him tragic. The *other*-directed audience sees this "fault," sympathizes perhaps, but does not follow. For an other-directed person bases conduct on what others want him to do and therefore does not hold to a course of rather obstinate individuality. Theoretically, tragedy is impossible in an other-directed society. The tragic hero finds himself fighting alone—the crowd has deserted him. Now one who throws himself away on a lost cause, we well know, is a fool—so much for tragic dignity.

These ways of looking at things—optimism, naturalism, and other-directedness—seem to be the main elements of the American climate of opinion that stand in the way of the success of the tragic hero and help account for the unenthusiastic response of audiences to him. Bearing in mind the distracting types previously described, we see why it is so easy for him to be mis-cast and a misfit, and why he has such a hard time.

IV

There remains a fact about the hero himself that, regardless of what the climate of opinion and perceptual images may be, is bound to affect the way he is received. I mean that he is not the man he used to be. Partly as a result of the naturalism already described, the tendency among artists is to pick smaller men as subjects of tragedy. The standard of better-than-average, used in the Athenian and Elizabethan classics, has been abandoned. Comparing any fair sample of modern characters with those of earlier periods will show that there has been a decline in the stature of the tragic hero. The thing could be proven in feet and pounds, if need be; Krutch has demonstrated it convincingly by comparing people like Oswald Alving and Hamlet. This means that, regardless of social climate and cultural images, we have a harder time admiring the tragic hero today. He is such an ordinary person, his weaknesses and faults are so evident, that it is often [412/413] hard to muster more than forgiveness for him. If we are to admire a Clyde Griffiths, a Blanche DuBois, an Emperor Jones, a Native Son, it must be all our own effort, so to speak; the artist has helped us but little—indeed, he may have so alienated us that we are unwilling to stay around for the funeral. Now (while this is entirely speculation), were tragic writers of today to choose clearly superior men as their subjects, we should have at least a favorable attitude toward them before the trouble started.

In short, the objective mediocrity of the modern hero combined with the unfavorable ethos and distracting cultural images make it very unlikely that an impression of grandeur will be produced when a man goes to pieces or blows his brains out before an American audience.

With such conditions working against the tragic hero, it is a wonder, indeed, that so many Americans do occasionally listen to his sombre lesson. While he cannot be said to be a popular type—and shows little signs of becoming one—he may serve by his presence to remind us, like an African mask in a modern living room, of insights that our ethos might otherwise hide. We test our perception on him, finding more often than not that he reflects themes of our own culture. Working like a prism, he scatters popular thought into its elements, showing its tendency to veer away from tragic insight to simpler modes of perception. But in so doing, he has utility for analyzing this thought. Enigma though he is—even if a fool in our eyes—he is, perhaps, capable of playing Touchstone for us.

Tragedy and the Common Man*

ARTHUR MILLER was born in New York City in 1915 and graduated from the Abraham Lincoln High School, Brooklyn, in 1932. He began his career as a dramatist while a student at the University of Michigan, where he won the Avery Hopwood Prize for his play *The Grass Still Grows* (1936). In 1938, when he graduated, he received the Theatre Guild National Award. In the next few years he worked for the Federal Theatre Project, wrote radio plays, and collected background material for the film *The Story of G.I. Joe*. In 1944 he published a commentary on the war, *Situation Normal*.

His first play to achieve a Broadway production, *The Man Who Had All The Luck* (1944), was a failure. In 1945 he published a novel, *Focus*, which had anti-Semitism as its theme. Success came to him in 1947 when *All My Sons* was awarded the Drama Critics' Circle Prize and the Pulitzer Prize. *Death of a Salesman* (1949) brought him the same awards and even higher critical praise. In 1950 Miller adapted Ibsen's *An Enemy of the People* for modern audiences. *The Crucible*, a play with the Salem witch-hunts as its subject, but with the current un-American activities investigations obviously glanced at, was produced in 1953. Since 1955, when he wrote two one-act plays, *A Memory of Two Mondays* and *A View from the Bridge*, there has been no new play from Arthur Miller.

The essay reprinted here, in which the dramatist attempts to justify on theoretical grounds his choice of a "common man" as tragic hero in *Death of a Salesman*, has stimulated a great deal of critical controversy, though a number of the ideas expressed in it date back at least as far as the eighteenth century.

In this age few tragedies are written. It has often been held that the lack is due to a paucity of heroes among us, or else that modern man has had the blood drawn out of his organs of belief by the skepticism of science, and the heroic attack on life cannot feed on an attitude of reserve and circumspection. For one reason or another, we are often held to be below tragedy—or tragedy above us. The inevitable conclusion is, of course, that the tragic mode is archaic, fit only for the very highly placed, the kings or the kingly, and where this admission is not made in so many words it is most often implied.

I believe that the common man is as apt a subject for tragedy in its highest sense as kings were. On the face of it this ought to be obvious in the light of modern psychiatry, which bases its analysis upon classic formulations, such as the Oedipus and Orestes complexes, for instances, which were enacted by royal beings, but which apply to everyone in similar emotional situations.

More simply, when the question of tragedy in art is not at issue, we never hesi-

*Arthur Miller, "Tragedy and the Common Man," *New York Times*, February 27, 1949, Sec. 2, pp. 1, 3.

tate to attribute to the well-placed and the exalted the very same mental processes as the lowly. And finally, if the exaltation of tragic action were truly a property of the high-bred character alone, it is inconceivable that the mass of mankind should cherish tragedy above all other forms, let alone be capable of understanding it.

As a general rule, to which there may be exceptions unknown to me, I think the tragic feeling is evoked in us when we are in the presence of a character who is ready to lay down his life, if need be, to secure one thing—his sense of personal dignity. From Orestes to Hamlet, Medea to Macbeth, the underlying struggle is that of the individual attempting to gain his "rightful" position in his society.

Sometimes he is one who has been displaced from it, sometimes one who seeks to attain it for the first time, but the fateful wound from which the inevitable events spiral is the wound of indignity, and its dominant force is indignation. Tragedy, then, is the consequence of a man's total compulsion to evaluate himself justly.

In the sense of having been initiated by the hero himself, the tale always reveals what has been called his "tragic flaw," a failing that is not peculiar to grand or elevated characters. Nor is it necessarily a weakness. The flaw, or crack in the character, is really nothing—and need be nothing, but his inherent unwillingness to remain passive in the face of what he conceives to be a challenge to his dignity, his image of his rightful status. Only the passive, only those who accept their lot without active retaliation, are "flawless." Most of us are in that category.

But there are among us today, as there always have been, those who act against the scheme of things that degrades them, and in the process of action everything we have accepted out of fear or insensitivity or ignorance is shaken before us and examined, and from this total onslaught by an individual against the seemingly stable cosmos surrounding us—from this total examination of the "unchange-

able" environment—comes the terror and the fear that is classically associated with tragedy.

More important, from this total questioning of what has previously been unquestioned, we learn. And such a process is not beyond the common man. In revolutions around the world, these past thirty years, he has demonstrated again and again this inner dynamic of all tragedy.

Insistence upon the rank of the tragic hero, or the so-called nobility of his character, is really but a clinging to the outward forms of tragedy. If rank or nobility of character was indispensable, then it would follow that the problems of those with rank were the particular problems of tragedy. But surely the right of one monarch to capture the domain from another no longer raises our passions, nor are our concepts of justice what they were to the mind of an Elizabethan king.

The quality in such plays that does shake us, however, derives from the underlying fear of being displaced, the disaster inherent in being torn away from our chosen image of what and who we are in this world. Among us today this fear is as strong, and perhaps stronger, than it ever was. In fact, it is the common man who knows this fear best.

Now, if it is true that tragedy is the consequence of a man's total compulsion to evaluate himself justly, his destruction in the attempt posits a wrong or an evil in his environment. And this is precisely the morality of tragedy and its lesson. The discovery of the moral law, which is what the enlightenment of tragedy consists of, is not the discovery of some abstract or metaphysical quantity.

The tragic right is a condition of life, a condition in which the human personality is able to flower and realize itself. The wrong is the condition which suppresses man, perverts the flowing out of his love and creative instinct. Tragedy enlightens—and it must, in that it [1/3] points the heroic finger at the enemy of man's freedom. The thrust for freedom is the quality in tragedy which exalts. The revolutionary questioning of the stable environment is what terrifies. In no way is the common man debarred from such thoughts or such actions.

Seen in this light, our lack of tragedy may be partially accounted for by the turn which modern literature has taken toward the purely psychiatric view of life, or the purely sociological. If all our miseries, our indignities, are born and bred within our minds, then all action, let alone the heroic action, is obviously impossible.

And if society alone is responsible for the cramping of our lives, then the protagonist must needs be so pure and faultless as to force us to deny his validity as a character. From neither of these views can tragedy derive, simply because neither represents a balanced concept of life. Above all else, tragedy requires the finest appreciation by the writer of cause and effect.

No tragedy can therefore come about when its author fears to question absolutely everything, when he regards any institution, habit or custom as being either everlasting, immutable or inevitable. In the tragic view the need of man to wholly realize himself is the only fixed star, and whatever it is that hedges his nature and lowers it is ripe for attack and examination. Which is not to say that tragedy must preach revolution.

The Greeks could probe the very heavenly origin of their ways and return to confirm the rightness of laws. And Job could face God in anger, demanding his right and end in submission. But for a moment everything is in suspension, nothing is accepted, and in this stretching and tearing apart of the cosmos, in the very action of so doing, the character gains "size," the tragic stature which is spuriously attached to the royal or the highborn in our minds. The commonest of men may take on that stature to the extent of his willingness to throw all he has

into the contest, the battle to secure his rightful place in his world.

There is a misconception of tragedy with which I have been struck in review after review, and in many conversations with writers and readers alike. It is the idea that tragedy is of necessity allied to pessimism. Even the dictionary says nothing more about the word than that it means a story with a sad or unhappy ending. This impression is so firmly fixed that I almost hesitate to claim that in truth tragedy implies more optimism in its author than does comedy, and that its final result ought to be the reinforcement of the onlooker's brightest opinions of the human animal.

For, if it is true to say that in essence the tragic hero is intent upon claiming his whole due as a personality, and if this struggle must be total and without reservation, then it automatically demonstrates the indestructible will of man to achieve his humanity.

The possibility of victory must be there in tragedy. Where pathos rules, where pathos is finally derived, a character has fought a battle he could not possibly have won. The pathetic is achieved when the protagonist is, by virture of his witlessness, his insensitivity or the very air he gives off, incapable of grappling with a much superior force.

Pathos truly is the mode for the pessimist. But tragedy requires a nicer balance between what is possible and what is impossible. And it is curious, although edifying, that the plays we revere, century after century, are the tragedies. In them, and in them alone, lies the belief—optimistic, if you will, in the perfectibility of man.

It is time, I think, that we who are without kings, took up this bright thread of our history and followed it to the only place it can possibly lead in our time—the heart and spirit of the average man.

On Social Plays*

This essay is the fullest statement **ARTHUR MILLER** has made of his belief that the dramatist must be "committed"—that his plays must have some direct relevance to the social and moral problems of his age. Miller continues here the questioning of modern values that he began in *Death of a Salesman*, and asserts his position as a traditional dramatist writing, with the Greeks, in "the main stream" of drama.

A Greek living in the classical period would be bewildered by the dichotomy implied in the very term "social play." Especially for the Greek, a drama created for public performance had to be "social." A play to him was by definition a dramatic consideration of the way men ought to live. But in this day of extreme individualism even that phrase must be further defined. When we say "how men ought to live " we are likely to be thinking of psychological therapy, of ridding ourselves individually of neurotic compulsions and destructive inner tendencies, of "learning how to love" and thereby gaining "happiness."

It need hardly be said that the Greek dramatist had more than a passing interest in psychology and character on the stage. But for him these were means to a larger end, and the end was what we isolate today as social. That is, the relations of man as a social animal, rather than his definition as a separated entity, was the dramatic goal. Why this should have come to be is a large historical question which others are more competent to explain, as several already have. For our purposes it will be sufficient to indicate one element in the life of classical Greece that differs so [1/2] radically from anything existing in the modern world as to throw a bright light on certain of our attitudes which we take for granted and toward which we therefore are without a proper perspective.

The Greek citizen of that time thought of himself as belonging not to a "nation" or a "state" but to a *polis*. The polis were small units, apparently deriving from an earlier tribal social organization, whose members probably knew one another personally because they were relatively few in number and occupied a small territory. In war or peace the whole people made the vital decisions, there being no profession of politics as we know it; any man could be elected magistrate, judge, even a general in the armed forces. It was an amateur world compared to our stratified and specialized one, a world in which everyone knew enough about almost any profession to practice it, because most things were simple to know. The thing of importance for us is that these people were *engaged,* they could not imagine the good life excepting as it brought each person into close contact with civic matters. They were avid argufiers. Achilles was blessed by the gods with the power to fight well and make good speeches. The people had a special sense of pride in the polis and thought that it in itself distinguished them from

*Arthur Miller, "On Social Plays," Introduction to *A View from the Bridge* (New York: The Viking Press, 1955), pp. 1-15.

the barbarians outside who lived under ty-
rannies.

The preoccupation of the Greek drama
with ultimate law, with the Grand Design,
so to speak, was therefore an expression
of a basic assumption of the people, who
could not yet conceive, luckily, that any
man could long prosper unless his polis
prospered. The individual was at one with
his society; his conflicts with it were, in
our terms, like family conflicts the opposing sides of which nevertheless shared
a mutuality of feeling and responsibility.
Thus the drama written for them, while
for us it appears wholly religious, was
religious for them in a more than mystical
way. Religion is the only way we have
any more of expressing our genuinely
social feelings and concerns, for in our
bones we as a people do not otherwise
believe in our oneness with a larger
group. But the religiousness of the Greek
drama of the classical [2/3] time was
more worldly; it expressed a social concern, to be sure, but it did so on the part
of a people already unified on earth rather
than the drive of a single individual toward personal salvation. The great gap
we feel between religious or "high"
emotion and the emotions of daily life
was not present in their mass affairs. The
religious expression was not many degrees
higher for them than many other social expressions, of which their drama is the most
complete example.

It is necessary to add that as the polis
withered under the impact of war and
historical change, as commerce grew
and a differentiation of interest separated man from man, the Greek drama
found it more and more difficult to stand
as a kind of universal mass statement
or prayer. It turned its eye inward, created more elaborated characterizations, and
slowly gave up some of its former lofti-
ness. Men, as H.D.F. Kitto has said in
The Greeks, replaced Man in the plays.
Nevertheless, to the end the Greek drama
clearly conceived its right function as
something far wider than a purely private
examination of individuality for the sake
of the examination or for art's sake. In

every dramatic hero there is the idea of
the Greek people, their fate, their will,
and their destiny.

In today's America the term "social
play" brings up images which are his-
torically conditioned, very recent, and, I
believe, only incidentally pertinent to a
fruitful conception of the drama. The
term indicates to us an attack, an arraignment of society's evils such as Ibsen
allegedly invented and was later taken
up by left-wing playwrights whose primary interest was the exposure of capi-
talism for the implied benefit of socialism or communism. The concept is tired
and narrow, but its worst effect has been
to confuse a whole generation of playwrights, audiences, and theater workers.

If one can look at the idea of "social
drama" from the Greek viewpoint for one
moment, it will be clear that there can
be only either a genuinely social drama
or, if it abdicates altogether, its true opposite, the antisocial and ultimately anti-
dramatic drama. [3/4]

To put it simply, even oversimply, a
drama rises in stature and intensity in
proportion to the weight of its application
to all manner of men. It gains its weight
as it deals with more and more of the
whole man, not either his subjective or
his social life alone, and the Greek was
unable to conceive of man or anything
else except as a whole. The modern playwright, at least in America, on the one
hand is importuned by his most demanding audience to write importantly, while
on the other he is asked not to bring onto
the stage images of social function, lest
he seem like a special pleader and therefore inartistic. I am not attempting a defense of the social dramas of the thirties,
most of which were in fact special plead-
ings and further from a consideration of
the whole man than much of the antisocial drama is. I am trying only to project a right conception of what social
drama was and what it ought to be. It is,
I think, the widest concept of drama
available to us thus far.

When, however, a contemporary dramatist is drawn for but a moment toward a

concept of form even remotely Greek, certain lacks become evident—a certain abyss even begins to appear around him. When you are writing in the name of a people unified in a self-conscious and rather small band, when you yourself as a writer are not an individual entrepreneur offering wares to a hostile market place but a member of a group who is in other ways no different from the rest —when, in short, the dramatic form itself is regarded as inevitably a social expression of the deepest concerns of all your fellow men—your work is bound to be liberated, freed of even the hypothesis of partisanship, if only because partisanship cannot thrive where the idea of wholeness is accepted. Thus in such a situation what we call social matters become inseparable from subjective psychological matters, and the drama is once again whole and capable of the highest reach.

If one considers our own drama of the past forty years in comparison with that of classical Greece one elemental difference—the difference which seems to me to be our crippling [4/5] hobble—will emerge. The single theme to which our most ambitious plays can be reduced is frustration. In all of them, from O'Neill's through the best of Anderson, Sidney Howard, and the rest, the underlying log jam, so to speak, the unresolvable paradox, is that, try as he will, the individual is doomed to frustration when once he gains a consciousness of his own identity. The image is that of the individual scratching away at a wall beyond which stands society, his fellow men. Sometimes he pounds at the wall, sometimes he tries to scale it or even blow it up, but at the end the wall is always there, and the man himself is dead or doomed to defeat in his attempt to live a human life.

The tragic victory is always denied us because, I believe, the plays cannot project with any conviction what the society, in the playwrights' views at any rate, has failed to prove. In Greece the tragic victory consisted in demonstrating that the polis—the whole people—had discovered some aspect of the Grand Design which also was the right way to live *together*. If the American playwrights of serious intent are in any way the subconscience of the country, our claims to have found that way are less than proved. For when the Greek thought of the right way to live it was a whole concept; it meant a way to live that would create citizens who were brave in war, had a sense of responsibility to the polis in peace, and were also developed as individual personalities.

It has often seemed to me that the Soviet Russians have studied classical Greece and have tried to bridge with phraseology profound differences between their social organization and that of Greece, while demanding of their writers what in effect is a Greek social drama. The word "cosmopolitan," as Kitto points out, was invented in Greece when the small polis were disintegrating, and when the drama itself was beginning to turn inward, away from the largest questions of social fate to the fate of individuals alone. It was invented to describe a new kind of man, a man whose allegiance was not primarily to his [5/6] society, his polis, but to others of like mind anywhere in the world. With it goes an intimation—or more—of skepticism, of self-removal, that presages the radical separation of man from society which the American drama expresses ultimately through themes of frustration. To supplant the polis and allegiance to it, the Soviets have a thousand kinds of social organizations, and, for all one knows, the individual Russian might well feel a sense of connection with civic affairs which the West does not afford its citizens. The crucial difference, however, is that only the most theoretical Russian can trace the effects, if any, of his personality upon the policies of his country, while the Greek could literally see what he had done when he made his speech and swayed or failed to sway his fellow men.

Thus the Russian drama after the Revolution, much as ours, is a drama of frustration, the inability of industrialized men to see themselves spiritually completed through the social organization.

But in the Soviet case the frustration is not admitted; it is talked away in large phrases having to do with a victory of the people through tragic sacrifice. The fact remains, however, that nowhere in the world where industrialized economy rules—where specialization in work, politics, and social life is the norm—nowhere has man discovered a means of connecting himself to society except in the form of a truce with it. The best we have been able to do is to speak of a "duty" to society, and this implies sacrifice or self-deprivation. To think of an individual fulfilling his subjective needs through social action, to think of him as living most completely when he lives most socially, to think of him as doing this, not as a social worker acting out of conscientious motives, but naturally, without guilt or sense of oddness—this is difficult for us to imagine, and when we can, we know at the same time that only a few, perhaps a blessed few, are so constructed as to manage it.

As with Greece, so with us—each great war has turned men further and further away from preoccupation with Man and drawn them back into the family, the home, the private life and [6/7] the preoccupation with sexuality. It has happened, however, that at the same time our theater has exhausted the one form that was made to express the private life —prose realism. We are bored with it; we demand something more, something "higher," on the stage, while at the same time we refuse, or do not know how, to live our private lives excepting as ego-centers. I believe it is this paradox that underlies the kind of struggle taking place in the drama today—a struggle at one and the same time to write of private persons privately and yet lift up their means of expression to a poetic—that is, a social—level. You cannot speak in verse of picayune matters—at least not on the stage—without sounding overblown and ridiculous, and so it should be. Verse reaches always toward the general statement, the wide image, the universal moment, and it must be based upon wide concepts—it must speak not merely of men but of Man. The language of dramatic verse is the language of a people profoundly at one with itself; it is the most public of public speech. The language of prose is the language of the private life, the kind of private life men retreat to when they are at odds with the world they have made or been heirs to.

The social drama, then—at least as I have always conceived it—is the drama of the whole man. It seeks to deal with his differences from others not *per se,* but toward the end that, if only through drama, we may know how much the same we are, for if we lose that knowledge we shall have nothing left at all. The social drama to me is only incidentally an arraignment of society. *A Streetcar Named Desire* is a social drama; so is *The Hairy Ape,* and so are practically all O'Neill's other plays. For they ultimately make moot, either weakly or with full power, the ancient question, how are we to live? And that question is in its Greek sense, its best and most humane sense, not merely a private query.

The social drama, as I see it, is the main stream and the antisocial drama a bypass. I can no longer take with ultimate seriousness a drama of individual psychology written for its own [7/8] sake, however full it may be of insight and precise observation. Time is moving; there is a world to make, a civilization to create that will move toward the only goal the humanistic, democratic mind can ever accept with honor. It is a world in which the human being can live as a naturally political, naturally private, naturally engaged person, a world in which once again a true tragic victory may be scored.

But that victory is not really possible unless the individual is more than theoretically capable of being recognized by the powers that lead society. Specifically, when men live, as they do under any industrialized system, as integers who have no weight, no *person,* excepting as either customers, draftees, machine tenders, ideologists, or whatever, it is unlikely *apere entirely*

(and in my opinion impossible) that a dramatic picture of them can really overcome the public knowledge of their nature in real life. In such a society, be it communistic or capitalistic, man is not tragic, he is pathetic. The tragic figure must have certain innate powers which he uses to pass over the boundaries of the known social law—the accepted mores of his people—in order to test and discover necessity. Such a quest implies that the individual who has moved onto that course must be somehow recognized by the law, by the mores, by the powers that design—be they anthropomorphic gods or economic and political laws—as having the worth, the innate value, of a whole people asking a basic question and demanding its answer. We are so atomized socially that no character in a play can conceivably stand as our vanguard, as our heroic questioner. Our society—and I am speaking of every industrialized society in the world—is so complex, each person being so specialized an integer, that the moment any individual is dramatically characterized and set forth as a hero, our common sense reduces him to the size of a complainer, a misfit. For deep down we no longer believe in the rules of the tragic contest; we no longer believe that some ultimate sense can in fact be made of social causation, or in the possibility that any individual can, by a heroic effort, make **[8/9]** sense of it. Thus the man that is driven to question the moral chaos in which we live ends up in our estimate as a possibly commendable but definitely odd fellow, and probably as a compulsively driven neurotic. In place of a social aim which called an all-around excellence—physical, intellectual, and moral—the ultimate good, we have set up a goal which can best be characterized as "happiness"—namely, staying out of trouble. This concept is the end result of the truce which all of us have made with society. And a truce implies two enemies. When the truce is broken it means either that the individual has broken out of his ordained place as an integer, or that the society has broken

the law by harming him unjustly—that is, it has not left him alone to be a peaceful integer. In the heroic and tragic time the act of questioning the-way-things-are implied that a quest was being carried on to discover an ultimate law or way of life which would yield excellence; in the present time the quest is that of a man made unhappy by rootlessness and, in every important modern play, by a man who is essentially a victim. We have abstracted from the Greek drama its air of doom, its physical destruction of the hero, but its victory escapes us. Thus it has even become difficult to separate in our minds the ideas of the pathetic and of the tragic. And behind this melting of the two lies the overwhelming power of the modern industrial state, the ignorance of each person in it of anything but his own technique as an economic integer, and the elevation of that state to a holy, quite religious sphere.

What, after all, are our basic social aims as applied to the individual? Americans are often accused of worshiping financial success, but this is, first of all, not an American monopoly, and, second, it does not as a concept make clear what is causing so much uneasiness and moral pain. My own belief, at any rate, is that America has merely arrived first at the condition that awaits every country that takes her economic road without enforcing upon every development of industrial technique certain quite arbitrary standards of value. **[9/10]**

The deep moral uneasiness among us, the vast sense of being only tenuously joined to the rest of our fellows, is caused, in my view, by the fact that the person has value as he fits into the pattern of efficiency, and for that alone. The reason *Death of a Salesman*, for instance, left such a strong impression was that it set forth unremittingly the picture of a man who was not even especially "good" but whose situation made clear that at bottom we are alone, valueless, without even the elements of a human person, when once we fail to fit the patterns of efficiency. Under the black shadow of that gigantic necessity, even the drift of some psychoanalytic practice is toward the fitting-in, the training of the individual whose soul has revolted, so that he may once again "take his place" in society—that is, do his "work," "function," in other words, accommodate himself to a scheme of things that is not at all ancient but very new in the world. In short, the absolute value of the individual human being is believed in only as a secondary value; it stands well below the needs of efficient production. We have finally come to serve the machine. The machine must not be stopped, marred, left dirty, or outmoded. Only men can be left marred, stopped, dirty, and alone. Our pity for the victim is mixed, I think. It is mixed with an air of self-preserving superiority—we, thank God, know how to fit in, therefore this victim, however pitiful, has himself to thank for his fate. We believe, in other words, that to fit into the patterns of efficiency is the ultimate good, and at the same time we know in our bones that a crueler concept is not easy to arrive at.

Nor may the exponents of socialism take heart from this. There is no such thing as a capitalist assembly line or drygoods counter. The disciplines required by machines are the same everywhere and will not be truly mitigated by old-age pensions and social-security payments. So long as modern man conceives of himself as valuable only because he fits into some niche in the machine-tending pattern, he will never know anything more than a pathetic doom. [10/11]

The implications of this fact spread throughout our culture, indeed, throughout the culture of the industrialized parts of the world. Be it in music, literature, drama, or whatever, the value of a work is, willy nilly, equated with its mass "acceptance," i.e., its efficiency. All the engines of economic law are, like the mills of the gods, working toward that same end. The novel of excellence which could once be published without financial loss if it sold two or three thousand copies

can no longer be published, because the costs of production require that every book sell at least ten, twelve, or fifteen thousand copies. The play that might have been produced at a decent profit if it could fill half a house for a few months can no longer be produced, for the costs of production require a play to draw packed houses from the first night.

When one has the temerity to suggest that the Greek theater was subsidized, that so much of the world's great music, art, and literature was stubbornly patronized by people who found honor in helping to bring beauty onto the earth, one is not quite suspect, to be sure, but the suggestion nevertheless has an unreal air, an air of being essentially at odds and possibly in dangerous conflict with some unspoken sense of values. For we do believe that a "good" thing, be it art or toothpaste, proves its goodness by its public acceptance. And at the same time we know, too, that something dark and dreadful lies within this concept.

The problem, then, of the social drama in this generation is not the same as it was for Ibsen, Chekhov, or Shaw. They, and the left-wing playwrights of the thirties who amplified their findings and repeated their forms, were oriented either toward an arraignment of some of the symptoms of efficiency men or toward the ultimate cure by socialism. With the proliferation of machine techniques in the world, and the relative perfection of distributing techniques, in America first and the rest of the world soon, the time will shortly be upon us when the truth will dawn. We shall come to see, I think, that Production for Profit [11/12] and Production for Use (whatever their relative advantages—and each has its own) leave untouched the problem which the Greek drama put so powerfully before mankind. How are we to live? From what fiat, from what ultimate source are we to derive a standard of values that will create in man a respect for himself, a real voice in the fate of his society, and, above all, an aim for his life which is neither a private aim for a private life nor one which sets him below the machine that was made to serve him?

The social drama in this generation must do more than analyze and arraign the social network of relationships. It must delve into the nature of man as he exists to discover what his needs are, so that those needs may be amplified and exteriorized in terms of social concepts. Thus, the new social dramatist, if he is to do his work, must be an even deeper psychologist than those of the past, and he must be conscious at least of the futility of isolating the psychological life of man lest he fall always short of tragedy, and return, again and again and again, to the pathetic swampland where the waters are old tears and not the generative seas from which new kinds of life arise.

It is a good time to be writing because the audience is sick of the old formulations. It is no longer believed—and we may be thankful for it—that the poor are necessarily virtuous or the rich necessarily decayed. Nor is it believed that, as some writers would put it, the rich are necessarily not decayed and the poor necessarily the carriers of vulgarity. We have developed so democratic a culture that in America neither the speech of a man nor his way of dressing nor even his ambitions for himself inevitably mark his social class. On the stage social rank tells next to nothing about the man any more. The decks are cleared. There is a kind of perverse unity forming among us, born, I think, of the discontent of all classes of people with the endless frustration of life. It is possible now to speak of a search for values, not solely from the position of bitterness, but with [12/13] a warm embrace of mankind, with a sense that at bottom every one of us is a victim of this misplacement of aims.

The debilitation of the tragic drama, I believe, is commensurate with the fracturing and the aborting of the need of man to maintain a fruitful kind of union with his society. Everything we learn, everything we know or deem valuable for

a man to know, has been thrown into the creation of a machine technology. The nuclear bomb, as a way of waging war, is questioned only now—because we have it, because we have invented it: not before both sides knew how to make it. Both sides have the bomb and both sides have the machine. Some day the whole world will have both and the only force that will keep them from destructive use will be a force strange to machine psychology, a force born of will—the will of man to survive and to reach his ultimate, most conscious, most knowing, most fulfilled condition, his fated excellence.

History has given the social drama its new chance. Ibsen and Shaw had to work through three acts to prove in the fourth that, even if we are not completely formed by society, there is little left that society does not affect. The tremendous growth in our consciousness of social causation has won for these writers their victory in this sense: it has given to us a wider consciousness of the causes that form character. What the middle of the twentieth century has taught us is that theirs was not the whole answer. It is not enough any more to know that one is at the mercy of social pressures; it is necessary to understand that such a sealed fate cannot be accepted. Nor is courage alone required now to question this complex, although without courage nothing is possible, including real dramatic writing. It is necessary to know that the values of commerce, values which were despised as necessary but less than noble in the long past, are now not merely perversely dominant everywhere but claimed as positive moral goodness itself. The question must begin to be asked; not whether a new thing will work or pay, [13/14] not whether it is more efficient than its predecessor, more popular, and more easily accepted; but what it will do to human beings. The first invention of man to create that response in all nations was the atomic bomb. It is the first "improvement" to have dramatized for even the numbest mind the question of value. Over the past decade this nation and this world have been gripped by an inner debate on many levels, a debate raised to consciousness by this all-destroying "improvement." Alongside it is the "improvement" called automation, which will soon displace workers who mass-produce in industry. The conquest of poverty and hunger is the order of the day; the refusal of the dark peoples to live in subjection to the white is already a fact. The world, I think, is moving toward a unity, a unity won not alone by the necessities of the physical developments themselves, but by the painful and confused re-assertion of man's inherited will to survive. When the peace is made, and it will be made, the question Greece asked will once again be a question not reserved for philosophers and dramatists; it will be asked by the man who can live out his life without fear of hunger, joblessness, disease, the man working a few hours a day with a life-span probability of eighty, ninety, or perhaps a hundred years. Hard as it is for most people, the sheer struggle to exist and to prosper affords a haven from thought. Complain as they may that they have no time to think, to cultivate themselves, to ask the big questions, most men are terrified at the thought of not having to spend most of their days fighting for existence. In every sphere, and for a hundred hard reasons, the ultimate questions are once again becoming moot, some because without the right answers we will destroy the earth, others because the peace we win may leave us without the fruits of civilized life. The new social drama will be Greek in that it will face man as a social animal and yet without the petty partisanship of so much of past drama. It will be Greek in that the "men" dealt with in its scenes—the psychology and characterizations—will be more than ends in themselves and once [14/15] again parts of a whole, a whole that is social, a whole that is Man. The world, in a word, is moving into the same boat. For a time, their greatest time, the Greek people were in the same boat—their polis. Our drama, like theirs, will, as it must, ask the same questions, the largest ones. Where are we going now that we are together? For, like every act man commits, the drama is a struggle against his mortality, and meaning is the ultimate reward for having lived.

The Timeless World of a Play*

THOMAS LANIER ("Tennessee") WILLIAMS was born in Columbus, Mississippi, in 1914; his father was a shoe salesman and his mother the daughter of an Episcopalian clergyman. In 1927 the family moved to St. Louis, Missouri, and from 1931 to 1933 Williams attended the University of Missouri, but financial difficulties forced him to leave college and work in the shoe factory where his father was employed. It was at this time that he first felt the urge to write; but the monotony of his job and the frustration of his creative desires soon produced a nervous breakdown. When he had recovered he enrolled, in 1936, at Washington University, transferring after a year to the University of Iowa, where he received the B.A. degree in 1938. He then travelled the country, obtaining employment where he could, much of it menial work, but all the time writing plays and poetry. His first minor success as a dramatist came when he was awarded a prize for *American Blues,* a series of one-act plays dealing with the depression, but his first full-length play to receive professional production, *Battle of Angels* (1940), failed at its Boston opening. His talent was rewarded, however, by a Rockefeller Fellowship, which enabled him to carry on writing, although he continued wandering across the country. While he was in Hollywood as a script writer, in 1943, he wrote *The Glass Menagerie,* which became his first commercial success when it was produced on Broadway in 1945, winning him the New York Drama Critics' Circle Prize as the best new play of the year. Much of his own experience with his family in St. Louis is embedded in the play. Critical acclaim and popular approval came more readily after this: *A Streetcar Named Desire* (1947) and *Cat on a Hot Tin Roof* (1955) secured for him not only two more Critics' Circle Prizes, but two Pulitzer Prizes as well. In addition to several one-act plays, Williams also wrote between 1947 and 1955 *Summer and Smoke* (1948), *The Rose Tattoo* (1950), and *Camino Real* (1953). He has followed these with *Orpheus Descending* (a revised version of *Battle of Angels,* 1957), *Suddenly Last Summer* (1958), *Sweet Bird of Youth* (1959), and *Period of Adjustment* (1960), besides several additional shorter plays.

The present essay, which formed the Introduction to Williams' comedy *The Rose Tattoo,* is the only explicit statement he has published of his theory of dramatic art, though he occasionally replies to his critics in letters to newspapers and has been interviewed on television programs. "The Timeless World of a Play" is reprinted here complete: the marks of ellipsis (". . .") are the author's punctuation.

Carson McCullers concludes one of her lyric poems with the line: "Time, the endless idiot, runs screaming 'round the world." It is this continual rush of time, so violent that it appears to be screaming, that deprives our actual lives of so much dignity and meaning, and it is, perhaps more than anything else, the *arrest*

*Tennessee Williams, "The Timeless World of a Play," Introduction to *The Rose Tattoo* (New York: New Directions, 1951), pp. vi-xi.

of time which has taken place in a completed work of art that gives to certain plays their feeling of depth and significance. In the London notices of *Death of a Salesman* a certain notoriously skeptical critic made the remark that Willy Loman was the sort of man that almost any member of the audience would have kicked out of an office had he applied for a job or detained one for conversation about his troubles. The remark itself possibly holds some truth. But the implication that Willy Loman is consequently a character with whom we have no reason to concern ourselves in drama, reveals a strikingly false conception of what plays are. Contemplation is something that exists outside of time, and so is the tragic sense. Even in the actual world of commerce, there exists in some persons a sensibility to the unfortunate situations of others, a capacity for concern and compassion, surviving from a more tender period of life outside the present whirling wire-cage of business activity. Facing Willy Loman across an office desk, meeting his nervous glance and hearing his querulous voice, we would be very likely to glance at our wrist watch and our schedule of other appointments. We would not kick him out of the office, no, but we would certainly *ease* him out with more expedition than Willy had feebly hoped for. But suppose there had been no wrist watch or office clock [vi/vii] and suppose there had *not* been the schedule of pressing appointments, and suppose that we were not actually facing Willy across a desk—and facing a person is *not* the best way to *see* him!—suppose, in other words, that the meeting with Willy Loman had somehow occurred in a world *outside* of time. Then I think we would receive him with concern and kindness and even with respect. If the world of a play did not offer us this occasion to view its characters under that special condition of a *world without time,* then, indeed, the characters and occurrences of drama would become equally pointless, equally trivial, as corresponding meetings and happenings in life.

The classic tragedies of Greece had tremendous nobility. The actors wore great masks, movements were formal, dance-like, and the speeches had an epic quality which doubtless were as removed from the normal conversation of their contemporary society as they seem today. Yet they did not seem false to the Greek audiences: the magnitude of the events and the passions aroused by them did not seem ridiculously out of proportion to common experience. And I wonder if this was not because the Greek audiences knew, instinctively or by training, that the created world of a play is removed from that element which makes people *little* and their emotions fairly inconsequential.

Great sculpture often follows the lines of the human body: yet the repose of great sculpture suddenly transmutes those human lines to something that has an absoluteness, a purity, a beauty, which would not be possible in a living mobile form.

A play may be violent, full of motion: yet it has that special kind of repose which allows contemplation and produces [vii/viii] the climate in which tragic importance is a possible thing, provided that certain modern conditions are met.

In actual existence the moments of love are succeeded by the moments of satiety and sleep. The sincere remark is followed by a cynical distrust. Truth is fragmentary, at best: we love and betray each other not in quite the same breath but in two breaths that occur in fairly close sequence. But the fact that passion occurred in *passing*, that it then declined into a more familiar sense of indifference, should not be regarded as proof of its inconsequence. And this is the very truth that drama wishes to bring us . . .

Whether or not we admit it to ourselves, we are all haunted by a truly awful sense of impermanence. I have always had a particularly keen sense of this at New York cocktail parties, and perhaps that is why I drink the martinis almost as fast as I can snatch them from the tray. This sense is the febrile thing that hangs in the air. Horror of insincerity, of *not meaning*, overhangs these affairs like the cloud of cigarette smoke and the hectic chatter. This horror is the only thing, almost, that is left unsaid at such functions. All social functions involving a group of people not intimately known to each other are always under this shadow. They are almost always (in an unconscious way) like that last dinner of the condemned: where steak or turkey, whatever the doomed man wants, is served in his cell as a mockingly cruel reminder of what the great-big-little-transitory world had to offer.

In a play, time is arrested in the sense of being confined. By a sort of legerdemain, events are made to remain *events,* rather than being reduced so quickly to mere *occurrences.* The audience can sit back in a comforting dusk to watch a [viii/ix] world which is flooded with light and in which emotion and action have a dimension and dignity that they would likewise have in real existence, if only the shattering intrusion of time could be locked out.

About their lives people ought to remember that when they are finished, everything in them will be contained in a marvelous state of repose which is the same as that which they unconsciously admired in drama. The rush is temporary. The great and only possible dignity of man lies in his power deliberately to choose certain moral values by which to live as steadfastly as if he, too, like a character in a play, were immured against the corrupting rush of time. Snatching the eternal out of the desperately fleeting is the great magic trick of human existence. As far as we know, as far as there exists any kind of empiric evidence, there is no way to beat the game of *being* against *non-being,* in which non-being is the predestined victor on realistic levels.

Yet plays in the tragic tradition offer us a view of certain moral values in violent juxtaposition. Because we do not participate, except as spectators, we can view them clearly, within the limits of our emotional equipment. These people on the stage do not return our looks. We do not have to answer their questions nor make any sign of being in company with them, nor do we have to compete with their virtues nor resist their offenses. All at once, for this reason, we are able to *see* them! Our hearts are wrung by recognition and pity, so that the dusky shell of the auditorium where we are gathered anonymously together is flooded with an almost liquid warmth of unchecked human sympathies, relieved of self-consciousness, allowed to function . . .

Men pity and love each other more deeply than they permit themselves to know. The moment after the phone has [ix/x] been hung up, the hand reaches for a scratch pad and scrawls a notation: "Funeral Tuesday at five, Church of the Holy Redeemer, don't forget flowers." And the same hand is only a little shakier than usual as it reaches, some minutes later, for a highball glass that will pour a stupefaction over the kindled nerves. Fear and evasion are the two little beasts that chase each other's tails in the revolving wire-cage of our nervous world. They distract us from feeling too much about things. Time rushes toward us with its hospital tray of infinitely varied narcotics, even while it is preparing us for its inevitably fatal operation . . .

So successfully have we disguised from ourselves the intensity of our own feelings, the sensibility of our own hearts, that plays in the tragic tradition have begun to seem untrue. For a couple of hours we may surrender ourselves to a world of fiercely illuminated values in conflict, but when the stage is covered and the auditorium lighted, almost immediately there is a recoil of disbelief. "Well, well!" we say as we shuffle back up the aisle, while the play dwindles behind us with the sudden perspective of an early Chirico painting. By the time we have arrived at Sardi's, if not as soon as we pass beneath the marquee, we have convinced ourselves once more that life has as little resemblance to the curiously stirring and meaningful occurrences on the stage as a jingle has to an elegy of Rilke.

This modern condition of his theater audience is something that an author must know in advance. The diminishing influence of life's destroyer, time, must be somehow worked into the context of his play. Perhaps it is a certain foolery, a certain distortion toward the grotesque, which will solve the problem for him. Perhaps it is only restraint, putting a mute on the strings that would like to break all bounds. [x/xi] But almost surely, unless he contrives in some way to relate the dimensions of his tragedy to the dimensions of a world in which time is *included*—he will be left among his magnificent debris on a dark stage, muttering to himself: "Those fools . . ."

And if they could hear him above the clatter of tongues, glasses, chinaware and silver, they would give him this answer: "But you have shown us a world not ravaged by time. We admire your innocence. But we have seen our photographs, past and present. Yesterday evening we passed our first wife on the street. We smiled as we spoke but we didn't really see her! It's too bad, but we know what is true and not true, and at 3 a.m. your disgrace will be in print!"

PART THREE
REVIEWS AND CRITICISM

Review of *Death of a Salesman**

BROOKS ATKINSON (1894-   ) retired as senior drama critic for *The New York Times* in 1960. He had reviewed plays and written on the theatre for the *Times* since 1926, except for the war years, when he was foreign correspondent in China and Russia. In 1947 he received a Pulitzer prize for journalism (for his war reports). He has written travel books, a study of Henry Thoreau, and a book about the theatre, *Broadway Scrapbook* (1948).

Even the people who have had nothing to do with the production of Arthur Miller's "Death of a Salesman" take a kind of platonic pride in it. What Mr. Miller has achieved somehow seems to belong to everybody. For he is writing as an American with an affectionate understanding of American family people and their family problems; and everybody recognizes in his tragic play things that they know are poignantly true. Although Mr. Miller is the author, he does not dissociate himself from his simple story of an ordinary family. He participates by recording it with compassion.

Discarded in his old age from the only world he knows, Willy Loman, the worn-out salesman, crawls into his grave where he thinks he is worth more to his family than he would be if he were still tinkering around the house. But Mr. Miller does not blame Willy, his sons, his boss or the system, and he draws no moral conclusions. In the space of one somber evening in the theatre he has caught the life and death of a traveling salesman and told it tenderly with a decent respect for Willy's dignity as a man.

In "All My Sons" two seasons ago Mr. Miller was arguing a moral point; like an efficient craftsman, he constructed his drama to reach a conclusion. That was a first-rate piece of work by an author of high convictions. But without being precious or self-conscious, "Death of a Salesman" is a creative work of art in which the form is so completely blended with the theme that you are scarcely aware of the writing. You accept it as a whole—play, acting, directing and scene designing fused into a unit of expression.

From the technical point of view Mr. Miller has accomplished some remarkable things in this drama. Without moving scenery, he has covered the past and present of Willy's itinerant career in Brooklyn, New York and Boston, recorded the separate careers of his two sons and the neighbors, touched on the problems and personality of Willy's boss and introduced some imagery from Willy's separate dream-world.

At one time, this would have been highly daring and experimental in the theatre. We once had a jargon for things like these—"expressionistic," "constructivist," "centrifugal." But "Death of a Salesman" belongs in none of the categories. It is a fresh creation in a style of its own. Mr. Miller has mastered his material and turned it directly into the grievous life of an affable man.

Strictly speaking there is a moral basis for the catastrophe in the last act. Willy

*Brooks Atkinson, Review of *Death of a Salesman*, New York Times*, February 20, 1949, Sec. 2, p. 1.

has always believed in something that is unsound. He has assumed that success comes to those who are "well liked," as he puts it. He does not seem to be much concerned about the quality of the product he is selling. His customers buy, he thinks, because they like him—because he is hale and hearty and a good man with jokes.

Out of sheer physical exuberance he rears his son, Biff, in the same tradition. Biff is popular, too. Willy indulgently overlooks Biff's easy going cheating in school and petty pilfering from the contractor next door. So long as Biff plays good football, wins games, gets his name in the newspapers and makes friends Willy thinks that he will succeed in life and carry on the jovial Loman tradition.

But these are the most unsubstantial things in a life. Although Biff is well liked, he is flunked out of school because he is not interested in studying. Although he is as good hearted as his father, he never gets over his habit of stealing, which finally lands him in jail. Willy has staked his whole happiness on Biff's success, but Biff is a failure.

And the unsubstantial quality of his own success catches up with Willy in his old age. The formula of personal popularity no longer works. The competition of chain stores has eliminated the personal element. Willy's friends are old or dead. Willy is old himself. He no longer has the physical gusto for slapping people on the back and breaking down resistance with good fellowship. He cannot stand the nervous strain of driving his car. Willy has lost his usefulness to the business world because he has founded a career on things that are ephemeral. He and Biff are good fellows and good animals—strong, full of fun and carefree. But they live in a world of golden illusion and they founder on reality in the end.

Not that Mr. Miller is holding them up as bad examples. On the contrary he knows that they are good men—especially Willy, who has never had a mean thought in his life. Out of sheer good nature he has gone cheerfully down a dead end street, always devoted to his family and carelessly sure of himself. Although his two boys do not understand him, they love him. His wife not only loves him but understands him thoroughly. Mr. Miller is not writing about ideas but about human beings, whom he is sufficiently modest to be able to value properly. And the tragedy of "Death of a Salesman" is almost unbearable in the last act because Mr. Miller has drawn the portrait of a good man who represents the homely, decent, kindly virtues of a middle-class society.

By common consent, this is one of the finest dramas in the whole range of the American theatre. Humane in its point of view, it has stature and insight, awareness of life, respect for people and knowledge of American manners and of modern folkways. From the technical point of view, it is virtuoso theatre. It brings the whole theatre alive.

Although Elia Kazan has done some memorable jobs of direction in the past few years, he has never equaled the selfless but vibrant expression of this epic drama which has force, clarity, rhythm and order in the performing. Without being fastidious, the performance has taste. Jo Mielziner's skeletonized setting is a brilliant design, tragic in mood, but also selfless and practical. Alex North has composed a stirring interpretive score which, like the direction and scenery, has the grace to melt unobtrusively into the work as a whole.

The acting is superb, particularly in Mildred Dunnock's warmly devoted portrait of the wife and Arthur Kennedy's turbulent, anxious playing of Biff. Although the part of the bewildered salesman is fully developed in Mr. Miller's writing, Lee J. Cobb brings a touch of human grandeur to the acting. He keeps it on the high plane of tragic acting— larger than the specific life it is describing. Willy is not a great man, but his tragedy is great, partly because of the power and range of Mr. Cobb's acting.

When Willy's life collapses, a whole world crashes because Mr. Cobb fills the play with so much solid humanity. In terms of the business world Willy is insignificant. But in terms of life he is a hero. Like Mr. Miller, Mr. Cobb knows what Willy is worth, and so do all of us.

Review of *Death of a Salesman**

GEORGE JEAN NATHAN (1882-1958), noted for his witty style, was a drama critic from 1905 until his death. He was author of a large number of books on dramatic and theatrical topics, the last of which was *The Theatre in the Fifties* (1953). Each year from 1942 to 1951 he collected his reviews, in revised and enlarged versions, in a *Theatre Book of the Year*. Thus he had the advantage of taking into account the opinions of his fellow-critics during the preceding year, and of giving more mature thought to his subject than is usually possible in a hastily written review.

W. H. Auden has thus differentiated between them: "Greek tragedy is the tragedy of necessity; that is, the feeling aroused in the spectator is 'what a pity it had to be this way'; Christian tragedy is the tragedy of possibility, 'what a pity it was this way when it might have been otherwise.' "

The definition again is found to be snugly appropriate to Miller's work and evidently no one appreciates its aptness more than he does. But where other playwrights often have usurped to themselves the Christian pity, he, though doubtless he experiences it himself, prefers to leave it to his audience. Therein lies one of his play's chief merits, for it does succeed in substantially evoking both an immediate and a lingering compassion not alone for the life its protagonist lived but for the life he might have lived in its stead, and with none of the more usual playwright's hard insistence.

There are other merits. The writing is simple; there is [**279/280**] no slightest pretentiousness; and, though the play, because of its basic disorganized expressionistic form, is susceptible of strained effect, little sense of strain is felt by its auditors. There is, moreover, none of the heavy striving for lyric tone common to the plays of prosy writers who seek to conceal their prosiness in something they choose to imagine is poetry, yet something of a poetic tinge nonetheless at times issues from it. And, finally, though it misses the spiritual exaltation that is the requirement of fine tragedy and though its end effect is rather acute depression, it triumphs over itself by virtue of the uncompromising honesty of its emotion.

That the play must have a considerable internal force becomes apparent when one considers that it registers the effect it has registered in spite of several confounding production elements. Though Elia Kazan, aided greatly by Mielziner's imaginative setting, has directed admirably the physical flow of the tragedy, his direction of the vocal is often so bad that its intrinsically gentle spirit has a difficult time in establishing itself. Lines that should be read quietly are so shouted and yelled that it seems at times he is determined to make the play a melodrama in spite of itself. There are moments, indeed, when the melodramatic screaming becomes so loud that it is next to impossible to make out what the father or his two

George Jean Nathan, Review of *Death of a Salesman*, in *The Theatre Book of the Year, 1948-1949* (New York: Alfred A. Knopf, Inc., 1949), pp. 279-285.

sons are talking about and not to feel that Lincoln J. Carter will pop in at any minute with a scene showing the father in his automobile racing against the tooting New York, New Haven and Hartford on one of his selling trips to Boston.

There is, too, the casting of Lee Cobb as the salesman doomed by false standards and self-deception to humiliation and failure. I can well understand the wisdom of avoiding the conventional in casting the role not with the Donald Meek type of actor but with one of strength and size, since the theatrical effect of tragic decline is thereby heightened. But Cobb is so bullish not merely in physical person but, more disastrously, in elemental grain and spirit that one feels, wrongly to be sure, that the playwright is arbitrarily pulling him into the picture and that, were the [280/281] character left on its own, his life would have taken a decidedly different course. And there are, as well, several additional points in the staging which take unhappy advantage of the author. The direction resorts to such obvious stuff as indicating the now aged salesman's once younger nature by having him jovially kick up his heels in a gazazka, his love of his elder son by causing him so to overdo camaraderie in pawing embraces and hearty yawping that he seems less the potential figure in a tragedy than a one-time understudy for Sam Bernard in *The Rich Mr. Hoggenheimer,* and his pretence of bravery in the face of consciousness of defeat by such a bellowing as was never equalled by the late Melbourne MacDowell, a booming mountebank if ever there was one, as the Duke de Gonzague. Some of my colleagues, I note, have described Cobb's performance as "tremendous." It is. As a boiler explosion.

That the play is weakened not only by such things but by Kazan's favorite occasional melodramatic emphasis on the box-office's behalf is clear. One periodically gets much the impression one would have got if they had brought in Paul Armstrong and Wilson Mizner to pepper up a play like *Our Town.* But the innate silent power of Miller's script, the reticence of

much of his writing, and the intermittent excellent flashes of imagery—such, for one example, as the memory of road drummers "riding on a smile and a shoeshine"—combine to make one sufficiently oblivious of the disturbances and to react to the whole as the author hoped.

Henry Arthur Jones once observed that "unless drama is touched with a sense of eternity, wrapped 'round with the splendor of heroism, and imbedded in what is primary and of everlasting import, the mere reproduction on the stage of the commonplace details of everyday life must always be barren, worthless, and evanescent." There is much to be said for the definition. *Death Of A* [sic] *Salesman,* by it, does not measure up, does not measure up by a very considerable margin, to a tragedy of real artistic stature. Its touch with a sense of eternity is but flicking; there is in it little splendor of heroism; it is imbedded but sketchily in what [281/282] is primary and of everlasting import; and it reproduces merely the commonplace details of everyday life. But it remains not barren, nor worthless, nor, possibly, evanescent, because it touches these commonplace details with a sense of deep and pitiful recognition, because there is splendor of a sort not in any heroism but in its very human cowardice, and because, at least for the time one is in its presence, what may not be primary and of everlasting import is made out of one's immediate won sympathy to seem so.

Whenever a critic, reviewing a play of some pretensions to quality, employs the word "melodrama" in a derogatory sense, other critics who are extreme in their regard for the play are certain to take him acidly to task with the now familiar remark that, since melodrama is the tone of to-day's world, it is asinine to use the term in condemnation of it. The gentlemen seem to overlook three small points. First, the fact that melodrama seems to be the present world's chief characteristic does not necessarily justify it as a chief characteristic of dramatic or any other art. Secondly, there are various kinds of melodrama and the melodrama that the critic has in mind in the instance of the play he is considering is the kind which in the interests of theatricalism raises its head at debatable moments. Where, in a word, completely honest characters would comport themselves with some intellectual, psychological and emotional reserve, the characters purely for the sake of theatrical effect are abritrarily made to dive off the Brooklyn bridge and hold up a mail train. And, thirdly, the melodrama is resorted to in order to lend a surface excitement to what a better dramatist might make even more exciting through emotional and physical reserve.

Sometimes the melodrama, which, incidentally, is the easiest of all dramatic forms to master, is unintentional on the part of a playwright, who confuses it with inner intensity of theme and character. Sometimes, when intentional, it gets out of hand and so supervises character that the latter explodes into nothingness from spontaneous combustion. And, sometimes, of course, it is well considered and completely and properly in key. But much more often in [282/283] the work of various American playwrights, whether deliberately or not deliberately, it has the air of an exclamation point inserted into what is essentially a passive sentence, the aspect of red-painted fingernails on a small girl child, and the sense of pulling the lever of a street corner fire-box and bringing on the engines, hook-and-ladders and hose carts in a false alarm. It is, in short, frequently a youngster's loud "boo" designed to startle other youngsters, a little boy's Indian whoop hopeful of scaring his quietly amused father. And it also, even when there is nothing intrinsically wrong with it, is sometimes so whimsically out of the immediate surroundings that it sounds something like the major domo of Buckingham Palace elegantly answering the telephone and exclaiming, "Why, yes, of course, Mrs. Greenberg."

This was the kind of melodrama that, among other things, made Miller's widely admired previous play, *All My Sons*, strike me as an inferior performance. I have already in the directly preceding volume of these annals spoken of the dubiety of his character drawing in that play, as well as of other elements in it that were open to skepticism. Since this subsequent play, *Death Of A Salesman*, is clear of all such defects, it is gratifying to hear Miller confess that he himself now sees the faults of *All My Sons* and equally encouraging to observe that some of those critics who were most enthusiastic about it now also see it, belatedly, as having been what they admit was a "contrived job."

As will be remembered, *All My Sons* was a dramaturgically conventional play of the rococo "well-made" species. Commenting on it, Miller says, "The conventional play form forces the writer to siphon everything into a single place at a single time, and squeezes the humanity out of a play. Why shouldn't a play have the depth, the completeness, and the diversity of a novel? I felt I had to perfect conventional technique first and *All My Sons* was an exercise."

Death Of A Salesman is no such exercise; it is the result of profit from trial and error, and not merely in respect to [283/284] dramaturgy. There is complete honesty in most of the characters; there is absolute honesty in contemplation of its theme as against the sense of fabrication one had in the case of *All My Sons*; and there is, unlike in that play, a minimum of theatrical compromise. Even in the few instances where one feels that perhaps Miller operates to avoid a possible monotony by including episodes of some forced theatrical color, the episodes themselves—as, for example, the scene in which the sons entertain their father in a Sixth Avenue corner saloon fabulously equipped with champagne service—somehow do not seem altogether too removed from truth. And the point of view throughout, in its challenge of popular conceptions, is strikingly intelligent. The popular credos that nothing is more valuable to a man than being liked; that sincere, hard work is bound to reap its ultimate reward; that children, even if they conceal the fact, have an inborn love for their parents; that loyalty is always a virtue; and that only the incompetent fail in this world—such beliefs, with no show of facile cynicism, Miller punctures. His tragedy of the little man has in it also, if obliquely, a little something of the tragedy of much bigger men, whether successes or failures by the world's standards.

In a preface to the published play, Mr. Miller goes to considerable lengths to justify his belief that the tragedy of the little man may be quite as exalted dramatically and artistically as that of the classic kings and emperors. He need not have gone to so much trouble. It may be, but there are two points which, seemingly in the interests of his own play, he chooses to overlook. Save the little man have something of a mind, which Mr. Miller's protagonist has not, his tragedy, while it may be moving, is in finality without universal size and is like the experience we suffer in contemplating on the highways a run-over and killed dog, undeniably affecting but without any profound significance. The tragedy, accordingly, becomes that not of a full-winged human being but merely that of a mindless clod, at once pitiful and touching but lost from the outset in the maelstrom of inevitable circumstance. And his strug- [284/285] gle against his surroundings becomes not cumulatively holding but obviously foredoomed, since there is no share of intellect even modestly to assist him. Great tragedy is the tragedy of man's mind in strong conflict with the stronger fates; minor tragedy that of mindless man already beaten by them.

The second point is the language in which tragedy is written. The fall of kings calls for a splendor of prose or poetry, otherwise it may be quite as unimpressive as the fall of little men. But the tragedy of the little man, to be as impressive as that of a king, calls as well for such treatment. It is not the story of and the reasons for a ruler's tragic end that remain in our hearts and memories but the flights of language through which they are related. Commonplace language, though it may be exactly suited to the tragedy of the underdog, may make for first-rate theatre but scarcely for first-rate and overwhelming drama.

In defence of his point of view, Mr. Miller concludes, "It is time, I think, that we who are without kings took up this bright thread of our history and followed it to the only place it can possibly lead in our time—the heart and spirit of the average man."

We are not without kings, though they may not wear the royal purple. We have men of heart and spirit—and also mind. They are or may be the meat of important tragedy. The average man's, the common man's, tragedy, save it be laid over and lifted above itself with the deceptive jewels of English speech, can be no more in the temple of dramatic art than the pathetic picture of a lovable idiot lifting his small voice against the hurricane of the world.

Review of *Death of a Salesman**

ELEANOR CLARK (1913-   ), American novelist, short-story writer, and essayist, has contributed a number of commentaries on the Broadway scene to *Partisan Review*, which is one of the leading critical magazines, noted for its incisive and uncompromising writing on American cultural and social life.

It would seem that the success of Arthur Miller's, or Elia Kazan's, "Death of a Salesman" has been due largely to the feeling of depression with which one makes for the exit. The idea is that anything that can make you feel that glum must be good, true and above all important—and publicity aside, it must be admitted that this culturally lace-curtain notion has a few things to support it these days at the Morosco. These are, notably, a superb performance by Lee Cobb as the salesman, a beautifully flexible and elegant stylization of a small Brooklyn house by Jo Mielziner, and a production so slick and fast that you have hardly the time or the presumption to question it. Unfortunately, however, it becomes necessary to question just what it is that gives the play its brilliant down-in-the-mouth effect, since it would surely be hard for any but its most insensitive admirers to deny that although they came out from it stuffed full of gloom, they were strangely lacking in a sense either of pity or of illumination.

They have seen a good, or good enough, man driven to suicide, a family in despair, an illusion shattered, and a portrayal of American life that should, it seems, have given them the sharpest pang of all; they have been expressly invited to indulge the tragic sense and to carry away a conception of man's fate as though from a production of "Oedipus Rex", and what they have carried away

instead is just that curious, rankling gloom. As the salesman's wife puts it after he has thrown himself under a train: "I can't cry. I want to cry, but I can't." If an honest poll could be taken it might well turn out that a large majority of these admirers, including the critics, had been secretly telling themselves not only after the play but during it that they were not really bored, just a little tired that night. Or was it perhaps that the tragic sense with all it has undergone from the facts of recent times needs now some entirely different, some unimaginably new appeal, and this was too much to ask [631/632] of a play?—better be grateful for this. But of course there is no reason to be grateful for something that pretends to be what it is not, and the fact of the matter is that these secret whisperings, if they occurred, were well justified. The play, with its peculiar hodge-podge of dated materials and facile new ones, is not tragedy at all but an ambitious piece of confusionism, such as in any other sphere would probably be called a hoax, and which has been put across by purely technical skills not unlike those of a magician or an acrobat.

Up to a point this might be considered no more than the usual operation of the second-rate mind as glamorized by Broadway. But there is a particular twist to the matter this time, which helps to explain how a subject that in its general

*Eleanor Clark, Review of *Death of a Salesman*, Partisan Review*, XVI (June, 1949), 631-635.

lines was run ragged fifteen or twenty years ago should be able to turn up now as a vehicle for such large claims and such ponderous emotionalizing.

Certainly as representing the false dream aspect of American society Mr. Miller's salesman offers nothing very original. The old gag about the install-ment-plan frigidaire ("Once in my life I'd like to own something outright before it's broke") are [sic] evidently still good for a laugh, and there is always a pocket of pathos reserved for the mortgage, but things have been sadder and funnier be-fore. A slightly fresher breeze does blow at moments. Willy Loman calls for a genuine smile or two with his distinction between being "liked" and being "well-liked," and the perception behind this is accurate enough, even though in context it becomes one of the half-truths typical of the play. Willy's rock-bottom faith has been in the capacity to get along with people, to "make a good impression"; it is with this faith that he slides to old age and ruin while his brother Ben, who appears in some well-staged flashbacks, piles up a fortune in Alaska, and because of it at the end he is still pushing his favorite son Biff toward a failure worse than his own, the irony, as presented, ly-ing not so much in the failure as in the denial of the man's true nature and talents along the way. Willy liked to work with his hands and had been happy when he was making a cement porch; and Biff, who had been happy as a ranch-hand in the West, has at the time of the play rest-lessly driven himself back home. In the end, after the suicide, it is the flashy son Hap, content with cheap success and easy women, who speaks of the salesman's dream as having been "good." Biff knows better—the dream was rotten though he speaks of his father nevertheless as a "prince"—and the wife knows better still; Willy was as good "as many other people." In short, he is the common man, and something or other has gone terribly wrong. The point is, what and why. [632/633]

At first blush the answer seems fairly simple. Willy has a fatal flaw. He lives in a dream world; he can't face reality; he has always had excuses for his own failures ("the shop was closed for inven-tory") and has ruined Biff's life by in-dulging him all through his childhood in any whim including theft. It is a good theme. But it turns out not only that the author is saying a good deal more than this, but that he is also either very un-clear as to his further meanings, or very anxious to present them and evade re-sponsibility for them at the same time. It is, of course, the capitalist system that has done Willy in; the scene in which he is brutally fired after some forty years with the firm comes straight from the party line literature of the 'thirties, and the idea emerges lucidly enough through all the confused motivations of the play that it is our particular form of money economy that has bred the absurdly false ideals of both father and sons. It emerges, however, like a succession of shots from a duck-blind. Immediately aft-er every crack the playwright withdraws behind an air of pseudo-universality, and hurries to present some cruelty or mis-fortune due either to Willy's own weak-ness, as when he refuses his friend's offer of a job after he has been fired, or gratuitously from some other source, as in the quite unbelievable scene of the two sons walking out on their father in the restaurant. In the end, after so much heaping of insult on injury, all one really knows about Willy Loman is that if the system doesn't kick him in the teeth he will do it himself—a well-known if weari-some tendency, that in itself might have dramatic possibilities, but that is neither particularly associated with salesmen nor adapted to the purposes of this play.

What it does lend itself to in this case is an intellectual muddle and a lack of candor that regardless of Mr. Miller's conscious intent are the main earmark of contemporary fellow traveling. What used to be a roar has become a whine, and this particular piece of whining has been so expertly put over that it has been able to pass for something else, but behind all the fancy staging the old basic clumsiness and lack of humor are there. To be sure there are a few moments of ordinary Broadway sprightliness, as in the matter of the ice-box, or Hap's little performance with the girls in the restaurant, but these are in passing.

The crucial scenes, like the general conception, are all heavily dead-pan, to an extent that floors the talents of every actor in the play but Mr. Cobb; Cameron Mitchell and Arthur Kennedy as the two sons do as well as possible with the script but both are driven by it at various points to over-act, and Mildred Dunnock in the part of the wife is obliged to keep up a tension of high-pitched nobility that would wear [633/634] out one's tragic sense long before the end even if nothing else did. As for the clumsiness, it shows not only in the large aspects of the play but, rather surprisingly considering the general technical excellence of the job in a number of small ones too. That the much-stressed point of Willy's being deprived of working with his hands, and of his pride in that, is not a specific reflection on the money standards which are central to the play's action, but as remarked on by many writers over the last hundred years, has to do with modern mechanized society in whatever form, could perhaps be passed over. But nothing excuses the triteness and pseudo-psycho-analytic nature of the Boston scene, dragged in to explain Biff's failures, though he would have been far better perceived as a contemporary character without it. It is also annoying not to know what the salesman sells, and whether or not the insurance is going to be paid after his death, and to have the wife say in her final speech that they were just getting out of debt, with no previous explanation of how, and when in fact we have just seen Willy getting further into debt.

These are details, but they indicate something of the speciousness of the play, which manages at every point to obscure both the real tragedy and the real comedy of the material. Willy is presumed to be losing his mind because he talks to himself, which permits the long series of flashbacks that give the play its illusion of liveliness, a form of madness that can at least, in the case, be called convenient; but all of us have seen and probably most of us have experienced delusions wilder and more illuminating than this. In the picture of Biff's unhappy restlessness Mr. Miller gives an impression of contemporaneity, but that is all; the true malaise of men of thirty now is a great deal more terrible than what happens to anyone in this play, and would not be a subject for a Broadway success. And so on. The play is made of such semi-perceptions, as can easily be appreciated by a glance at Eudora Welty's story, "Death of a Traveling Salesman," published some years ago.

There are of course many possible approaches to the character of the salesman, and Miss Welty was humble in hers, but she succeeded nevertheless in some twenty pages in creating a figure of loneliness and haunting futility that conveys a truly tragic sense, and remains as a clear, echoing symbol in the mind. The story makes no claims, it says only what it has to say, at its own sure quiet pace, and its limitations are never violated, but it strikes deep and has been deeply felt and so they become irrelevant. If one chooses to take it that way, this is as strong a condemnation as one could wish of one of the abnormal, humanly stultifying aspects of our society, as represented by one of its most [634/635] victimized as well as victimizing characters; and yet the effect, with all its continuing vibrations of meaning, has been achieved by nothing but a simple juxtaposition of a moment of the salesman's life with a pattern of simple, almost primitive love. There is no sound of whining here. It may be that this salesman too would have enjoyed working with his hands, but he is incapable of it; when his car rolls into a ditch another man has to haul it out for him, and he goes to his death in a dumb despair at the thought of that other man's life.

As against as strong and unpretentious a piece as this, Mr. Miller's use of his material seems even more unpleasantly pompous, and above all, flat. It can hardly have occurred to anyone to use such a word as, for instance, suggestiveness in connection with it. Everything is stated, two or three times over, all with a great air of something like poetry about it but actually with no remove, no moment of departure from the literal whatever; through scene after snappy scene the action ploughs along on a level of naturalism that has not even the virtue of being natural. A jumble of styles is maintained, with borrowings from the movies, the ballet and the Greeks, and at moments of particular significance the colloquial but unimagized language of the play becomes a trifle more genteel —"I search, and I search, and I search, and I can't understand," Willy's wife says after his suicide, though she has been foreseeing it and explaining it from the beginning of the play. But such tricks, however skillfully worked, are no substitute for real impact, and can only momentarily hide the fact that this is a very dull business, which departs in no way that is to its credit from the general mediocrity of our commercial theater . . . .

Review of *Death of a Salesman**

HAROLD CLURMAN (1901-   ), director and critic, has been actively associated with the American theatre since 1924. In 1931 he helped to found the Group Theatre and achieved considerable success with his direction of the plays of Clifford Odets. He tells the story of this theatre and its contribution to American drama in *The Fervent Years* (1945). Recent plays that he has produced or directed include Arthur Miller's *All My Sons,* Carson McCullers' *The Member of the Wedding,* William Inge's *Bus Stop,* Jean Giraudoux's *Tiger at the Gates,* Jean Anouilh's *Waltz of the Toreadors,* and Tennessee Williams' *Orpheus Descending.* He has written on the theatre for *Tomorrow* magazine (1946-1952), the *New Republic* (1949-1952), and (since 1953) for the *Nation. Lies Like Truth* (1958) is a collection of his essays on the theatre.

Arthur Miller's *Death of a Salesman* is one of the outstanding plays in the repertory of the American theatre. That its theme is not, strictly speaking, new to our stage—Arthur Richman's **[68/69]** *Ambush* (1921), J. P. McEvoy's *The Potters* (1923), Elmer Rice's *The Adding Machine* (1923), George Kelly's *The Show-Off* (1924), Clifford Odets' *Awake and Sing* and *Paradise Lost* (1935) being in this respect its antecedents—does not in any way lessen its effect or significance. The value of *Death of a Salesman* lies in the fact that it states its theme with penetrating clarity in our era of troubled complacency.

Death of a Salesman is a challenge to the American dream. Lest this be misunderstood, I hasten to add that there are two versions of the American dream. The historical American dream is the promise of a land of freedom with opportunity and equality for all. This dream needs no challenge, only fulfillment. But since the Civil War, and particularly since 1900, the American dream has become distorted to the dream of business success. A distinc-

tion must be made even in this. The original premise of our dream of success—popularly represented in the original boy parables of Horatio Alger—was that enterprise, courage and hard work were the keys to success. Since the end of the First World War this too has changed. Instead of the ideals of hard work and courage, we have salesmanship. Salesmanship implies a certain element of fraud: the ability to put over or sell a commodity regardless of its intrinsic usefulness. The goal of salesmanship is to make a deal, to earn a profit—the accumulation of profit being an unquestioned end in itself.

This creates a new psychology. To place all value in the mechanical act of selling and in self-enrichment impoverishes the human beings who are rendered secondary to the deal. To possess himself fully, a man must have an intimate connection with that with which he deals as well as with the person with whom he deals. When the connection is no more than an exchange of commodities, the man himself ceases to be a man, becomes a commodity himself, a spiritual cipher.

*Harold Clurman, Review of *Death of a Salesman,* in *Lies Like Truth. Theatre Reviews and Essays* (New York: The Macmillan Company, 1958), pp. 68-72.

This is a humanly untenable situation. The salesman realizes this. Since his function precludes a normal human relationship, he substitutes an imitation of himself for the real man. He sells his "personality." This "personality," now become only a means to an end—namely, the consummated sale—is a mask worn so long that it soon comes to be mistaken, even by the man who [69/70] wears it, as his real face. But it is only his commercial face with a commercial smile and a commercial aura of the well-liked, smoothly adjusted, oily cog in the machine of the sales apparatus.

This leads to a behavior pattern which is ultimately doomed; not necessarily because of the economic system of which it is the human concomitant, but quite simply because a man is not a machine. The death of Arthur Miller's salesman is symbolic of the breakdown of the whole concept of salesmanship inherent in our society.

Miller does not say these things explicitly. But it is the strength of his play that it is based on this understanding, and that he is able to make his audience realize it no matter whether or not they are able consciously to formulate it. When the audience weeps at *Death of a Salesman*, it is not so much over the fate of Willy Loman—Miller's pathetic hero—but over the millions of such men who are our brothers, uncles, cousins, neighbors. The lovable lower-middle-class mole Willy Loman represents is related to a type of living and thinking in which nearly all of us—"professionals" as well as salesmen—share.

Willy Loman never acknowledges or learns the error of his way. To the very end he is a devout believer in the ideology that destroys him. He believes that life's problems are all solved by making oneself "well liked" (in the salesman's sense) and by a little cash. His wife knows only that he is a good man and that she must continue to love him. His sons, who are his victims, as he has been of the false dream by which he has lived, draw different conclusions from his failure.

The younger boy, Hap, believes only that his father was an incompetent (as do many of the play's commentators), but he does not reject his father's ideal. (It is to be noted that in a very important sense Willy Loman is sympathetic precisely because of his failure to make himself a successful machine.) The older boy, Biff, comes to understand the falsity of his father's ideal and determines to set out on a new path guided by a recovery of his true self.

There are minor flaws in *Death of a Salesman*, such as the constant pointing to a secret in the older brother's past which is presumed to be the immediate cause of his moral breakdown—the secret turning out to be the boy's discovery of his father's [70/71] marital infidelity. There is validity in this scene as part of the over-all picture of the father-son relationship. A shock such as the boy sustains here often serves to propel people into the unexplored territory of their subconscious, and may thus become the springboard for further and more basic questioning. Miller's error here is to make the boy's horror at his father's "deceit" appear crucial rather than contributory to the play's main line.

Some people have objected that the use of the stream-of-consciousness technique—the play dramatizes Willy's recollection of the past, and at times switches from a literal presentation of his memory to imaginary and semisymbolic representation of his thought—is confusing, and a sign of weakness in the author's grasp of his material.

These objections do not impress me. The limitations of *Death of a Salesman* are part of its virtues. The merit in Miller's treatment of his material lies in a certain clean, moralistic rationalism. It is not easy to make the rational a poetic attribute, but Miller's growth since *All My Sons* consists in his ability to make his moral and rationalistic characteristics produce a kind of poetry.

The truth of *Death of a Salesman* is conveyed with what might be compared to a Living Newspaper, documentary accuracy. With this there is a grave probity and a sensitivity that raise the whole beyond the level of what might otherwise have seemed to be only agitation and propoganda. Other playwrights may be more colorful, lyrical and rich with the fleshed nerves and substance of life; Miller holds us with a sense of his soundness. His play has an ascetic, slate-like hue, as if he were eschewing all exaggeration and extravagance; and with a sobriety that is not without humor, yet entirely free of frivolity, he issues the forthright commandment, "Thou shalt not be a damn' fool!"

Elia Kazan's production is first rate. It is true to Miller's qualities, and adds to them a swift directness, muscularity and vehemence of conviction. If any further criticism is in order I should say the production might have gained a supplementary dimension if it had more of the aroma of individual characterization, more intimacy, more of the quiet music of specific humanity—small, as the people in the play are small, and yet suggestive of those larger truths their lives signify. [71/72]

Mildred Dunnock as the mother embodies the production's best features: its precision, clarity, purity of motive. Someone has said that the part might have been more moving if it had been played by an actress like Pauline Lord with all the magic overtones and "quarter-tones"

of her subtle sensibility. Concretely such a suggestion is, of course, irrelevant, but it points to a need I feel in the production as a whole more than to Miss Dunnock's particular performance.

Lee Cobb as the salesman is massively powerful and a commanding actor every step of the way. Yet I cannot help feeling that Cobb's interpretation is more akin to the prototype of a King Lear than to Willy Loman. What differentiates Willy from some similarly abused figure is his utter unconsciousness—even where the author gives him conscious lines—his battered pride, querulous innocence, wan bewilderment even within the context of protest and angry vociferation.

Cameron Mitchell as the younger son is eminently likable, but for the play's thesis he ought also to be something of a comic stinker. Arthur Kennedy, who plays the older son, is a truly fine actor, who loses some of his edge because the general high pitch of the production forces him to blunt his natural delicacy.

Jo Mielziner's scene design seems to me too complex in shape and too diverse in style to be wholly satisfactory for a functional set or for beautiful decoration. Neither this nor any of the other faults that may have been found in *Death of a Salesman* prevent it from remaining a cardinal event not only of this season but of many a long year in the American theatre.

Arthur Miller's Collected Plays*

WILLIAM J. NEWMAN is Professor of Government at Boston University; *Twentieth Century* is a long-established British periodical. This review is particularly interesting as an attempt to clarify the peculiarly American qualities of Miller's plays for British readers.

Arthur Miller says in his introduction to *Arthur Miller's Collected Plays* that his plays are plays of ideas, that a play without ideas is no play at all. Consequently he spends much of the space of his long introduction telling the reader what ideas he has tried to present in his drama. It is a useful thing to do. Being a playwright who works closely with the pragmatic content of his plays it has been easy to see what each play means but not what his plays mean. Now that his drama as a whole has been put before the reader and he has told us what it means to him it is possible to see what he is doing.

One thing he does not do. He does not write political plays. As he says,

A play cannot be equated with a political philosophy. . . . There is no political program—any more than there is a theory of tragedy—which can encompass the complexities of real life. . . .

One may wonder at Miller's refusal to understand the purpose of a theory and to see that it exists exactly to encompass complexities, and still recognize that this point of view has its value. It not only negates the attempts of those who aim to put him on their side of politics, but it also gives him and his audience freedom to see the plays in a broader context than that of ideology. But his refusal of the criticism and concepts of ideology and theory does not lead to the vice of well-meaning but fuzzy ideas; quite the contrary, he is freed for the precision which comes from the use of American images which he has manipulated into a viable dramatic form. The source of his plays in these images is a cause of strength and weakness, but whatever the case they make his plays potent in their effect; an [491/492] American has only to read the following to have the uncomfortable feeling that everything is about to be told:

It [*The Death of a Salesman*] grew from images of futility—the cavernous Sunday afternoons polishing the car. Where is that car now? And the chamois cloths carefully washed and put up to dry, where are the chamois cloths?

He details a good many other images of futility, but this one is enough. What a subject to bring up—those chamois cloths, those Sunday afternoons. They have only to be mentioned to bring back whole scenes of the emptiness peculiar to America; Willy Loman is a *real* ghost.

In the face of such precise evocations many things can be said, but talk about the existence or absence of political or social attitudes is not one of them. Yet Miller certainly is what is now commonly called a committed playwright. He is not committed in the sense of trying to push new ideas into the defenceless heads of his audience. He even sees an ironic and unresolvable conflict between a new idea

*William J. Newman, "Arthur Miller's Collected Plays," Twentieth Century, CLXIV (November, 1958), 491-496.

and drama or any idea and drama. His aims are set low, for all he wants to do is present ideas which are already 'in the air': 'each of these plays . . . was begun in the belief that it was unveiling a truth already known but unrecognized as such.' Yet this concept of the rôle of the dramatist is a commitment as worthy as any other; and if it tends to make an author wary of abstractions—of theory—it can also give him the power of fascinating his audience.

But what is the nature of this commitment? If Miller says that he is a dramatist of ideas in the tradition of Ibsen, then what are his ideas?

Although there is no fundamental 'philosophical' view which can be derived from Miller's plays, there is nevertheless a persistent and continuing problem which gives him the raw material of his plays and the means of expressing his ideas. It is a problem which enables Miller to narrow down the situation of universal man to the concrete situation of a particular American man. The relationship of the American father and son and of both to the American family in the American 'situation' provides him, not with his themes, but with the raw material of tensions and conflicts between human beings. (Note how uninteresting and undeveloped the women are in Miller's plays; they witness the drama but have little to contribute to it.) For Arthur Miller it is not just the salesman which is interesting and which he is discussing, but the salesman as a family man; Willy Loman's greatest and most immediate failure was not his failure to sell whatever it was he was selling, but as a man in relationship to his son, a failure of love. His significance comes from the *fact* of the American family—the fact of those awful chamois cloths—and its failure. Miller evidently has some need for such a [492/493] factual basis for his drama for he records in his introduction how his earlier (unpublished) plays were diffuse for lack of 'cause and effect, hard actions, facts, the geometry of relationships.'

What kind of 'hard actions, facts' does the family in America provide for Arthur Miller? The American family, it should be understood, is excellent material not only for a humorist but for someone who takes life seriously, for it is a constantly fragile, constantly disintegrating attempt to create a personal framework of affection and loyalty in a world where class, institutional and local loyalties have been reduced to a minimum or do not exist at all. Richard Hoggart has claimed that Auden left Britain for America because British life was too cozy. Whatever American life is, it is not cozy; there are none of the institutional—and family—protections which give the British middle class at least a semblance of security, of 'place' in a society. The American family not only serves the usual functions of a family, but more than elsewhere becomes a last-ditch stand to erect a *place* of affection and certainty, of refuge from the wider and brutal world of impersonality. The existentialist attempt to *found* oneself takes many forms, but for the American middle-class man it is above all else the family. The other important social group in America, the business unit, is by nature insecure, for within it the individual is always in danger of falling out; he is always under ruthless pressure; business 'friends' are notoriously unable—even if willing—to help when help is needed, a Rotary club is simply a mask for cutthroat business competition, while social class is an escalator which takes one up or down depending on the play of the cards.

The poor American male, if he is not to be left desolate, must establish solidarity through and within the family; hence it is that everything must be done for the family, that all the actions of the husband in the wider world are thought of in terms of what it will do for the family; nothing must be allowed to stand in the way of maintaining the tenuous stability of the family in a world devoted to inhuman relationships, and, if the result is often to make the male the slave of the family, that is a price he chooses and pays willingly. The American businessman is not selfish; there is no one who is more of a self-made sacrifice. Yet the sacrifice is considered worth while, because only within the family in America is there a chance of affection and place in return for sacrifice.

Thus the accuracy of Keller's poignant cry in *All My Sons* when he is revealed to his son as corrupt.

MOTHER: Joe, Joe. . . . It don't excuse it that you did it for the family.
KELLER: It's got to excuse it!
MOTHER: There's something bigger than the family to him.
KELLER: Nothin' is bigger. . . . (desperately, lost). For you, Kate, for both of you, that's all I ever lived for. [**493/494**]

But this American family is founded out of thin air; it has no tradition of itself, no social support (quite the contrary, all the forces of society work against it); it is usually the creation of two persons who do not know each other's past, who come from different geographical areas and social classes, who have different ideas and creeds, and whose children move to different cities and different ideas. In short, it lacks almost every element of continuity; the very conditions of American life which dictate the peculiar aim of the American family also condemn it to the failure of achieving that aim. It is this failure which Arthur Miller has described in his plays. If the American family is a desperate effort in the face of social loneliness ('loneliness is socially meaningful in these plays') , its very desperation provides the facts for an analysis of man in America and elsewhere.

The substance of Miller's plays is therefore bottomed on a particular American experience. In each of his plays (with the exception of *The Crucible* which is explicitly political in intent) the central situation centres around a child-father relationship in which the child is at an age when it is about to break loose from the family; in each case the father is faced with the consequent breakdown of the family-world he had tried to create;

in each case the conflict between the child and father takes place in terms of the wider world breaching the walls of protection the father had built around the family; in each case the father is corrupt and is revealed to be corrupt by his child; and in each case this corruption leads the father to choose death as the penalty for destroying his own ideal. The pattern is so strictly followed—even in the curtain raiser, *A Memory of Two Mondays*, where the warehouse gang acts as the family to Bert—that it is clear that the failure of these families has given the central focus of Miller's work so far.

The meaning of that failure lies in the destruction of the family as a bulwark against social loneliness by the very values which caused its creation. Keller, in *All My Sons*, makes a corrupt profit in the war because if he did not the economic basis of the family would have disappeared, but his corruption turns his son against him and destroys the family. Willy Loman, in *The Death of the Salesman,* lives by corrupt values because that is all he knows; thus he kills the whole purpose which the family held for him, the love of Biff. And finally, Eddie, in *A View from the Bridge* represents an ultimate and a logical end of love within the family—incest. (It is significant that Eddie is a working-class figure; such a conclusion to the middle-class ideal of a family is best located elsewhere than on the middle-class hearth.) The avid, single-minded pursuit of love within the family causes the corruption which destroys the family. What is implicit in all the other plays becomes manifest through Eddie's brutal sense of logic; the family itself is threatened by the love which created it. Yet, what else is possible in America? What other [**494/495**] possibility was there for Keller, Willy and Eddie, in a society dogged by social loneliness?

But Miller tells us in his introduction that these are free men, making a free choice. It may be that they demanded too much from the family, that the strain was too great, that society was at fault in forcing this strain. Nevertheless they were men who did not, in Miller's words, 'settle for half'. Willie, for example, is cruelly treated as a salesman and is driven into obscenity and corruption by his society; still he stands as a man who, eventually at least, knew what he did and who took the consequence as a free choice.

In making this claim for his heroes Miller is stating the theme for which the crises within his families is the occasion. It is the theme of the commitment, not of Arthur Miller, but of his heroes. Miller's attitude towards Willy is symptomatic of all his plays (including *The Crucible*): to Miller, Willy 'is actually a very brave spirit who cannot settle for half but must pursue his dream of himself to the end.' And Miller tells us that the price that Willy and Keller and Eddie pay is a conscious one. If Willy's values are those of the success ethic, he is none the less aware, Miller claims, of his 'separation from values that endure'; he is 'no dumb brute heading mindlessly to his catastrophe.'

It is in the freedom of Miller's heroes to make a commitment like that of Eddie, who makes a 'sacrifice of himself for his conception . . . of right, dignity and justice,' that Miller's own commitment to the free man can be found.

The idea of the hero . . . is incompatible with a drama whose bounds are set in advance by the concept of an unbreakable trap. . . . [Man's] will is as much a fact as his defeat. . . . An innate value, an innate will does in fact posit itself as real. . . . A new poem will appear because a new balance has been struck which embraces both determinism and the paradox to will.

Miller goes on to say that his plays attempt to prove 'that we are made and yet are more than what made us.' That is his aim and commitment. But does he

achieve his aim? Does the lack of a theory which he dislikes so much prevent him from driving his point home, from portraying his heroes as truly free men?

One may be an admirer of Miller's compassionate grasp of American and human fact and still wonder if such is not the case. Philip Toynbee's request that Miller write a play about a conscious, articulate hero is, to be sure, beside the point; a conscious hero who explains the whole thing to the audience is easy to draw. Yet the question remains: does Miller succeed in the difficult trick, taking a Willy Loman and showing him to be a free man?

For a free choice to be made it is not necessary that a Willy Loman be aware of all the nuances of his decision; most of humanity doesn't [495/496] know all that it has chosen and, if it does, it certainly doesn't when it chose. But it is necessary for the audience to know what choice the hero has made. Does an audience of a Miller play know that? Yes, and for this reason. If we are not showing an Orestes storming off the stage as he calls on the flies to follow him (one Orestes a generation is enough), we are *shown* courage. We are not shown a hero debating his moment of decision, but we are *shown* a man who knows the consequences of what he has done and who is not afraid of them. It would be easy for Miller's heroes to contract out, to 'settle for half'; evasion, too, is a free choice. And that is the choice with which Miller's heroes are faced, whether to 'settle for half' or not. When their families fail and disintegrate they know that they have failed; and then they *choose* the consequences. Miller shows that men are free because they have courage. For there is no deterministic law saying that a man has to be courageous.

Our Colossal Dad*

This essay is a review of Arthur Miller's Collected Plays and of Joseph Wood Krutch's The American Drama Since 1918 (revised edition, 1958). Traditionally all book reviews in The Times Literary Supplement are anonymous.

Arthur Miller abandons the reticent security of the author's box and in a long introduction to his *Collected Plays* tells of his fortunes and intentions as a playwright. The exposition in which he handles the first person with his usual masculine detachment is as carefully constructed as any of the plays it precedes. Success in the theatre came to him only after a struggle in the mid-1940s, up to which time he had written eight or nine plays that were never produced in the professional theatre. He calls these "desk-drawer plays" and resurrects them:

I had begun with a play about a family, then a play about two brothers caught on either side of radicalism in a university, then a play about a psychologist's dilemma in a prison where the sane were inexorably moving over to join the mad, a play about a bizarre ship's officer whose desire for death led him to piracy on the seas, a tragedy on the Cortes-Montezuma conflict, and others.

Whatever may have been wrong with them, it is a list of real conflicts on the strength of which Henry James would undoubtedly have recognized someone with a nose for a subject. *The* subject, however, still eluded him and he was approaching thirty, and wondering whether to quit unrewarded ambition. His next play, *The Man Who Had All the Luck*, proved exceedingly difficult to write.

I had heard the story of a young man in a mid-western town who earned the respect and love of his town and great personal prosperity as well, and who, suddenly and for no known reason, took to suspecting everyone of wanting to rob him, and within a year of his obsession's onset had taken his own life.

Again a more than promising notion, but doomed because the essential *donnée* was missing; in struggling with its composition, though, Mr. Miller mercifully arrived at the moment of truth which at long last released his talent into the light of day.

What I saw, without laboring the details, was that two of the characters, who had been friends in the previous drafts, were logically brothers and had the same father. Had I known then what I know now I could have saved myself a lot of trouble. The play was impossible to fix because the overt story was only tangential to the secret drama its author was quite unconsciously trying to write. But in writing of the father-son relationship and of the son's search for his relatedness there was a fullness of feeling I had never known before; a crescendo was struck with a force I could almost touch. The crux of *All My Sons*, which would not be written until three years later, was formed; and the roots of *Death of a Salesman* were sprouted.

He had arrived by the long way round at the theme which not only gives a unity to all his subsequent work but also puts him in a single perspective with his great predecessor in the American theatre, Eugene O'Neill, and in the still more august distance with Ibsen. None of Mr. Miller's earlier plays had been dynamically charged with the great reproach of "O my Papa!"; from now on he becomes the playwright of a corrupt

*"Our Colossal Dad," *Times Literary Supplement* (London), August 29, 1958, p. 482.

paternal morality. Something is radically wrong with—to borrow out of context Mr. Auden's phrase—our colossal Dad.

In O'Neill the image had been carefully set apart from the present time so that it glowed with a patriarchal grandeur. Whatever his shortcomings now, Ephraim Cabot in *Desire Under the Elms* has won the hardest victory of all, that of conquering the intractable soil of New England before the play begins and we can never forget the fact. The father figures who dominate the first two plays in Mr. Miller's volume are clothed in no such garments of primeval privilege. They are to be seen not in the context of the Old Testament, Sophocles and Freud, but of books such as Mr. Walter Lowen's *You and Your Job*. It is not in themselves that they are thus or thus, but in the manner in which they have coped with the problem of getting on in society. They are quite shamelessly, or perhaps one should say quite unconsciously, "other-directed."

To a playwright preoccupied with a social code of values, Ibsen's *Pillars of the Community* and other of his earlier plays would obviously appear as a landmark, and Mr. Miller makes no secret of his dependence on "the tired model" (as Mr. Walter Kerr calls Ibsen in his plea for more poetry in the American theatre). Ibsen taught him, he confesses, how to see life as a process of evolutionary development and how to forge a play upon "factual bedrock." In *All My Sons* he made almost too correct and neat an adaptation of the master's technique. Joe Keller, the small-time war profiteer, is a much less complex character than Karsten Bernick, though both criminally endanger human life by peddling a shoddy product. Joe, "a man among men," was instrumental in supplying defective cylinder heads for use in military aircraft during the war. Far from being a "pillar" of the community, only by a characteristic show of brazenness that is brilliantly recalled does he succeed in gaining re-acceptance by the community after his exoneration by the

court, where he had succeeded in laying the blame for the deed on his weak-willed partner. Ibsen-wise we watch the past catching him up, the foul deed rising into the light of the present and the full realization of its social implications in the last-minute, if long-foreseen, revelation that one of the aircraft fitted with his dud cylinder-heads has been responsible for the death of his own son. *All My Sons* is a well-made, but exhaustible play, designed to yield its whole content the first time it is seen, which it does. It also suffers by comparison with the model in that the whole crime occurred in the past, and the present action merely consists in its revelation. The unrealized *The Man Who Had All the Luck* seems on paper at least to have had the richer theme.

To have a father who sells defective goods to the Government in wartime faces his son with a problem which is appalling but also simple: somehow he must summon the courage to repudiate him, and this is what at the end of the play we watch Chris Keller doing. (It was hearing of a daughter who denounced her father in similar circumstance, Mr. Miller tells us, that first gave him his idea.) But to have a father with an incurably defective view of reality faces his sons with a problem that is by no means simple (though in the last extremity just as appalling). This is the problem with which Willy Loman's two sons find themselves faced in *Death of a Salesman* and Mr. Miller explores it with a richness of mood and emotion that was a great advance on *All My Sons*. He devised in the setting of the salesman's apartment with its broken boundaries and transparent walls a stage picture that could both happily encompass the quotidian and also wryly make a silent instantaneous transition from present to past.

Music significantly completes the effect. "A melody is heard, played upon a flute. It is small and fine, telling of grass and trees and the horizon. The curtain rises." In this opening stage direction we hear, though we do not yet realize it, the ancestral memory of the salesman's father whom he hardly remembers, pioneer-symbol of a wide open and friendly America. Willy's father, though a flute-maker, belonged in fact to the world of O'Neill's primitives.

Father was a very great and a very wild-hearted man. We would start in Boston, and he'd toss the whole family into the wagon, and then he'd drive the team right across the country; through Ohio, and Indiana, Michigan, Illinois, and all the Western states. And we'd stop in the towns and sell the flutes that he'd made on the way. Great inventor, Father. With one gadget he made more in a week than a man like you could make in a lifetime.

Father was with his golden tremolo harmonious to the social scheme of his time; he seems to have passed on some of his determination to his elder son, Ben, who is cunningly placed in the pattern of the play as a fugitive reproach, a hint of a wrong turning to Willy. In him the father's successful flute has been replaced by only a loud mouth, a fluency for a kind of bullying pep talk to which reality all too quickly gives the vivid lie.

Instead of highlighting father's grandeur the play is beautifully saturated with a sense of his littleness and the littleness of his values, exemplified by his pride in watching his two sons spend a Sunday afternoon polishing his car. Mr. Kerr would surely admit that it is in such touches which evoke the quotidian with such startling familiarity rather than a concentration upon mere extravagance or eccentricity of language that we find the "poetry" of the theatre. In the introduction Mr. Miller pitches a bit, as they say, in trying to relate Willy to Oedipus and "the tragic victory," suggesting that our sense of tragedy resides in our consciousness of the universal law broken by the hero, and that Willy has broken the tacit, modern law which says that "a failure in society and in business has no right to live." True, but the old perennial law of Know Thyself is more fundamental. A salesman is a peculiarly felicitous contemporary symbol of a man who does not know himself ("A salesman is got to dream, boy. It comes with the territory"), but in fact members of any profession—playwrights, editors, philosophers, school-masters, critics, to take a handful at random—may as we know just as easily suffer from the affliction, and hence become suffused in pathos. Do not all tragic characters, Hamlet and Solness, Phèdre and the Three Sisters, have in common sufficient clarity of mind to perceive the logic of their situation even though they may fail to resolve it?

The argument has a crucial relevence to Mr. Miller's work because he is especially concerned with putting people on the stage who are not accustomed to articulate logically about the most important decisions that confront them in their lives. It may be objected that in *The Crucible*, a remarkable re-creation of the theocratic forces (an historical instance of defective paternal authority) at work in Salem in the seventeenth century that led to the malicious imaginings of evil children being taken as legal evidence on the strength of which innocent people were put to death, the universal abeyance of the discriminating faculty is the point at issue. *The Crucible* succeeds so well for most of the time through, as much as anything, its vigorous solution of the language problem—the tone is in period but not archaic—that the objection there may be sustained. The play seems likely at any rate to outlive the more recent historical instance of hysteria with which it was coupled.

It is in *A View from the Bridge* that the fallen father reaches the extremity in Mr. Miller's theatre of bodily strength combined with intellectual frailty. To drive home the tragedy of Eddie Carbone, the Brooklyn longshoreman who has a passion, secret even from himself, for his niece, Mr. Miller provides him with an articulator, the lawyer Alfieri, a weakness which the London dramatic critics pounced on to a man. The split between the act of violence with which the powerful play ends and the affirmation of identity the hero is said to make is complete. Eddie dies by his own knife with which he meant to kill one of his own kind, and it is left to Alfieri to say before the curtain falls, ". . . he allowed himself to be wholly known and for that I think I will love him more than all my sensible clients." Wholly known by everyone except himself, he means. By the end he has really done no more than lose his temper; but rather than try to affix pedagogic labels to an immensely vital play, it is much more to the point to consider the skill and sureness with which Mr. Miller presents us with the immigrant community, a closed primitive society obedient to its own laws and taboos lodged within the State, to which authority it owes final allegiance. The forebears of the characters in this play were those Sicilian peasants whose wretched poverty, huge capacity for grief, and volatile explosiveness Pirandello set down at first-hand in his short stories. Beneath the surface of the American way of life they still retain these characteristics, and in the play friction arises not from a clash of character but from generation against generation: Eddie's "the guy ain't right" is true not for the implied reason but because he is ready to immerse himself completely in the new element, just as for the girl Catherine, whom both of them love, stenography opens up the possibility of a whole new world.

Social transition is a difficult thing to catch in the theatre and Mr. Miller throughout the whole volume is acutely conscious of it. In his high fidelity to the texture of his characters' lives, most often their working lives, he creates a sense of the whole social structure of American life. Take, he says, in a one-act play new to this country, people as they really are, not in some fashionable Van-Drutenesque apartment but in the shipping room of a large auto-parts warehouse and consider the men and women for whom this grimy building is both an imprisoning place of work and a romantic escape from home. *A Memory of Two Mondays* is a minor variation on the theme of finding one's place and holding it in the great industrial hierarchy, and it is to be hoped that we shall some time have the opportunity to judge its effectiveness in performance.

If at times a romantic light may glimmer in the fact of going out to work, the social vision of these plays is wholly urban and unromantic. Mr. Miller seems quite happy to leave it to the makers of musicals to pastoralize the American way of life. Apparently he does not think of himself, and does not like to be thought of, as a pessimist, but, be that as it may, in his plays falling in love is never presented as the answer to the problem of self-discovery in a society where the individual counts in proportion to his bank statement. He stages a man's world in which the women are nearly all helpless victims or onlookers.

The redeeming force here is the strength by which the individual is able to grip hold of his own bootlaces and lift himself out of the rat-race. "Workers of the world, separate!—you have nothing to lose but your rose-tinted contact lenses," might be the burden of his song, and it is a new one for the American theatre. Mr. Joseph Wood Krutch as its official historian can be referred to in his *The American Drama since 1918* for the pre-war picture, but his effort to bring the book up to date by including a chapter on the post-war period has not been successful in an all too skimpily revised edition. Mr. Miller is allowed approximately three pages: not enough for a dramatist whose concern about the individual's difficulty to discover his identity in an overmechanized society which has permanently damaged father's outlook is one which has passed on to the brightest of *les jeunes* in the British theatre to-day. Mr. Osborne, Mr. Bolt, and—more recently still—Mr. Shaffer have each brought father's problem, and his sons', nearer home. In his fierce concentration on Willy Loman's failure Mr. Miller raised the question of freedom in terms that owe nothing to metaphysics and at the same time won a new freedom for the theatrical image.

A Matter of Hopelessness in *Death of a Salesman**

This radio program was made up of excerpts from several interviews recorded by Phillip Gelb, a member of the Department of Speech at Hunter College. (The complete interview with Arthur Miller was printed in the *Educational Theatre Journal*, X [October, 1958], 190-202, under the title "Morality and Modern Drama"; it is valuable for the opinions that Miller expresses on other dramatists, on the American social and political scene, and on some of his own plays, notably *The Crucible* and *A View from the Bridge*.) Richard Watts is drama critic for the *New York Post*, John Beaufort for the *Christian Science Monitor*, Martin Dworkin for *Progressive* magazine; David W. Thompson is Professor of Speech and Theatre Arts at the University of Minnesota.

GELB: This series is concerned with "Ideas and the Theatre," and we feel Arthur Miller is qualified both as a thinker and as a dramatist. Actually, I think he also qualifies as a kind of prophet. He is a prophet in the sense that he warns us of the possible bitter harvest that may be reaped from our present limited ways; he calls attention to the moral and ethical decisions that must be made; and he dramatizes the problem and the need for individuality and will. These may well prove to be the ultimate meanings of hope. But why hope? *Death of a Salesman* is generally thought to be Mr. Miller's most important play; is it an affirming one? Let's refresh our memories.

WATTS: The title, *Death of a Salesman*, has the virtues not only of being striking and provocative, but also of telling forthrightly what the drama is about. Mr. Miller is describing the last days of a man who is forced to face the terrible fact that he is a failure; that his vague ideal of success has crumbled; that his sons, on whose .respect and success he has counted, have only contempt for him. With the utter collapse of Willy Loman's world, there is nothing for him to do but die. The story is as simple as that, and there is such truth in it that it is hard to see how any sensitive playgoer can fail to find something of himself in the mirror that it holds up to life. Only the most fatuous observer could think of *Death of a Salesman* as a propaganda play, and yet it manages to go so deeply into contemporary values that it becomes a valid and

*"A Matter of Hopelessness in *Death of a Salesman*. A Symposium with Arthur Miller, Richard Watts, John Beaufort, Martin Dworkin, David W. Thompson and Phillip Gelb (Moderator)," *Tulane Drama Review*, II (May, 1958), 63-69. Printed by the *Tulane Drama Review* in revised form from the radio series *Ideas and the Theatre*, produced by the University of Minnesota radio station, KUOM, for the tape network of the National Association of Educational Broadcasters under a grant from the Educational Television and Radio Center.

frightening social criticism. Mr. Miller looks upon the salesman ideal of success with an angry but discerning eye, and he sees its hollowness and treachery. Poor Willy Loman, who thought that for a successful salesman popularity and good fellowship were all and tried to [63/64] teach his sons what he believed was his wisdom, is a completely credible victim of a prevailing code as the encroachment of old age destroys its shabby plausibility. Set down with frank emotions (this) play is, I suspect, something to make strong men weep and think.

GELB: Mr. Watts, that was an excerpt from your review of the play when it first opened in 1949; do you think the play still stands up?

WATTS: Oh yes, I think so. The curious thing about this play is that it really was a tragedy for extroverts. The more extroverted people were that went to it, the more they seemed to be moved by it. Usually with a tragedy here, the wives drag their protesting husbands along and the husbands have an awful time and the wives cry. But I saw again and again that it would be the husband who would be moved by *Death of a Salesman*. He would see something of himself in it. He would get far more out of it usually than his wife did.

GELB: If *Death of a Salesman* is so starkly pessimistic, what is so special about it?

DWORKIN: The play is special and Miller's most meaningful work, because he really hit something deep in America when he made that play. The great American idea of the salesman goes back to the old Yankee trader of the Sam Slick type and exists today in the modern huckster who doesn't carry a suitcase or a sample-kit but sells, and in selling he has to take a part of what is human and make it marketable and put a price on it. I consider this Miller's greatest play because his own great skill, his dramatic sense, his artistry, gets beyond his argument so successfully. He has some severe criticisms to make of our society, and yet *Death of a Salesman* criticizes without be-

ing propaganda because the characters are so real. The play is an illustration of that paradoxical problem, that so often emerges when discussing works of art, in which the more valid the particularity gets, the more universal it is an exemplification. Willy Loman comes to represent a certain danger, a certain menace, a certain integral nature in salesmanship in general, because he is so much a particular Willy Loman and not simply a slogan out of the 1930's. He represents a condition where a man necessarily has to go out into space with nothing but a smile and a shoe shine and that packet of samples he is selling and get that order! This strange man, out in space, completely divorced from the fundamental productive processes which manufacture the merchandise that he is selling, not quite the friend and not quite the enemy and not quite the instrument of the people to whom he is selling, somehow, this strange intermediary must sell himself in order to sell things.

BEAUFORT: I am not sure I agree here. I do not believe Willy Loman is a tragic character. I think that he is a sad character. I think he is a vicious character. The trouble with Willy Loman, as a figure in dramatic tragedy, is that he never starts with any ideals to begin with. He is a man who, from the very beginning of the play, says it is a question of whether you're liked or whether you're well-liked. He encourages his sons to steal and cheat. He has no moral values at all.

GELB: But what if one asks, isn't this Americana? Isn't this the common man?

BEAUFORT: It's one phase of Americana; but if Willy Loman truly represented the whole mass of American civilization of today, I think that the country would be in a terrible state. I just can't accept Willy Loman as the average American citizen. I can accept him as a specimen of a certain aspect of society. We all know that people like Willy Loman exist, and Miller has every right to write about him. I'm perfectly willing to accept him as a dramatic character on the stage; but I will not for a minute accept Willy Loman as the American "Everyman." I think that is nonsense.

GELB: What reasons are there for people doing things in our mid-twentieth century other than to be liked or well-liked or to realize more material benefits? I suppose what I'm asking is how much of an influence, if any, do you think the moral and spiritual factors are in our time?

BEAUFORT: I think they're still very substantially influential. I'm not a social historian; I'm not a sociologist. All I'm willing to say is that I believe that for the most part the people in the United States are motivated by many such things or other and many finer things than Willy Loman was motivated by: love of country, religious principles, and ethical values . . . I mean you only have to consider in any situation the response of the American people to a disaster and the need for help to see that we are not an indifferent people. We are a concerned people. Oh, I don't mean to say that we never manifest indifference, we do; but all I'm trying to say is [65/66] that you couldn't, at least I couldn't, accept Willy Loman as the reflection of the mean of American society in terms of the individual citizen. It just wouldn't be possible.

GELB: Arthur Miller, how valid and pertinent are Mr. Beaufort's observations?

MILLER: The trouble with Willy Loman is that he has tremendously powerful ideals. We're not accustomed to speaking of ideals in his terms; but, if Willy Loman, for instance, had not had a very profound sense that his life as lived had left him hollow, he would have died contentedly polishing his car on some Sunday afternoon at a ripe old age. The fact is he has values. The fact that they cannot be realized is what is driving him mad—just as, unfortunately, it's driving a lot of other people mad. The truly value-less man, a man without ideals, is always perfectly at home anywhere . . . because there cannot be a conflict between nothing and something. Whatever negative qualities there are in the society or in the en-

vironment don't bother him, because they are not in conflict with what positive sense one may have. I think Willy Loman, on the other hand, is seeking for a kind of ecstasy in life, which the machine.civilization deprives people of. He's looking for his selfhood, for his immortal soul, so to speak. People who don't know the intensity of that quest, possibly, think he's odd. Now an extraordinary large number of salesmen particularly, who are in a line of work where a large measure of ingenuity and individualism are required, have a very intimate understanding of this problem. More so, I think, than literary critics who probably need strive less after a certain point. A salesman is a kind of creative person (it's possibly idiotic to say so on a literary program, but they are), they have to get up in the morning and conceive a plan of attack and use all kinds of ingenuity all day long, just the way a writer does.

GELB: What about this, Mr. Miller? John Beaufort made the statement that if Willy Loman represented the whole mass of American civilization today, the country would be in a terrible state. He would not for a moment accept Willy Loman as an average American man.

MILLER: Well, it's obvious that Willy Loman can't be an average American man, at least from one point of view; he kills himself. That's a rare thing in society, although it's more common than one could wish. But this "being average" is beside the point. As a matter of fact, the standard of averageness is hardly valid. It tells neither whether a character is a truthful character, as a character, nor a valid one. It's ridiculous. Hamlet isn't a typical Elizabethan either. Horatio probably is. What's the difference? It has no point unless we are not talking about literature but about patriotism. I did not write *Death of a Salesman* to announce a new American man, or an old American man. Willy Loman is, I think, [66/67] a person who embodies in him some of the most terrible conflicts running through the streets of America today. A Gallup poll might not indicate that they are the majority conflicts; I think they are; but then what is the difference?

GELB: Earlier, Martin Dworkin said that he feels the play makes a statement about the average American man because Willy Loman is such a particular Willy Loman. Do you feel that the best way to present a universal is in terms of a really specific story?

MILLER: It is the best way! It is the hardest way, too! The ability to create the universal from the particular is not given to many authors, nor to any single author many times. You have to know the particular in your bones to do this. But it is the best way. As the few plays that are repeatedly done over generations and centuries show, they are generally, in our Western Culture anyway, those plays which are full of the most particular information about the people.

GELB: What about this question of hope and hopelessness? I mean, is there a chance to make the positive value in drama dramatic? Or is drama, by its very nature, only an attack upon things?

MILLER: Not only drama, but literature in general—and this goes back a long, long distance in history—posits the idea of value, of right and wrong, of good and bad, high and low, not so much by setting forth, but by showing so to speak, the wages of sin. In other words, when, for instance in "Death of a Salesman" [*sic*], we are shown a man who dies for the want of some positive, viable human value, the play implies—and it could not have been written without the author's consciousness that the audience did believe something different. In other words, by showing what happens where there are no values, I at least, assume that the audience will be compelled and propelled toward a more intense quest for the values that are missing. I am assuming always that we have a kind of civilized sharing of what we would like to see occur within us and within the world. I think that the drama, at least mine, is not so much an attack but an exposition of "the want." This kind of drama can be done only if the audience itself is constantly trying to supply what is missing.

GELB: Although critic John Beaufort and playwright Arthur Miller seem to be in some disagreement over the character of Willy Loman, I think it is even more significant to note that Mr. Beaufort, in his earlier comments, came up with the very conclusion that Mr. Miller wanted from his play—the conclusion that there is a better way than Willy's way, that we can act on more meaningful values. In other words, John Beaufort supplies some of what Arthur Miller seems to be suggesting as the missing moral links between the *Death of a Salesman* and the Life of a Man. The day I first interviewed Arthur Miller was shortly after the Russians had launched the first satellite. This led me to ask Mr. Miller as to whether or not the various sciences, from nuclear physics to psy- [67/68] chology, hadn't made the contemporary artist's job too difficult by giving him too many facts and views to consider. Under this deluge of knowledge, weren't apathy, anxiety and cynicism the natural results? Could any creative writer take even most of the available information and insights into consideration and still write creatively?

MILLER: Well, whether it can be done remains for me or somebody else to prove. But let me put it this way: we're living, or I'm living anyway, with a great consciousness of the incredible force of objective thought. As we speak, there is an object flying around in the sky passing over this point every, I think it's one hundred and some minutes, which was put up there by thinking men who willed it to go up there. The implications of this are as enormous as any statement by or on the part of Zeus, or Moses, or Shakespeare, or any feeling man. Now, it may be a great bite to take, but I think the only thing worth doing (whether one can do it or not is an entirely different story, but aims are important) today in the theatre, from my point-of-view, is to synthesize the subjective drives of the human being with what is now demonstrably the case. Namely, that by acts of will he can and has changed the world. It is said that nothing is new under the sun. This is! It's right under the sun, and it's new! But it's only one of many things that are new. I've seen communities transformed by the act of a committee. I've seen the interior lives of people transformed by the decision of a company, or of a man, or of a school. In other words, it is old fashioned to simply go on asserting the helplessness of the individual.

GELB: You're not in the large "artistic" camp then of those who write of, by, and for despair.

MILLER: Well, for myself I can't write anything if I'm sufficiently unhappy. A lot of writers write best when they're most miserable. I suppose my sense of form comes from a positive need to organize life and not from a desire to demonstrate the inevitability of defeat and death.

GELB: Do you think this becomes a kind of final analysis of many issues in life—social, political, economic, psychological? You made a statement putting you on the side of life against death. Aren't many "final answers" dependent upon whether this is or is not a basic commitment?

MILLER: It is a commitment on my part. I don't see the point in proving again that we must be defeated. I didn't intend that in "Salesman." [*sic*] I was trying in "Salesman," in this respect, to set forth what happens when a man does not have a grip on the forces of live and has no sense of values which will lead him to that kind of a grip; but the implication of it was that there must be such a grasp of those forces—or else we're doomed. I was not, in other words, Willy Loman. I was the writer, and Willy Loman is there because I could see beyond him. [68/69]

THOMPSON: In summary then, "The curious thing" about Arthur Miller's *The [sic] Death of a Salesman* is, as Mr. Watts said, that it really is "a tragedy for extroverts." In older drama, for example in Moliere, a bumbling, simpleminded hustler is always a figure of fun. He is the object of satiric criticism. Mr. Miller does criticize his salesman but

earnestly, without a trace of the older comic view. And what is really curious is that the play, besides criticizing Willy Loman's dishonesty and vulgarity, asks that a great deal of sympathy and attention be paid to the failure himself. Willy is shown to be wrong in every respect of human decency but is still expected to be a great tragic figure. This asking for more sympathy than the facts seem to deserve is what gives, a certain sentimentality to the play. As Mr. Beaufort put it, "I think that Willy Loman is not a tragic character. I think that he is a sad character. I think he is a vicious character. The trouble with Willy Loman, as a figure in a dramatic tragedy, is that he never starts with any ideals to begin with . . . He has no moral values at all."

This word "values" set off the big controversy in today's program. In his reply to Mr. Beaufort's charge, Mr. Miller at first insisted that Willy Loman "has tremendously powerful ideals . . . The fact is that he has values . . . (he) is seeking for a kind of ecstasy in life." (One might note here in passing that the universal, primitive egotism of a child always leads to a generalized "seeking for a kind of ecstasy in life"—its worth depends entirely upon what specific values and forms mark that search, especially in adult life). Later, Mr. Miller seemed to contradict himself by saying that his play shows "what happens where there are no values," and that Willy Loman has "no sense of values" which will lead him to "a grip on the forces of life." This contradiction, of course, proves very little, except perhaps that Mr. Miller, fortunately for us, is a playwright and not a dramatic theorist.

There was, after all, general agreement among the participants as to Mr. Miller's important, even leading, position as a contemporary American dramatist. There was no denying that his *Death of a Salesman* is a powerful play giving a true-to-life portrayal of a certain type of American, who, as Mr. Dworkin said, is as old as the Sam Slick Yankee trader and as current as the modern huckster. If some of us, like Mr. Beaufort, feel the play is marred by a certain sentimentality in its demanding so much sympathy for Willy, this may only mean that we are neither salesmen or extroverts.

Perhaps in older, tougher days the subject of a foolish, childish salesman, plus Mr. Miller's keen sense of realistic detail, would have produced a biting social satire. Today, however, it is certainly not Mr. Miller's fault that his audience, composed mainly of hucksters, will accept criticism only in a sympathetic "tragedy for extroverts."

Confusion and Tragedy: The Failure of Miller's *Salesman**

RICHARD J. FOSTER (1928-   ), Assistant Professor of English at the University of Minnesota, has published a number of articles on modern literature and criticism. The essay on Arthur Miller, published here for the first time, was originally given as a lecture in the Freshman English Lecture Program at the University of Minnesota in 1959.

Sooner or later most discussions of the merits of Arthur Miller's *Death of a Salesman* turn to the question of the possibility of modern tragedy. Given the conditions of the modern world, the question runs, is it possible to write true tragedy in our time? Of course the very asking of the question sounds the negative. But there are likely to be answerers around who will invoke the names of certain moderns—Ibsen, or Strindberg, or O'Neill, or O'Casey, or even Arthur Miller—who are alleged to have made tragedies out of the common materials of modern life. And Miller himself, in response to commentators who have denied that *Salesman* is a tragedy, has vigorously affirmed, in an essay called "Tragedy and the Common Man," the right of his play, and the matter it is made of, to the epithet *tragic*. That both critic and playwright care so strongly about how the words *tragic* and *tragedy* are to be applied shows at the very least that the words carry a rather heavy charge of positive value. But there is also a theoretical question behind the question of value, and the differences between Miller and his critics can be accounted for at least partially on the basis of the difference between their "theories" of tragedy.

To put the matter very simply, Arthur Miller has a very general or very loose and vague theory of tragedy, or perhaps no clear theory at all, while the critics have a fairly definite one derived from a couple of thousand years of literary tradition. The traditional view of tragedy, founded very largely upon the principles of Aristotle and the practice of Sophocles and Shakespeare, assumes at least two prior essentials to be inherent in the materials of any tragic action. First, the hero must have "stature": this means that while he must in some way represent the general human condition, he must also be larger and grander than the norm —certainly in the inherent fineness and depth and energy of his mind and character, and perhaps also in his exterior societal role—so that his fall will have deep emotional consequence for the audience. Second, the world in which the tragic hero acts must be sensed as bounded or permeated by some meaningful and larger-than human order—call it a Moral Order, or the Natural Law, or Providence, or even Fate—which he in some way challenges or violates and which correspondingly exacts, but not without some sense of ultimate justice in the exaction, the tragic hero's life in consequence of that violation. The first part of this formula, the requirement of "stature" in the tragic hero, Miller's play obviously fails to live up to. Willy Loman is a childish and stupid human being, and his societal

*Richard J. Foster, "Confusion and Tragedy: The Failure of Miller's *Salesman*."

82

role of salesman is of only very minor consequence. And since one of the thematic intentions of the play is to present the picture of a world in which there can be no moral appeal to an order more profound than those of commerce and the machine, *Salesman* obviously cannot meet the second requirement either.

So by the test of tradition, *Death of a Salesman*, whatever else it may be, is no tragedy. But wait, Miller seems to say in "Tragedy and the Common Man," by the test of *feeling* it *is* tragedy. "The tragic feeling," he writes, "is evoked when we are in the presence of a character who is ready to lay down his life, if need be, to secure one thing—his sense of personal dignity." He mentions Orestes, Hamlet, Medea, and Macbeth as examples, and goes on to say that "in the tragic view the need of man to wholly realize himself is the only fixed star, and whatever hedges his nature and lowers it is ripe for attack and examination." Miller is affirming, then, a continuity in tragedy that is not dependent upon historical accidents: what counts is the tragic *sense,* not the mechanical details of an abstract formula for the tragic. In spite of history, Miller is saying, in *felt* significance *Death of a Salesman* is just as much a tragedy as Sophocles' *Electra* or Shakespeare's *Hamlet.* Putting aside formulas and abstractions, let us examine it on its own grounds—not only in the light of the *kind* of play it is ("bourgeois tragedy," with a pretty weighty tradition of its own behind it from Ibsen to Clifford Odets), but also in the more universal light of the truth and depth and integrity that we expect from any piece of real literature, regardless of its time or type.

Two things will strike us when we consider Miller's focal character, Willy Loman, and both of them are in Miller's favor. First, we cannot miss the force of Willy's imagination, the energy of his language, the ferocity of his hope and rage. (Miller uses the word "mercurial" to sum this up in his stage directions.) We *know* that Willy is a pathetic fool, but we nevertheless *feel* him vividly as

a vital human being. He may be mediocre, even barbaric, but he is not dull. And second, we cannot miss Willy's failure always to translate imagination and feeling into effective action. His continual inconsistencies, for example: Biff is both a "lazy bum" and "hard worker" to Willy in Act I, and in Act II Willy's advice to Biff on conducting his interview with Bill Oliver is that he should both "talk as little as possible" and "start off with a couple of . . . good stories to lighten things up." Willy says of himself at one point, and all in one breath, "I'm very well liked in Hartford. You know, the trouble is, Linda, people just don't seem to take to me." Willy's great intensity provides a recognizable touch, at least, of something like "stature." And perhaps his incoherence of mind and will resembles the "flaw" of nature or judgment usually borne by the traditional tragic hero. Like Hamlet—or at least the Hamlet that some of the critics think they see—Willy's personal tragedy is that he is inherently unable to bring himself to take the rational action necessary to save himself and put his world in order. But unlike Hamlet, Willy seems to have suffered his tragedy all his life. With reflections of the past playing continually over the present, Miller's play focuses on the end of that life when, ironically, the last opportunity for creative action remaining to Willy is the opportunity to destroy himself.

Death of a Salesman is a play remarkably lacking in action—which is not to say that it is a bad play for that reason. This lack of action, this continual dispersion of motive in Willy, is of course part of the play's theme. Intensity of feeling plus confusion of intellect yields paralysis of will. Willy's inability to act in any coherent way, an inability that the flashbacks show us is not confined only to Willy's old age, seems to be related directly to his inability to see the truth, or to his inability to distinguish between illusion and actuality, or to harmonize his dreams with his responsibilities. Charlie says to Willy, after Willy has been in effect fired by Howard, "The only thing you got in this world is what you can sell. And the funny thing is that you're a salesman, and you don't know that." Charley means that Willy is suffering because he is looking for a deeply human fulfillment in an activity which is conditioned not by what is human, but by goods and cash.

Charley himself see the "facts" of business and selling as they are, and he is thereby able to keep his practical sense and his humanity sharply distinguished, in balance, intact. But Willy, perhaps a greater personality than either Charley or Bernard, however much more childish and unintelligent he may be than they, has an incurable vision. It is a vision that Charley knows cannot be realized in selling, for it implies creativity, heroism, beauty, and wholeness: the creativity of Willy's father, the free and wandering inventor; the heroism of Ben, who tamed two continents and made them serve him; the beauty of Biff at seventeen—"a young god, Hercules . . . and the sun all around him"—receiving the cheers of the crowd at Ebbets Field; the wholeness of Dave Singleman, who, like an old king full of honor, could simply pick up the phone in his hotel room and command the respect and love of hundreds at the other end. Biff, who functions in the play as an amplification or reflection of Willy's problems, has been nurtured on Willy's dreams too. But he has been forced to see the truth. And it is the truth—his father's cheap philandering—in its impact on a nature already weakened by a diet of illusion that in turn paralyzes him. Biff and Willy are two versions of the idealist, or "dreamer" may be a better word, paralyzed by reality: Biff by the effects of disillusionment, Willy by the effects of the illusions themselves. This is how they sum themselves up at the end of the play, just before Willy's suicide: "Pop!" Biff cries, "I'm a dime a dozen, and so are you!" "I am not a dime a dozen!" Willy answers in rage. "I am Willy Loman, and you are Biff Loman!" And the tragedy—if it *is* tragedy —is that they are both right.

But why is it that Willy and Biff, both of them meant by Miller to be taken as men of potential, must be paralyzed and defeated? It seems to be a matter partly of psychological accident. Willy never had a real father, and his hard predatory older brother became his father-substitute. "Never fight fair with a stranger" was Ben's wisdom. And his faith—"When I was seventeen I walked into the jungle, and when I was twenty-one I walked out. And by God I was rich!" It seems also to be a matter partly of historical accident: times have changed. If ever there were days when essentially human values and loyalties prevailed in the world of selling, those days passed with old Dave Singleman and Willy's former boss. The business world is now run by cold young materialists like Howard, and though a wise realist like Charley may survive, there is no place in it for the all-too human dreamer and vulgarian, Willy Loman.

Psychology, history—these lead us to the third and most important cause of Willy's suffering, the great evil, the great villain of most modern writing in the realist vein—Society. Keeping in mind traditional tragedy and how it brings the audience's attention to bear on the relation between the tragic hero and the moral order implied in the background of his action, we see that Willy, unlike the traditional tragic hero, is meant to be seen as greater and better, at least in potential, than the world that destroys him. While the traditional tragic hero is felt to be in some way responsible to a moral order larger than himself, and fulfills that responsibility, sometimes with the overtones of sacrifice, even of "atonement," in the event, by losing his life, the hero of bourgeois tragedy tends to be better than the order—not a moral order now, but a merely mechanical social order—and is victimized by it. Willy Loman is potentially better than his world in that he has at least incipient values that are better than the world's values. Society's guilt, as it is projected in *Death of a Salesman*, lies in its not making available ways and means for a man like Willy to implement and realize those values, and in dooming him thus to frustration, paralysis, and ultimately destruction as a human being.

The values that seem to be represented in Willy, the "good" values that function in the play as implicit criticisms of society's "bad" values, are the familiar romantic ones: nature, freedom, and the body; free self-expression and self-realization; individualism and the simple life. Nature and the simple life are supposed to be announced in the play's opening flute music, which, Miller tells us in a stage direction, speaks "of grass and trees and the horizon." Willy's memories of the wistaria and elms around the house when the boys were young, his vague dream of having a farm in his old age, his symbolic attempts to plant seeds in the night, and Biff's rhapsodies about the bare-chested life and young colts and the western plains, are all overshadowed and threatened by the encroaching bulwarks of apartment houses and the costly and complicated machines that sap one's resources and won't perform their functions. Willy's life is a continuum of futile worry, and his garden is a shadowed and sterile plot where the life-giving sun can no longer get in. Though Biff was a "young god" and Willy a spokesman for toughness, Society seems to have stifled these goods too: Willy has become soft and fat; Biff and Happy, inhabitants of a world where "getting ahead of the next fella" is the prime goal, find their strength and energy turning into bullying; and all of them display a mistaken and self-defeating contempt for the mind.

Another category of value against which society militates has to do with the feelings, with love, with deep and full and natural human relationship. The real capacities for love of both Willy and his boys disperses itself in meaningless and trivial philanderings. Biff and Happy yearn fruitlessly to run a ranch or a business together—the *together* is what is important—and to marry decent girls with, as they put it, "substance," just as Willy dreams of a happy old age with his children and his children's children thriving happily around him. But sterility and disharmony obtain: the boys, growing older, do not marry, and Willy's hopes for his family explode with finality in the chaos of the terrible restaurant scene in Act II. The enemy of love, of course, is society's principle of "success"—getting ahead by competition, which is the impersonal opposite of love. It is significant that Willy's vision of fulfillment is made up of characters who stand alone—Willy's father, Brother Ben, Biff as a public hero, Dave Singleman—characters who have succeeded, who stand not with but above and beyond the rest of humanity, and who do not give love but receive it, and at an impersonal distance, from cheering crowds or from faceless respectful voices at the other ends of telephone lines. This vision, created and enforced by the norms of the competitive, success-centered society that Willy lives in, is a denial of the deeply personal and human capacities for love that are inherent in Willy's nature.

A final set of values implicit in Willy's character, and defeated by the circumstances in which he finds himself, are his unformed impulses toward two of the original American virtues—self-reliance and individualism of spirit. These virtues, implying basic self-sufficiency and personal creativity, *not* domination of others, are perhaps the pure forms underlying the corrupt and destructive societal imperatives of success and getting ahead. Willy has the self-reliant skills of the artisan: he is "good at things," from polishing a car to building a front porch, and we hear of his beloved tools and his dream of using them some day to build a guest house on his dreamed-of farm for his boys and their families to stay in. But self-reliance has collapsed, the tools rust, and Willy has become the futile and pathetic victim of a machine culture. And individualism has been translated and corrupted in Willy into a belief in the jungle value of privilege for the strong: he encourages his boys to steal, and he calls it initiative and their right.

So far I have assented to the strength and vitality of Willy's characterization and to the validity of the social and moral criticism that Miller makes of the world Willy lives in. If, then, the leading character and world of the play are made to interact in such a way as to engage our conviction, can we agree with Arthur Miller that, whatever the formula, the *feeling* evoked by *Death of a Salesman* succeeds in being "tragic"? I think we are likely to have to answer, No. All formulas for the tragic aside, when we say a play is tragic we are ascribing perhaps the highest literary value to it. We are saying that it is an instance of the most serious form of literature, and that it engages not only the emotions but also the intellect and the moral sense in their fullest and most profound state of awareness. This, I think, is what *Death of a Salesman* is not able to do. For to read it as literature betrays in it a softness, a damp sentimentality, an intellectual and moral confusion that destroys the effectiveness both of its moral themes and its central character. As I have said, in portraying the victimization by society of one of its members, *Death of a Salesman* functions as both a negative criticism of society and a positive assertion of counter-values. But one simply cannot look too closely at the values implied by the play without feeling real doubt as to what they amount to, nor at certain of the characters that embody them without feeling confusion, embarrassment, possibly even boredom.

Isn't there, for example, a weariness about certain easy stereotypes—Bernard, say, who because he is intelligent wears glasses and is poor at sports? (Or is it the other way around?) And if Biff is designed by Miller, as I think he is, to provide both lyric and intellectual perspectives on Willy's sufferings that crude Willy by himself cannot give us, doesn't he, through the thinness and the triteness of his type, fail in those very important functions? Biff is a very dull imitation of a Thirties literary stereotype—the sensitive, serious young man,

felt vaguely to be some sort of potential creative genius, who cannot find himself in a hardened world of machines and imperceptive materialists, and who, kept from his fulfillment by circumstance, ought either to be a poet or a potato farmer. Bluntly calling for a stock response from his audience, Miller makes Happy say, just after Biff has been explaining the beauty of new-born colts and Texas in the spring, "You're a poet, you know that, Biff? You're a—you're an idealist!" But how seriously can one respond to an idealist whose ideals are flabby clichés, or to a poet whose language is at best stock, at worst incoherent. (Biff cries out to his father, at one particularly intense moment in the play, "We should be mixing cement on some open plain, or—or carpenters." What is the quality either of the idealism or the poetry here?) And it is overpoweringly false and too patently convenient to have Bernard, as a mature man, declare to Willy that in spite of the cheating and the bullying he had always "loved" egotistical, musclebound, boring Biff. And this, we must remember, comes from the mouth of a young lawyer on his way to argue a case before the Supreme Court. I think the truest and most dramatically destructive words about Biff are said by Willy in a moment of honest pique for him, and of unwitting clear-sightedness for Miller: "Not finding yourself," Willy cries, with perfectly justifiable impatience, "at the age of thirty-four is a disgrace!"

But the vagueness and triteness of Biff's characterization and role is only a natural concomitant of the vagueness, perhaps also the triteness, of the romantic values—nature, the body, the feelings, individualism—that the play implicitly opposes to society's anti-humanism. And if these values seem to emerge from the play not as *ideas* but as rather perfunctorily paraded sentimental clichés, we doubt their reality and validity even more when we discover that they are strangely mingled with certain recognizable bourgeois values that Miller seems, with rather puzzling inconsistency, to approve almost without criticism. Linda, for example, is plainly a "good" character; and yet if we look at her honestly we see that she has as fine a set of Momist traits as Philip Wylie himself might have imagined. To what extent might Linda's placid mothering have been responsible for the collapse of Willy and his sons had she been created by a more conscious and complicated social observer than Arthur Miller—by Clifford Odets, for example. And then what of Bernard, the myopic puny bookworm who spent his boyhood as prime admirer and truckler-in-chief to Biff the bullying egoist. He is rewarded with the most valued of bourgeois successes—a place in the professions, and a top place at that—and he ultimately functions in the play, puzzlingly and surprisingly, I feel, as a norm of fulfillment (*success* in a *profession*) and decency (he is a family man). So who cares for all that talk of horses and carpentering and getting back to nature with these golden visions of the Supreme Court and Success and Suburbia floating before us in the shape of Bernard?

The theme of Success, while it undergoes criticism in the play, seems always to be before us—the idea of the romance of selling, for example, is articulated by solid Charley as well as by Willy—in some desirable, even worthy manifestation. In fact, the bourgeois religion of Success haunts *Death of a Salesman* throughout, and in the end pretty well defeats the values that all along Miller had seemingly wished to pit against it.

There are many fine elements in the play, of course, perhaps the finest of them Willy himself. In Willy, the pathetic bourgeois barbarian, Miller has made an intense and true character, perhaps a nearly great one, surely a greater one than Sinclair Lewis's mythic but rather flat Babbitt. Just as Willy is a humanly great character, there are humanly great scenes, too—like the powerful and devastating restaurant scene, which corresponds to the "catastrophe" of traditional tragedy. And while Miller is surely

no poet of the theatre, there are moments even of real expressive power. Though the writing is consistently bad—dull, cliché-ridden, vacuously corny—around Biff and what he stands for, Willy's talk always has great energy and validity; and his cry, "The woods are burning!", the emblem of his personal tragedy, is poetry, and as that it is memorable.

Willy's requiem, a kind of ritual elegy or coda in which, each in his own way, those who loved Willy pay tribute to him in death, is a graceful completing touch. Biff, having learned from his father's sacrifice, proclaims the mistakenness of Willy's ambitions, and will head west again; Happy, as if in duty to Willy's memory, will stay behind in the hope—probably futile—of licking the system on its own terms; Charley rhapsodizes the meaning and value that survives the defeat ("A salesman is got to dream, boy. It comes with the territory."); and Linda utters the simple human grief of one who, without thought, loved. A graceful touch structurally and tonally—that is it would have been so, a fitting recognition of the whole range of relevant human response to Willy's destruction, had the play that it completes and depends on for its significance been the intellectually coherent one it ought to have been. But appended to *Death of a Salesman* as it stands, the requiem lacks meaning; it is *only* a touch, a sentimental flourish, an exercise of dramatist's technique for its own sake.

Death of a Salesman's failure, then, lies in the failure of its intellectual content and order. So when the traditionalist critics protest that the play is not a tragedy they are right, but I think for the wrong reasons. And when Miller says it is tragedy because it creates tragic feeling, I think he is wrong, unless the audience he has in mind is an intellectually inadequate one. For the play fails simply because it is sentimental: and by that I mean that if we read it with the full awareness and intelligence that we try to bring to a great playwright like Shakespeare or a great novelist like Faulkner—or even to a good non-tragic dramatist like Shaw—we discover that Miller is relying not on ideas but on a frequently self-contradictory and often quite arbitrary melange of social and moral clichés and the stock emotional responses attached to them.

Miller once said in a panel discussion of his play that Willy Loman is "seeking for a kind of ecstasy in life, which the machine civilization deprives people of. He's looking for his selfhood, for his immortal soul, so to speak." I think that most tragic heroes in the tradition were doing something rather different from this—making hazardous decisions and taking action in consequence of them, action that elicited the scrutiny of, perhaps challenged, a greater moral order outside themselves. Miller's statement may explain why *Death of a Salesman* is so little like an action, so much like a prolonged cry—Linda's cry, perhaps, that "attention must be paid." And perhaps it is, very simply, this aim of expressing not an idea, but only an agony that keeps *Death of a Salesman* from being either a "tragedy" or a great piece of literature.

Review of *A Streetcar Named Desire**

GEORGE JEAN NATHAN. For biographical information, see the review of *Death of a Salesman* by George Jean Nathan, reprinted on page 57.

The play, which might well have been titled *The Glans Menagerie,* has been criticized in some quarters as an unpleasant one. The criticism is pointed. But the fact that a play is unpleasant, needless to say, is not necessarily a reflection on its quality. *Oedipus, Lear,* and *The Lower Depths,* to name only three out of many, are surely very far from pleasant, yet it is their unpleasantness which at least in part makes them what they are. There is a considerable difference between the unpleasant and the disgusting, which is the designation Mr. Williams' critics probably have in mind, and his play is not disgusting, as, for example, is scum like *Maid In The Ozarks* and *School For Brides.* The borderline between the unpleasant and the disgusting is, however, a shadowy one, as inferior playwrights have at times found out to their surprise and grief. Williams has managed to keep his play wholly in hand. But there is, too, a much more positive borderline between the unpleasant and the enlightening, and he has tripped over [163/164] it, badly. While he has succeeded in making realistically dramatic such elements as sexual abnormality, harlotry, perversion, venality, rape, and lunacy, he has scarcely contrived to distil from them any elevation and purge. His play as a consequence remains largely a theatrical shocker which, while it may shock the emotions of its audience, does not in the slightest shock them into any spiritual education.

Eight years ago, at the beginning of his career, Williams wrote a play called *Battle Of Angels,* which closed in Boston after a brief showing. It hinted at his preoccupation with sex in its more violent aspects, which continues in the present exhibit. It also, while not nearly so able a play, betrayed his apparent conviction that theatrical sensationalism and dramatic substantiality are much the same thing and that, as in the present case, one can handily pass the former off for the latter, and for something pretty artistic into the bargain, by gilding it with occasional literary flourishes accompanied by off-stage vibra-harps, flutes, and music boxes. The hanky-panky may work with a susceptible public, but not with the more ingressive criticism. There is a considerable difference between Wedekind and Wedekindergarten. To fashion any such festering materials into important drama it is essential that they be lifted out of life into a pattern larger than life, as, among others, Strindberg and his contemporary disciple, O'Neill, have appreciated. Williams in considerable part leaves them where he found them and deludes himself into a belief that he has made of the gutter a broad sea by now and then sailing in it little papier-mâché poesy boats, propelled by doughty exhalations.

Impressionistically, the play suggests a wayward bus occupied by John Steinbeck, William Faulkner and James Cain, all tip-

*George Jean Nathan, review of *A Streetcar Named Desire,* in *The Theatre Book of the Year,* 1947-1948 (New York: Alfred A. Knopf, Inc., 1948), pp. 163-166.

sy and all telling stories simultaneously, and with Williams, cocking his ear to assimilate the goings-on, as the conductor. Critically, it suggests that he is a little deaf and has not been able to disentangle what may be valid from the bedlam and assimilate it to possibly meritorious ends. Theatrically and popularly, however, the re-[164/165]sult will surely impress a lot of people, even such as will pretend for appearances' sake to be offended by what they allude to as its "strong meat" and who after seeing it will profess that they long for a breath of fresh, good, clean glue.

Like a number of his contemporaries, Williams seems to labor under the misapprehension that strong emotions are best to be expressed strongly only through what may delicately be termed strong language. I am not, you may be relieved to know, going to take up again the already over-argued question as to whether such language has any literary justification. I am as tired of the discussion as undoubtedly you are. But, justified or not in certain cases, it seems to me that in this specific instance he has at times used it not because it is vitally necessary but for purposes of startle and because his dramatic gifts do not yet include the ability to achieve the desired effect without easy recourse to such terminology. His writing—to fall back on a description I have used before—sometimes sounds altogether too much like a little boy proudly making a muscle.

The play centers on a Southern schoolteacher whose youthful marriage ended in tragedy when her homosexual husband committed suicide, who has vainly sought nepenthe in miscellaneous sex, and who has become an incurable neurotic with delusions of grandeur. It develops her amatory life with her sister's husband and with the latter's crony. And it ends with her mental disintegration and deposit in an asylum. That it holds one's interest is not to be denied. But it holds it much as it is perversely held by a recognizably fixed prizefight or a circus performer projected out of what appears to be a booming cannon by a mechanical spring device. It is, in other words, highly successful theatre and highly successful showmanship, but considerably less than that as critically secure drama.

In this general view of the play, I hope that no one will suspect that I am suscribing to such definitions as Jerome's "Ugliness is but skin-deep; the business of Art is to reveal the beauty underlying all things." Such sweet sentiments, though generally accepted as true, are much too [165/166] broad and sometimes faulty. The revelation of fundamental ugliness and depravity has been known to be not only the business of art but even occasionally its triumph. The form and style and manner of the revelation may be beautiful, but the revelation itself is not. A better definition might be that the business of art is to reveal whatever is basically true, whether beautiful or ugly, in terms of the highest æsthetic competence. The ugliness in Williams' play may in the definition of the Jeromes be only skin-deep, but the ability to prick deeper into it and draw from it the blood drops of common humanity, and in them a true count of dramatic art, is absent. It scarcely throws one off critical scent to quote in the program verse, by Hart Crane, about "the broken world," "the visionary company of love," and "its voice an instant in the world." It is not enough to substitute the ingenious stage magic of lights and music for the equally seductive but more definitely powerful magic of poetry. For what still mutinously forces itself upon one in this tale of a prostitute who would envelop hideous reality in the anodyne of illusion and supplant the world of pursuing lust with one of pure love is, save in a few valid scenes, the impression of a Pirandello theme dramatized by a hopeful aspirant to dramatic lyricism and which periodically—and I am not being as facetious as you may think—converts its characters into rampaging approximations to Harpo Marx.

Contributing greatly to the external successful aspects of the play are admirable direction by Elia Kazan and a uniformly excellent acting company in which, supported by Marlon Brando, Karl Malden and the rest, Jessica Tandy in the role of Forever Streetcar gives one of the finest performances observed locally in several seasons. Also helpful is Jo Miel-ziner's variant of his scenic design for the same authors' *The Glass Menagerie*, though one may wonder how he reconciles an acutely realistic lavatory with the rest of his fancifully imagined and dreamlike interior of a dwelling in the Vieux Carré.

Review of *A Streetcar Named Desire**

HAROLD CLURMAN. For biographical information, see the review of *Death of a Salesman* by Harold Clurman, reprinted on page 65.

The newest writing talent in the American theatre is that of Tennessee Williams. His *The Glass Menagerie* was a lyric fragment of limited scope but undeniable poignancy. Tennessee Williams' latest play—*A Streetcar Named Desire*—stands very [72/73] high among the creative contributions of the American theatre since 1920. If we had a national repertory theatre, this play would unquestionably be among the few worthy of a permanent place there. Its impact at this moment is especially strong, because it is virtually unique as a stage piece that is both personal and social and wholly a product of our life today. It is a beautiful play.

Its story is simple. Blanche Du Bois, a girl whose family once possessed property and title to position in the circle of refined Southern respectability, has been reduced to the lowest financial estate. She has taught English in a high school, but when we meet her she has apparently lost her job and has come to stay with her younger sister Stella in New Orleans. Blanche expects to find Stella living in an environment compatible with their former background, but finds instead that Stella is in the kind of neighborhood that playgoers call sordid, though it happens to be no worse than any of the places inhabited by the majority of American people. Blanche is shocked at these Elysian Fields (literally the name of this particular spot in New Orleans, just as the streetcar she took to reach it is actually called Desire). She is even more shocked by her sister's husband, an American of Polish origin, an ex-sergeant, a machine salesman, and a rather primitive, almost bestial person. Her brother-in-law resents and then suspects the girl's pretentious airs, particularly her obvious disdain of him. Slowly he (and we) discover the girl's "secret": after her family's loss of all its property, the death of the last member of the older generation, an unfortunate marriage at an early age to a boy who turned out to be a homosexual, and the boy's suicide, Blanche has become a notorious person, whose squalid affairs have made it impossible for her to remain in her home town. She meets a friend of her brother-in-law whom she wants to marry because he is a decent fellow, but her brother-in-law by disclosing the facts of the girl's life to her suitor wrecks her hopes. Drunk the night of his wife's labor, the brother-in-law settles his account with Blanche by raping her. She is ordered out of Stella's house, and, when Blanche tells the story of the rape she is thought to be mad and is finally conducted unprotesting to a public institution for the insane. [73/74]

Some of the reviewers thought Blanche Du Bois a "boozy prostitute," and others believed her a nymphomaniac. Such designations are not only inaccurate but reveal a total failure to understand the author's intention and the theme of the play. Tennessee Williams is a poet of frustration, and what his play says is that aspira-

*Harold Clurman, review of *A Streetcar Named Desire*, in *Lies Like Truth. Theatre Reviews and Essays* (New York: The Macmillan Company, 1958), pp. 72-80.

tion, sensitivity, departure from the norm are battered, bruised, and disgraced in our world today.

It would be far truer to think of Blanche Du Bois as the potential artist in all of us than as a deteriorated Southern belle. Her amatory adventures, which her brother-in-law (like some of the critics) regards as the mark of her inferiority, are the unwholesome means she uses to maintain her connection with life, to fight the sense of death which her whole background has created in her. The play's story shows us Blanche's seeking haven in a simple, healthy man and that in this, too, she is defeated because everything in her environment conspires to degrade the meaning of her tragic situation. . . . Her lies are part of her will-to-beauty; her wretched romanticism is a futile reaching toward a fullness of life. She is not a drunkard, and she is not insane when she is committed to the asylum. She is an almost willing victim of a world that has trapped her and in which she can find "peace" only by accepting the verdict of her unfitness for "normal" life.

The play is not specifically written as a symbolic drama or as a tract. What I have said is implicit in all of the play's details. The reason for the play's success even with audiences who fail to understand it is that the characters and the scenes are written with a firm grasp on their naturalistic truth. Yet we shall waste the play and the author's talent if we praise the play's effects and disregard its core. Like most works of art the play's significance cannot be isolated in a single passage. It is clear to the attentive and will elude the hasty.

Still, the audience is not entirely to blame if the play and its central character are not understood. There are elements in the production—chiefly in the acting— that make for a certain ambiguity and confusion. This is not to say that the acting and production are poor. On the contrary, they are both distinctly superior. The director, Elia Kazan, is a man of high theatrical [74/75] intelligence, a craftsman of genuine sensibility. . . . But

there is a lack of balance and perspective in the production of *A Streetcar Named Desire* due to the fact that the acting of the parts is of unequal force, quality and stress. To clarify this I must digress here and dwell a bit on the nature of acting in general. What is acting? What is its function in the theatre? How does it serve the goal of art, which is at all times to give flesh to essential human meanings? The digression, we shall see, may lead to a greater insight into the outstanding theatrical event under discussion.

A pedant might characterize the actor as a person endowed with the capacity to behave publicly and for purposes of play as though fictional circumstances were real. The actor knows that the lines he speaks and the action he performs are merely invention, just as he knows the objects he deals with on the stage— scenery, properties, lights—are parts of an artificial world. His acting consists in his ability to make all these things take on a new reality for himself and for his audience. Just as the first step in painting is the "imitation" of an object, so the actor "imitates" a series of human events that in terms of real life are no more true than the apple or flower or horse that we see in a painting.

The actor is himself an instrument, and, if he is able to look right in terms of what he is "imitating," his very presence on the stage is already an accomplishment. Yet we know that an actor of a convincing presence who merely reads his lines intelligibly offers us little more than information, which is the small change of the theatre. The actor who adds visual illustration to what he is saying (beating his breast to indicate anguish!) provides a sort of lamp whereby we read the play more comfortably, although at times the illustration if well chosen may give special illumination. The actor becomes creative only when he reveals the life from which the play's lines may have emerged, a life richer perhaps than the lines' literal significance. The creative actor is the author of the new meaning that a play acquires on the stage, the author of a personal sub-text into which the play's lines are absorbed so that a special aesthetic body with an identity of its own is born. . . . Just as the painter who merely sets down the image of an apple that looks like one is not an artist, so the [75/76] actor who merely "imitates" the surface impression that we might gather from a perusal of the play's text—an actor who does not create a life beyond what was there before he assumed his role—belies the art of the theatre.

The new meaning that the actor gives to the play emerges from what is popularly known as the actor's personality—not alone his physical "type," but the whole quality of his skill, emotion, insight, sensibility, character, imagination, spirit. These have an existence of their own, which the actor with the aid of the director must shape to the form of their interpretation or understanding of the problem they have set themselves for the play.

There are two things to be considered in any judgment of acting: the material of the actor himself and the use that the material has been put to in relation to the play as a whole. A very fine actor may utterly distort the intention of a play—that is, transform it with as much possibility of happy as of disastrous results. Bernard Shaw tells us that Duse was superior to Sudermann; it was her acting of that dramatist's play *Home* that made it a work of art. In Paris I saw the Laurette Taylor part in *The Glass Menagerie* very ably played in a way that robbed the character of all poetry. In my opinion, most of our highly regarded Hamlets are simply *readings* of the part but rather inferior acting or not acting at all. Katharine Cornell's Cleopatra may be said to have certain attractive aspects (no one need debate Miss Cornell's natural endowments), but, even aside from the question of physical qualifications, she creates nothing with the part, not only in the Shakespearean sense but within her own orbit. On the other hand, I have read that Michael Chekhov's Hamlet was not Hamlet (in the sense that there might be an "ideal" Hamlet) but that it was a true creation, albeit a very special one.

In *A Streetcar Named Desire* all the actors are good, but their performances do not truly convey Tennessee Williams' play. By virtue of its power and completeness the play pretty nearly succeeds in acting the actors, but the nature of the play's reception indicates a prevailing sentiment of excitement and glowing enthusiasm disassociated from any specific meaning.

Jessica Tandy's Blanche suffers from the actress's narrow [76/77] emotional range. One of the greatest parts ever written for a woman in the American theatre, it demands the fullness and variety of an orchestra. Miss Tandy's register is that of a violin's A string. The part represents the essence of womanly feeling and wounded human sensibility. Blanche lies and pretends, but through it all the actress must make us perceive her truth. She is an aristocrat (regardless of the threadbare myth of Southern gentility); she is an aristocrat in the subtlety and depth of her feeling. She is a poet, even if we are dubious about her understanding of the writers she names; she is superior by the sheer intensity and realization of her experience, even if much of what she does is abject.

If she is not these things, she is too much of a fraud to be worthy of the author's concern with her. If the latter is true, then the play would be saying something rather surprising—namely, that frank brutality and naked power are more admirable than the yearning for tenderness and the desire to reach beyond one's personal appetites. When Blanche appeals to her sister in the name of these values, Miss Tandy is unable to make it clear whether she means what she says and whether we are supposed to attach any importance to her speech or whether she is merely spinning another fantasy. It is essential to the play that we believe and are touched by what she says, that her emotion convinces us of the soundness of her values. All through the play, indeed, we must be captured by the music of the girl's martyred soul. Without this there is either a play whose viewpoint we reject or no play at all—only a series of "good scenes," a highly seasoned theatrical dish.

Marlon Brando, who plays Stanley Kowalski (Blanche's brother-in-law), is an actor of genuine power. He has what someone once called "high visibility" on the stage. His silences, even more than his speech, are completely arresting. Through his own intense concentration on what he is thinking or doing at each moment he is on the stage all our attention focuses on him. Brando's quality is one of acute sensitivity. None of the brutishness of his part is native to him: it is a characteristic he has to "invent." The combination of an intense, introspective, and almost lyric personality under the mask of a bully endows [77/78] the character with something almost touchingly painful. Because the elements of characterization are put on a face to which they are not altogether becoming, a certain crudeness mars our impression, while something in the nature of the actor's very considerable talent makes us wonder whether he is not actually suffering deeply in a way that relates him to what is represented by Blanche rather than to what his own character represents in the play. When he beats his wife or throws the radio out the window, there is, aside from the ugliness of these acts, an element of agony that falsifies their color in relation to their meaning in the play: they take on an almost Dostoevskian aspect.

For what is Stanley Kowalski? He is the embodiment of animal force, of brute life unconcerned and even consciously scornful of every value that does not come within the scope of such life. He resents being called a Polack, and he quotes Huey Long, who assured him that "every man is a king." He screams that he is a hundred per cent American, and breaks dishes and mistreats his women to prove it. He is all muscle, lumpish sensuality, and crude energy, given support by a society that hardly

demands more of him. He is the unwitting antichrist of our time, the little man who will break the back of every effort to create a more comprehensive world in which thought and conscience, a broader humanity are expected to evolve from the old Adam. His mentality provides the soil for fascism, viewed not as a political movement but as a state of being.

Because the author does not preach about him but draws him without hate or ideological animus, the audience takes him at his face value. His face value on the stage is the face of Marlon Brando as contrasted to that of Jessica Tandy. For almost more than two-thirds of the play, therefore, the audience identifies itself with Stanley Kowalski. His low jeering is seconded by the audience's laughter, which seems to mock the feeble and hysterical decorativeness of the girl's behavior. The play becomes the triumph of Stanley Kowalski with the collusion of the audience, which is no longer on the side of the angels. This is natural because Miss Tandy is fragile without being touching (except when the author is beyond being overpowered by an actress), and Mr. Brando is tough without being irredeemably coarse. [78/79]

When Kowalski tells his wife to get rid of Blanche so that things can be as they were (the author is suggesting that the untoward presence of a new consciousness in Kowalski's life—the appeal to forbearance and fineness—is a cruel disturbance and that he longs for a life without any spiritual qualms), the audience is all on Kowalski's side. Miss Tandy's speeches—which are lovely in themselves—sound phony, and her long words and noble appeals are as empty as a dilettante's discourse because they do not flow from that spring of warm feeling which is the justification and essence of Blanche's character.

One of the happiest pieces of staging and acting in the play is the moment when Kowalski, having beaten his wife, calls for her to return from the neighbor's apartment where she has taken momentary refuge. He whines like a hurt animal, shouts like a savage, and finally his wife descends the staircase to return to his loving arms. Brando has been directed to fall on his knees before his wife and thrust his head against her body in a gesture that connotes humility and passion. His wife with maternal and amorous touch caresses his head. He lifts her off her feet and takes her to bed. . . .

This, as I have noted, is done beautifully. Yet Brando's innate quality and something unresolved in the director's conception make the scene moving in a manner that is thematically disruptive. The pathos is too universally human (Kowalski at that moment is any man); it is not integrated with that attribute of the play which requires that Kowalski at all times be somewhat vile.

If Karl Malden as Blanche's suitor—a person without sufficient force to transcend the level of his environment—and Kim Hunter as Blanche's sister—who has made her peace with Kowalski's "normal life"—give performances that are easier to place than those of the two leading characters, it is not because of any intrinsic superiority to the other players. It is simply due to the fact that their parts are less complex. Miss Hunter is fairly good, Mr. Malden capital, but both appear in a sense to stand outside the play's interpretive problem. They are not struggling with a consciousness of the dilemma that exists in the choice between Kowalski's world and that of Blanche Du Bois. [79/80]

As creative spectators, we cannot satisfy ourselves at a play like *A Streetcar Named Desire* with the knowledge that it is a wonderful show, a smash hit, a prize winner (it is and will be all of these). It is a play that ought to arouse in us as much feeling, thought, and even controversy as plays on semipolitical themes; for it is a play that speaks of a poet's reaction to life in our country (not just the South) , and what he has to say about it is much more far-reaching than what might be enunciated through any slogan.

I have heard it said, for example, that Tennessee Williams portrays "ordinary" people without much sense of their promise, and reserves most of his affection for more special people—that minority which Thomas Mann once described as life's delicate children. I find this view false and misleading, but I would rather hear it expressed than to let the play go by as the best play of the season, something you must see, "great theatre."

If the play is great theatre—as I believe—it is precisely because it is instinct with life, a life we share in not alone on the stage, but in our very homes by night and day. If I have chosen to examine the production with what might seem undue minuteness, it is because I believe that questions of the theatre (and of art) are not simply questions of taste or professional quibbles, but life questions. I can think of no higher compliment to the director and actors of such a production than to take their work with utmost seriousness—even to the point of neglecting to make allowance for the difficulties attendant on the realization of so original a play on Broadway.

The Dilemma of Tennessee Williams*

HARRY TAYLOR. *Masses and Mainstream* (which since 1956 has changed its name to *Mainstream*) carried the following statement in the editorial column of its first number (March, 1948): "Our editorial viewpoint—though not necessarily the viewpoint of every contributor—is Marxist. . . . And we believe that the artist of integrity, insofar as he truthfully reflects these evils [of capitalism] will confirm in his esthetic achievement the Marxist science that points to socialism."

Tennessee Williams has written nine full-length plays and some twenty or more sketches and playlets. In 1939 he won the Group Theatre prize for a series of four one-acters, *American Blues.* In 1943 the Theatre Guild produced his *Battle of Angels;* but notwithstanding the combined talents of director Margaret Webster, Miriam Hopkins and Boston's Watch and Ward Society, the management did not find it good enough to bring to New York. Williams, however, could not be denied and came to Broadway with *The Glass Menagerie,* following it in the next season with *You Touched Me,* written in collaboration with Donald Windham and based on a story by D. H. Lawrence. Now, with *A Streetcar Named Desire,* he is firmly established as one of the best men of our theatre. He is only thirty-four and presumably has a long and important writing life before him. We are, therefore, at a good point—and so is he, for reasons which will develop—to appraise his work and to cast up his accounts if only to carry them over to the next white page on which the rest is yet to be written.

Artists may be placed in many categories but for our purpose I will describe them as falling into two: the artist who uses his experience and accumulated at- titudes and judgments to interpret material outside the intimate, personal facts of his life and the artist who uses this intelligence almost exclusively to interpret autobiographical material. I make no choice between these approaches: each is rich enough in content to stimulate the creative imagination of a Shakespeare or a Gorky. But the artist who uses the significant moments of his private life without re-subjecting them to the light of his total and most adult experience, limits the boldness and maturity of his art. However excellently he may depict the subjective memory of the dramatic moment, he is robbing it of force and penetration and even of truth [51/52] if he fails to let his latest maturity take the incident out of its singular shadow into the many faceted world of our common life.

And if, as in Williams' case, there was never more than a small patch of happy boyhood in a youth-time dominated by a developing family tragedy, by poverty and hard work and many menial jobs, his static stare will always give him back the same gloomy landscape in which even the small Eden seems a lying mirage and the relationship of forces remains fixed in an endless and cannibalistic assault of

*Harry Taylor, "The Dilemma of Tennessee Williams," *Masses and Mainstream,* I (April, 1948), 51-55.

the insensitively powerful upon the pathetic and defenseless. The more he stares at the incidents of his life, the more they are the same. He grows older, he knocks about on his own, he writes plays, he is welcomed and acclaimed; yet, curiously, he is still the traumatized youngster inexorably re-creating the pattern of his trauma, unable to break through to adult reality. That is why the characters he hates or fears or despises always win; while those to whom his sympathy is drawn invariably go down. In such a context there can be no conflict, no human dignity which is at the same time strong and healthy, and no future except for evil. And, indeed, for all their beauty of dialogue, atmosphere and characterization, this is a just description of Williams' plays.

Moreover, his static stare prevents his taking into account the factors that have brutalized his world. It is true that he is not unaware of these factors—and herein lies hope. In *Nitchevo*, a discarded old worker names the enemy, though even here we do not see it in action; we only see its end results, its victims in interaction. I have the impression that Williams can be positive and constructive in his daily citizenship. He abominates racial discrimination and fights it. He is for a national theatre. My last information is that he understands the necessities behind Henry Wallace's campaign. And yet his artistic philosophy remains where it was before he came of political age.

Some will say: Why bother Williams with the outer world or the enlargement of his view and of reality? Surely a man who can write *A Streetcar Named Desire* may be forgiven pessimism and the repetition, itself an effect of pessimism, that comes from always seeing the same things the same way. But that is precisely the reason for this appraisal. For it is my contention that Williams has been robbing himself as well as his audience of the full possibilities of his dramatic intelligence and, as we shall see, even of perfection of craft. [52/53]

Let us examine the three plays of his

which I have seen performed. Their elements are repeated throughout the body of his work. Even his collaborative adaptation of D. H. Lawrence's story seems to have been undertaken because it contained the salient features of his fixed material.

We will begin with *The Property Is Condemned*. In this twenty-minute sketch, almost a monologue, we meet a girl of fifteen. The child's unceasing flow of words re-creates for us the destructive reality of a broken home, parents gone, protective older sister recently dead of a venereal disease, she herself surreptitiously living in the house since lost to the bank, trading her body for food and excitement; and all this inextricably woven through with the wild fantasies of past glories and glamorous prospects made poignant by the innate knowledge that she is trapped.

In *The Glass Menagerie*, the protagonist is again the young daughter in a mean, disrupted home, in which, while her harridan mother lies about the golden past and assails the present and her beloved brother is preparing to desert them both for a dream seemingly beyond his strength, the girl, crippled and willess, peers out for a brief scene from among the perfect figurines which she has substituted for the world of reality—and then, hopelessly, sinks back again. There is a fourth in this new hand that Williams is dealing. He is a commonsensical man on whom the girl is forced to pin her last hope of love and understanding and return to sanity. When he fails her, her little animals close in. The play is patently an extension and enrichment of the character, environment and atmosphere of the sketch; indeed, of all its ingredients except, significantly, its outlook on life. The play even has a *semblance* of dramatic conflict, though the confrontations do not spring from the main theme.

In *Streetcar*, Blanche Du Bois, parents dead, homosexual husband an early suicide, ancestral mansion lost to the bank, driven out of her home town as a menace to the morals of schoolboys, on the crumbling edge of insanity, arrives at the last chance station of her life—the slum area two-room apartment of her newly-wed younger sister, Stella, and her uncouth Polish-American husband, Stanley Kowalski. Again, then, we have the frightened fugitive from a brutal reality, diaphanously gowned in what she hopes is an impenetrable cloth of glamorous deceits, pretensions and self-deceptions; we have the power- [53/54] less sibling who wishes to love and protect her; and in the person of one of Stanley's friends, Mitch, the stranger who may pull her to safety but fails her. To these tried elements, the author now brings a newly found craft of direct confrontation. For, seeing his home invaded by a creature utterly foreign to his experience, his routine disrupted, his relations with Stella assailed and endangered, Stanley ruthlessly attacks Blanche with the dreaded revelations of her existence, turns Mitch from her, criminally assaults the half-mad woman as if to prove her defenselessness before the urgent, insensitive realities of life, and, finally, having driven her clear off the edge of reason, summons the attendants of a mental institution to take her away.

Unquestionably, this last play is the one toward which the others were heading; toward which, in fact, all Williams' work has been heading. On the way he has picked up speed and power and definition, and the story now stands at what is probably dead end. And still, for all its enhanced movement and characterization and the rest of the eloquent testimony to his deepened mastery of theatre, Williams, as a direct consequence of his socio-philosophical position, has been unable to achieve conflict. Confrontations, yes, and savage, almost animal. Elia Kazan has projected them with so much clash and claw that we are momentarily bemused into believing them the real article of theatre. But there can be no conflict in a man's methodically beating a child to death. The prisoner of a view in which the dominant reality is monstrously destructive and implacable, Williams has once more opposed it with a poor, hazy-minded being already broken in the toils and armed only with obstinate illusions rather than with reasonable will.

Streetcar is an absorbing and beautifully written play and magnificently produced, but it is not a great play as most of our critics would have us believe. Great drama cannot emerge out of flight and hysteria, but arises from genuine conflict, an element that can only be generated by the writer's conviction that the battle is vital and that the means to wage it exist. Williams will write greatly only if he can re-examine reality and emotionally recognize what his intellect may already have grasped: that the forces of good in this world are adult and possess both the will and the power to change our environment.

He needs but the merest extraversion, the briefest glance at human [54/55] history to see these forces in operation. If today we shudder at the unparalleled malevolence of the war-making class, we need to understand that its viciousness is in direct ratio to its desperation at the prospect of losing power. Natural and human history is a constant dying of the old and entrenched, even while the new is struggling to take over.

This is no special plea for social plays. But surely the absence of the socio-historic periphery in the author's mind weakens his attack even on personal drama, depriving it of the aura of larger reality and of moral conviction.

Williams once wrote: "The one dominant theme in most of my writings, the most magnificent thing in all nature, is valor—and endurance." However he may believe this to be so, it is not true of his work. Only the passionate conviction of the value of human valor, endurance and dignity, and an understanding of the historic forces that embody these qualities can springboard his next greatest leap forward of craft and artistic stature. But first of all, of simple craft: the knowledge that great drama cannot be evoked from the opposition of will with non-will but only by the firmly engaged conflict of powerful wills.

Tennessee Williams*

FATHER DESMOND REID, S. J., is Director of the Marriage Courses given at the Catholic Workers' College, S.J., Dublin, Ireland, where he also lectures in sociology. He has long been interested in the theatre. *Studies*, published in Dublin, is "An Irish Quarterly Review of Letters, Philosophy and Science."

Thomas Lanier Williams was born in Missouri forty-five years ago. As clerk, lift-boy, telephone operator, waiter and cinema worker, he learned to observe people and to write about them. He wrote poetry, short stories and plays. He studied in the Universities of Missouri and Iowa and in Washington University. Now, as Tennessee Williams, he is a playwright of high talent. His own judgment that he is a minor dramatist who has written one or two major plays seems a modest one: he has not been uniformly brilliant but few of his works have failed to reflect glimpses, at least, of sure craftsmanship. He has won the annual New York Drama Critics' Circle Award three times, and twice the coveted Pulitzer Prize.

It is not, however, because of these successes that Tennessee Williams has become a much-discussed man, both inside and outside the theatre world. He has been the centre of enduring controversy; and each new play, almost indeed each new production of one of his plays, has whipped up that controversy. The main point at issue is the predominance of 'sex', and sexual aberration, in his work and the manner in which he treats it. His critics condemn him as bold and bawdy, often suggestive, sometimes indecent; to those who defend him he is a sincere artist impatient of superficiality and convention, a realist who depicts people as they

are: with their private hopes and fears and failings and failures.

That is but a broad statement of the opposing points of view. I shall discuss them more fully in the course of this article. Meantime we may note Tennessee Williams's reaction to the strife that surrounds him. He refuses to change his methods; he writes what he wants to write; and if theatre-goers do not like it they can stay away from his plays. Here are his own words:

Of course I know that I have sometimes presumed too much upon corresponding sympathies and interest in those to whom I talk boldly, and this has led to rejections that were painful and costly enough to inspire more prudence. But when I weigh one thing against another, an easy liking against a hard respect, the balance always tips the same way, and whatever the risk of being turned a cold shoulder, I still don't want to talk to people only about the surface aspects of their lives, the sort of things that acquaintances laugh and chatter about on ordinary social occasions.[1] **[431/432]**

Of this it may be observed in passing that many of his supporters seem to accord him much more than 'a hard respect', that 'a cold shoulder' hugely understates the attitude of his opponents

[431][1]From the Introduction (*Person-to-Person*) of *Cat on a Hot Tin Roof*. Except where otherwise noted, all quotations are from the editions of Tennessee Williams's plays published by Secker and Warburg, London. They are cited here by kind permission of the publishers.

*Desmond Reid, "Tennessee Williams," *Studies*, Winter, 1957, 431-446.

and that in their opinion a hard respect or even warm acclaim may be won at too great a price.

I have never seen one of Williams's plays on a stage. It may seem strange, then, to presume to discuss them with any degree of authority. As Williams himself has written: ' . . . a play in a book is only a shadow of a play and not even a clear shadow of it. . . . The printed script of a play is hardly more than an architect's blueprint of a house not yet built or built and destroyed.'[1] With that we will all, I think, agree. A play for the stage is what the dramatist writes; and he may fairly claim that his success or failure be judged from the stage presentation of his plays. But suppose one is interested rather in the content matter of the plays, searching for the author's lines of thought, for an underlying philosophy of life, for community of theme or character. Then the plays must be read and re-read and pondered. A performance on the stage is over in two or three short hours; one is left with impressions, with, perhaps, half-remembered lines of dialogue. Further, an actor or a director may by a personal interpretation heighten or lessen the force of phrase or situation. He may change or misrepresent the emphasis, and fail to convey what the dramatist intended. Admittedly in modern plays when characters are more sharply drawn there is less scope for individualistic interpretation— Hamlets are few nowadays; but to avoid anything of a misleading nature it is necessary to go to the sources, to the play in print. There acts and scenes and lines may be considered at leisure; you can turn back a page; you can make a note; you can compare and contrast; and when all is over you can form a fairer judgment.

*   *   *

The characters which Tennessee Williams puts before us are people in trouble. Usually they are people in desperate trouble: they are lonely, forgotten, poverty-stricken, misunderstood or despised, without hope of helping themselves and unhelped by others. He is remarkably faithful to this theme. Sometimes he crowds all the trouble on to the shoulders of one unhappy person; sometimes there are two or three, equally unhappy, whose lives and troubles intermingle; sometimes he leaves them at the curtain-fall with a dim ray of hope; more often there is none.

Blanche du Bois in *A Streetcar Named Desire* is perhaps Williams's most forlorn character. She has been a gentlewoman knowing wealth and ease; now she is destitute, an alcoholic, an ageing nymphomaniac. [432/433]
She scrabbles frantically for a hold, something with which to lift herself from the depths. She glimpses a breathless break in the clouds when Mitch is attracted to her, likes her and will, she realizes, ask her to marry him. But her tottering hopes crash forever when her brother-in-law, despising her and her airs of gentility and her ceaseless recalling of better days, tells Mitch of her past promiscuity. At the play's end she is taken, screaming, to a mental home.

Alma, in *Summer and Smoke*, is in her middle twenties: '. . . there is something prematurely spinsterish about her. An excessive propriety and self-consciousness is apparent in her nervous laughter; . . . people of her own age regard her as rather quaintly and humorously affected'. She has a father hopelessly unable to understand and help her, and a mother, 'a spoiled and childish girl who evaded the responsibilities of later life by slipping into a state of perverse childishness'.[1] Alma falls in love with John Buchanan. She insists on marriage, but he will not be tied by any such contract. After a long, disintegrating struggle with herself, unaided and unadvised, Alma can stand the strain no longer; she offers herself to John on his own terms. But it is too late: time and tragedy, and Alma, have changed John Buchanan. He is in love with and engaged to a younger girl. We leave Alma on the street with a passing stranger. She will almost surely end as another Blanche du Bois.

[432] [1]*Camino Real* in the Afterword.
[433] [1]*Summer and Smoke*, Part I, Scene I.

The Rose Tattoo presents to us Serafina delle Rose, shattered and slatternly after the death of her husband. Her dulled mind is shocked still more at the revelation of her husband's infidelity. Her meeting with another stray, Alvaro, opens the door to hope. Of their initial conversation Williams writes: 'Their fumbling communication has a curious intimacy and sweetness, like the meeting of two lonely children for the first time'.[2] In this play too we have the correlative unhappiness of Serafina's daughter, Rosa: young and wild and immoral, disgusted by her mother, avid for affection, for a man to love and who will love her.

And so the sad list grows: there is triple tragedy in *Cat on a Hot Tin Roof*, Big Daddy, a vigorous mountain of a man dying of cancer, Brick, his son, well on the way to being a confirmed dipsomaniac, and Maggie, Brick's wife, desperately trying to reach her husband through his unveiled contempt and indifference and fighting for a share of Big Daddy's fortune; *The Glass Menagerie* shows us Tom, chained to a nagging mother (du Bois-like in her dreams of earlier gentility and 'gentlemen callers' on Sundays) and a crippled sister, Laura. He deserts them in the end after cruelly raising their hopes of betterment by introducing Laura to a friend of his. A possible husband for the shy, reserved **[433/434]** girl? But the friend explains honestly that he cannot call again: 'I go out all the time with a girl named Betty. She's a home-girl like you, and Catholic, and Irish, and in a great many ways we—get along fine'. He leaves; and Tom leaves—for good; and the two women face a bleak future alone.

Still the list grows as the one-act plays add their quota of human beings crumbling under strain or loneliness: for example, poor deranged Miss Collins (*Portrait of a Madonna*—traces again of Blanche du Bois), Charlie Colton, the elderly salesman (*The Last of My Solid Gold Watches*) whose world, and business connections, have vanished, the derelict Little Man and his love for a cat, 'She isn't a fair-weather friend . . . She'd be

faithful to me' (*The Strangest Kind of Romance*), and the homeless, friendless little orphan girl (she is about thirteen) of *This Property is Condemned*.

There is about all this a terrible singleness of purpose. Always it is the waifs and strays and outcasts and misfits that claim Tennessee Williams's attention. In bringing their distress before us he serves them well. His writing is clear-sighted and remorseless. He is sincere in his belief that what he depicts is representative of the world about us, and, as he himself tells us, he is trying to drive home the screaming need of a world-wide human effort to know ourselves and each other a great deal better. To Williams his hapless characters are not merely the misfits of the world: they are typical human beings. They typify others similarly if not identically cudgelled by misfortune. The little world of a Williams play is a miniature of the great cruel world in which we, all of us, live. The squalid dwellings which are the homes of his characters symbolize the decay and corruption of our world.[1]

Although it is his aim to reflect reality, I wonder if the picture painted by Tennessee Williams is a complete one. That there are tension and trouble and violence in the world is beyond question. It is also true that some of the sufferers suffer and tread the downward path alone, unaided by any human hand. But is that the common lot of people in distress? Is every door shut against them and every head turned away? It is easy, I know, to view the matter through Irish spectacles. We are, taking us by and large, a kindly people; we will help, as a rule, when help is needed and when help we can. But we have not a corner in charity. Charity is a human virtue and sympathy for our fellow men is something ingrained in hu-

[433] [2] Act II, Scene I.
[434] [1] Here are some of the author's Production Notes. 'The dark, grim rear wall of the Wingfield tenement' (*The Glass Menagerie*); 'spindling pillars, sagging steps and broken rails' (*The Rose Tattoo*); 'the shabby room', 'the furnishings are dishevelled and old' (*The Long Goodbye*); 'There is an effect of sinister antiquity in the setting, even the flowers suggesting the richness of decay' (*Auto-Da-Fé*); 'the sagging porch', 'the loose boards', 'the rusty spout', 'the unkempt lawn' (*Baby Doll*).

man nature. In individuals these virtues may be blighted by a rotting selfishness. But they are as old as the world [434/435] itself and they die hard. I cannot feel that they are as yet dead or dying.

I do not, I think, misinterpret Tennessee Williams on this point. He is concerned about widespread decay of understanding and sympathy. The title, *This Property is Condemned,* refers directly to the tumbledown house that is the only home known to Willie the orphan girl. There she lives alone. Clearly, at the play's end, we are intended to apply the phrase to the child herself. What her subsequent life will be is sadly obvious. But Williams would have us apply the phrase also to the world at large: it too is a property that is condemned.

The crazy plaza of *Camino Real* is his scarifying conception of our world. It is peopled by pitiable wrecks and those who can but will not help them: there are sex-ridden men and women, cheats, profiteers, military guards to enforce a mocking law. Only death and removal in the Streetcleaners' barrel awaits those in the Camino Real. It is a condemned property; and so, too, are those, all of them, who have the unhappiness to dwell within it. Tennessee Williams does not exclude humour from this or other of his plays, but the over-riding effect is one of gloom and despair.

A more accurate likeness is drawn by John Steinbeck in *The Grapes of Wrath* or by Michael Vincente Gazzo in another modern play, *A Hatful of Rain.* Steinbeck's is an angry book. He tells a fearsome story of a dispossessed community, thousands of people hunted and haunted by hunger and cold and dereliction. At the end of his last page he leaves them still homeless, foodless and workless. But all along the way, on endless journeys, through unceasing want and privation, kindness travelled with them. Those who had a little shared with fellow-sufferers who had nothing. When one of the travellers died, all mourned. The troubles of one were the troubles of all. There were instances, too, of fellow-feeling from outside their own shabby ranks—a canteen girl sold for a cent two nickel-apiece candies to two hungry little boys. This spirit lightens the whole book in biting contrast to the greed and cruelty of the landowners and land-grabbers so powerfully indicted by Steinbeck.

A Hatful of Rain makes the same point in a different, more confined, way. Here we have four people: a young man, a drug addict, his wife and his father who are unaware of this, and his brother who has known and has tried to help him from the start. Twice a day now Johnny needs a 'shot'; he has no money left; neither has Polo, the brother. Johnny struggles to keep his secret from his wife and his bouncy, respectable father. Inevitably he collapses under the strain and they learn the ugly truth. At once the family ranks close; other, lesser troubles are forgotten; they will all help Johnny.

Tennessee Williams could not have given us either of these stories. When reading *Summer and Smoke* for the first time I reached the scene [435/436] where Alma returns to John Buchanan. She can no longer live without him:

> One time I said 'no' to something. . . . But now I have changed my mind, or the girl who said 'no', she doesn't exist any more, she died last summer—suffocated in smoke from something on fire inside her. No, she doesn't live now. . . . I said, 'But what about your pride?'—She said, 'Forget about pride whenever it stands between you and what you must have!' And then I said, 'But what if he doesn't want me?' I don't know what she said then. I'm not sure whether she said anything or not—her lips stopped moving—yes, I think she stopped breathing.[1]

There I was interrupted, before John gave his answer. But I knew what that answer must be. Tennessee Williams would not countenance a happy ending for Alma. Although John's views on marriage have changed, she must suffer a final blow: John is engaged to another girl.

This consistent refusal to salt the lives of his characters with a little legitimate happiness or a little human aid sounds a

[436] [1] *Summer and Smoke.* Part II, Scene II.

false note in Williams's plays. Of his leading characters, too, only Stella and (to a lesser extent) Mitch of *A Streetcar Named Desire* and Jack (*The Rose Tattoo*) seem to be balanced human beings. Stella is a flower in the Williams wilderness: she is normal. She feels deeply for her sister, Blanche; but, for all his coarseness and for all the roughness of their life together, she loves her husband. She will not allow Blanche to wreck their marriage. There are surely as many Stellas in the world as there are Blanches. Tennessee Williams would have given us a more complete picture had he reflected that fact in his plays.

*   *   *

It is remarkable that although Williams writes consistently of suffering humanity there is little anger in his writing. Here too he differs from Steinbeck. Clearly, much of the sorrow that surrounds his heroes and heroines is occasioned by the acts or omissions, wilful or unconscious, of their acquaintances. But Williams does not waste time with the culprits. His whole attention is given to the sufferers, and he is himself always gentle and understanding with them. He is pitiless in exposing their weaknesses, but he is compassionate with them. He is on their side. He fights their battles.

This gentle compassion strikes me as the most noteworthy characteristic of Tennessee Williams. It permeates his work. It is rooted in the understanding he has for the fears and motives of his characters. He sees how straitened, almost ensnared, they are by circumstance. Faith-[436/437] fully and in detail he puts their plight before his audience or his readers; and so powerfully does he write that he can hardly fail to communicate to viewers or readers his own sense of immense pity.

It is unnecessary to point to isolated lines that illustrate this compassionate approach. It is the very stuff of which the plays are woven. Williams writes:

These people on the stage do not return our looks. We do not have to answer their questions nor make any sign of being in company with them, nor do we have to compete with their virtues nor resist their offenses. All at once, for

this reason, we are able to see them! Our hearts are wrung by recognition and pity, so that the dusky shell of the auditorium where we are gathered anonymously together is flooded with an almost liquid warmth of unchecked human sympathies, relieved of self-consciousness, allowed to function. . . .[1]

He is extraordinarily skilful in building up a scene to a point where our sympathy is called forth unrestrainedly. Again and again in *Cat on a Hot Tin Roof* he does it. We feel for Big Mama as she reels under Big Daddy's verbal onslaughts, for Brick trying desperately to conceal from Big Daddy the reason for his drinking, for Big Daddy himself hugely exulting in the fact that he has not got cancer—when all the time, we know, he has; when he learns the truth 'his face crumbles like broken yellow plaster about to fall into dust'. In switching our sympathy from one character to another Williams is a master.

Individuals claim our compassion in most of the other plays: Serafina and Blanche, Laura (*The Glass Menagerie*), The Little Man, The Little Girl, and so on. In *Baby Doll*[2] we feel for Aunt Rose and Archie, even (a tribute to Williams's dexterity) for spoilt Baby Doll and vengeful Silva.

Unhappily, just as Tennessee Williams exaggerates the universality and aloneness of suffering humanity, so too does he push his compassion too far. He is on sure ground when he states that he has never met a person he could not love, provided he understood that person. To understand and to sympathize and to love are right and good things. It is when Williams goes further that we must part company with him: individuals have taken right or wrong paths not by choice but by necessity, driven willy-nilly by themselves, their circumstances and their antecedents. That is a morally indefensible doctrine. It is the most dangerous element in Tennessee Williams's works.

It should be said that he does not expressly approve in the plays of immoral

[437] [1] *The Rose Tattoo* in the Introduction, *The Timeless World of a Play.*
[437] [2] The film script was based largely on Williams's one-act play, *27 Wagons Full of Cotton.*

conduct. But I do not, I think, read him incorrectly in [437/438] saying that his 'necessity' doctrine and his avowed disbelief in 'guilt' must imply condonation of the offences his plays reveal. In addition, he is at such pains to pile agony on agony, cornering his tortured little people, that our sympathy tends to flower into the judgment, 'I don't blame them for what they did'.

In the plays we find the implied suggestion, based on compassion, that Williams's men and women are not responsible for their immoral behaviour. They are unhappy weary people. They fall into two groups: some whose present plight is the result of earlier excesses (mainly of a sexual nature) to which they were driven by circumstances; they are now to be pitied, but who, understanding the stresses to which they surrendered, will blame them for what they did? To this group belong, for example, Blanche du Bois and Bertha (*Hello from Bertha*). The second is a larger and more varied group: we see the circumstances working on the characters, the vain search for relief and, finally, the fall. Here we have Serafina and Rosa and Alma and Brick; Big Daddy belongs to this class too, though his is a somewhat different situation: freed after years from the fear of cancer, he is going to live again, he is a lusty old man bent on celebrating. And Alvaro, lonely for so long, with only love and affection to offer 'on hot days and cold days in this lonely old world' will sin with Serafina. And Silva (*Baby Doll*), hated as 'a man with foreign blood', his cotton gin burnt down by Archie Meighan, will talk bitterly of the

evil spirits that haunt the human heart and take possession of it, and spread from one human heart to another human heart the way that a fire goes spreading from leaf to leaf and branch to branch in a tree till a forest is all aflame with it —the birds take flight—the wild things are suffocated—everything green and beautiful is destroyed.

So Silva will take revenge on stupid old Archie by seducing Archie's stupid but desirable young wife. And again (the implied suggestion is) who, understanding,

will blame these people. They crave for and surely they deserve a little release, a little happiness, a little self-assertion.

There is here, obviously, question of moral standards. Williams himself writes that 'The great and only possible dignity of man lies in his power deliberately to choose certain moral values by which to live . . .'[1] But what are these 'certain' moral values? Is each man to choose his own? Or is each man to strive to measure up to the objective norm of the natural law and its precepts? or the revealed law of God, the Ten Commandments which apart from being God's rules of life enshrine fundamental principles without which men cannot live together? Not many of the Williams characters seem to profess acceptance of the [438/439] natural law or the revealed law of God. That may not be the dramatist's fault: he portrays the world as he sees it, and he sees a materialistic, immoral world. So Big Daddy and Maggie and Brick and Alvaro and Stanley Kowalski and others are little, if at all, influenced by moral considerations.

And yet they are responsible for their actions. They are human beings with freedom of choice; they can choose to do or omit this, to do this or that; they are not children or sleepwalkers or lunatics; as human beings they can distinguish between right and wrong. Whatever their troubles, as long as they retain the ability to reason and to choose they are responsible for what they do. Stress of circumstance, environment, antecedents may weaken their defences and lessen their culpability. But they remain free to accept or decline. For pathological cases, clearly, full allowance must be made. Exceptionally, too, repeated offences forming a habit of sinful conduct can so undermine a person's moral fibre that now each individual failure may not be morally imputable. I would say that this applies to Blanche du Bois as Williams depicts her. But even here we ought to remember that the earlier offences, which led to the forming of the habit, may have been im-

[438] [1]*The Rose Tattoo*, in the Introduction.

putable and should not be made little of.

This is not a new doctrine. It does not set an impossible standard. Neither does it fail to take account of strain and weaknesses which do in fact lessen without removing imputability.[1] But it would seem that Tennessee Williams does not accept this teaching. I believe that he is sincere in this. He does not parade his characters as models to be imitated. To him they are accusing ghosts—accusing his audiences who, through lack of charity and understanding, have had a share in putting them, or others like them, where they now are.

Mrs. Hardwicke-Moore, the central character of *The Lady of Larkspur Lotion*, is another desperate, broken-down woman. Her landlady, Mrs. Wire, will no longer be fobbed off with the threadbare excuse that she is expecting money from her Brazilian rubber plantation:

MRS. WIRE: You with your Brazilian rubber plantation. That coat-of-arms on the wall that you got from the junk-shop—the woman who sold it *told* me! One of the Hapsburgs! Yes! A titled lady! . . .
WRITER: Stop badgering this unfortunate little woman! Is there no mercy left in the world anymore? What has become of compassion and understanding? Where have they all gone to? Where's God? Where's Christ? What if there *is* no Brazilian rubber plantation? [439/440]
MRS. HARDWICK-MOORE: I tell you there is, there *is!*
WRITER: What if there is no rubber king in her life! There *ought* to be rubber kings in her life! Is she to be blamed because it is necessary for her to compensate for the cruel deficiencies of reality by the exercise of a little—what shall I say?—God-given—imagination?
   . . .   .
MRS. WIRE: I'll ask you to please stop spitting me in the face those high-flown speeches. . . .[1]

Mrs. Hardwicke-Moore is—any sufferer? Mrs. Wire is—any member of Williams's audience? The Writer is—surely, Tennessee Williams himself? This plea for understanding might be inserted into any of his plays, and his query 'Is she to be blamed. . . .' be repeated, changing the compensation seized on by Mrs. Hardwicke-Moore to something more serious than the exercise of imagination.

Powerfully, then, Williams evokes our compassion. But he must not blind us to the fact that the sins we see *are* sins—free offences against the divine law, be it revealed or contained in the natural law.

*   *   *

The elements in Tennessee Williams's plays to which most people take exception are his use of 'strong language', dialogue about intimate sexual matters, and suggestive situations. It is not at all easy to indicate where the line should be drawn in this connection. Some things unquestionably should not be discussed or done in public on a stage; others, equally undoubtedly, are allowable. But there is a middle group which will always pose problems: is *this* immoral, or suggestive, or indecent, or obscene? Has the borderline been crossed?

We may set aside from the present discussion the pornographer. He is a sex pedlar. He may seek to avoid unqualified condemnation and perhaps prosecution by adroit handling of his shabby wares, but his purpose is to sell his cake because of the spice it contains. It is unnecessary to comment on the morality of his writing.

Here we consider a writer with a different aim. A playwright is concerned, as an artist, to present a slice of life or of human experience. He presents for our observation a few or several people. In the little section of their life which we view 'sex' has a place. They may be married or unmarried; they talk about sex and their sexual problems; they giggle or guffaw at sexy jokes and smutty stories; consistent with the action of the play and with the circumstances in which they find [440/441] themselves, they are drawn towards sexual intimacies; there are scenes of 'love' and seduction leading at times to fornication or rape or other crimes to be committed offstage or after the fall of the curtain. All these things happen in real life. People circumstanced as are the

[439][1]For fuller treatment of this matter, see *Criminal Responsibility and Punishment* by Michael Connolly, S.J., in *Studies*, Autumn, 1957.
[440][1]*The Lady of Larkspur Lotion* in *27 Wagons Full of Cotton and other one-act plays* by Tennessee Williams, published by John Lehmann, London.

characters in the play are so tempted, and many succumb to the temptation. And the dramatist, concerned with reality, depicts these things with fidelity.

What is his purpose in so doing? It may vary:

(a) he may have no purpose beyond the representation of life as he sees it;

(b) primarily or secondarily he may seek by showing forth evil in all its ugliness to develop in his audience an aversion for it;

(c) again primarily or secondarily he may aim at stirring the consciences of his audience: to shock or startle them into realization that in real life, by act or omission, they may have been a contributory cause, partial perhaps or indirect, of others' sinning as do the characters in his play.

If I read him correctly, Tennessee Williams's work combines the first and third of these.

To what extent is all this allowable? We face here a problem that has long been debated. The matter is governed by moral principles that are old and wise and based on discerning knowledge of human nature. They are as sound today as they were centuries ago; and they cannot with impunity be disregarded. It should be obvious that it is necessary to avoid two extremes. The first of these would sweep away any restriction on the dramatist's licence. In this 'progressive' view, sexual matters may be treated in an uninhibited manner as is any other less inflammatory facet of human life. The dramatist as an artist is above morality. To take cognizance of it would cramp his artistic expression. Surely this is false. The dramatist is a man; as such he is subject to the laws of human nature; to temper his writing, to respect the laws that govern him and all mankind cannot impair his work as an artist. On the contrary his work must thus be enhanced, completed and rendered more valuable.

The second extreme, with almost equal rashness, would exclude all treatment of so delicate a matter from stage or novel or screen. It would cast, in the name of

reverence, a cloak of silence about the whole subject of sex. In so doing it would, unwittingly and ironically, help to perpetuate the misguided impression that over even legitimate lovemaking and marriage relations there hangs a dark and dirty cloud. Marriage and [441/442] related topics are sacred things. They are indeed worthy of reverence. But reverence does not demand puritanical silence.

To come back now to the three elements mentioned: 'strong language', dialogue about intimate sexual matters, and suggestive situations. To attempt an assessment of the allowability or otherwise of individual lines or incidents or scenes in individual plays would be a hopeless task within the confines of a study such as this. I cannot quote extracts, and anyway to filch from their context a number of lines would be unfair. Here, however, are some general observations.

'Strong language' can vary in quality and strength. The nautical profanities of Long John Silver in *Treasure Island* are scarcely objectionable. The bloody-and-damn type of expletive (as in, say, *The Shadow of a Gunman*) at worst may leave some people uncomfortable. But the use of other words, of anatomical slang and of phrases involving the Holy Name are out of place and objectionable on the stage, as they are in real life. In this connection I would find fault with, for example, *Cat on a Hot Tin Roof*. Language of this sort may contain little that incites to positive sin. If used repeatedly and immoderately, however, it can lower the moral tone of a person, a group—or a nation.

'Smutty' talk and stories and remarks are generally inadmissible. But a qualification must be made. It is accepted that the moral danger involved in such conversation depends on the condition and temperament of the persons who converse. There is an obvious difference between the casual banter of married people and the furtive tale-swapping of adolescents. It is worth noting, too, that those who indulge in this kind of talk are careful, by and large, to do so only in relatively small and private groups. Most people of sane and normal upbringing (even those private offenders) are repelled by such conversation on a stage. There will always be the few who take delight in this more public badinage, just as there will always be the stupid irritating giggle at any reference, however inoffensive and well-intentioned, in theatre or cinema, to marriage or child-bearing or similar subjects. Morality apart, there is something peculiarly distasteful about presenting this kind of thing as part of a theatrical entertainment for large groups of men and women of varying age, upbringing and maturity.

I cannot see that Tennessee Williams's plays would have suffered unduly had he curbed his characters in this matter. His dramatic sense, his power in building up atmosphere and his incisive, repetitive dialogue do not depend on this doubtful assistance. Specifically, by way of example, his Elephant Story in the Broadway version of *Cat on a Hot Tin Roof* (Act III) is vulgar and offensive. In fairness it may be said that, for the most part, Williams's 'smutty' lines are not dragged in; they *fit* in; they are in character. But that does not wholly justify them. [442/443]

More serious discussion of sexual affairs may be less offensive. Here there is no poking fun at matters sacred. There is rather honest exploration of a difficult situation or problem. Presentation and delicacy of touch are of first importance; and again, 'realists' and 'art' advocates notwithstanding, there is room for and need of judicious reticence. A husband and wife may discuss their marital intimacies or difficulties in the privacy of their room. But there may well be serious moral dangers to watchers and listeners when that discussion takes place in a 'private' room on a public stage. A tremendous amount depends on the content and tone of the conversation, as on the quality of the audience: what is fit food for adults can be poison for younger people.

In *Summer and Smoke* (Part II, Scene VIII) we find Alma Winemiller and John

Buchanan discussing love. John delivers a long speech: 'Hold still! Now listen here to an anatomy lecture. You see this chart . . .' (he is a doctor), and he goes on to discourse of the three birds on the anatomical tree: all hungry, one for truth, one for food, one for love. Alma, he tells her, has fed the first and third birds with 'nothing but hand-me-down notions—attitudes—poses!' Here is Alma's answer:

> So that is your high conception of human desires. What you have here is not the anatomy of a beast, but a man. And I— I reject your opinion of where love is, and the kind of truth you believe the brain to be seeking! There is something not shown on the chart.
>
> JOHN: You mean the part that Alma is Spanish for, do you?
>
> ALMA: Yes, that's not shown on the anatomy chart! But it's there just the same, yes, there! Somewhere, not seen, but there. And it's *that* that I loved you with— that! Not what you mention! . . .

This is worth noticing because it is one of the rare instances of a Williams character conceding that there is more to human love than bodily enjoyment. He makes the point finely if briefly here (it arises equally briefly elsewhere in the play); he is open but neither vulgar nor indelicate. One might wish, however, that he had chosen a more balanced protagonist than Alma for the spiritual side of the discussion. All through the play her problem is the same: to stick to her principles, certain of their soundness, or to yield to John. Ironically, when she would finally capitulate, John has switched to her way of thinking. Her fall is sadly pointed by the fact that she has helped to spiritualize his outlook—just as in *The Prisoner* Brigid Boland's Cardinal, disgraced beyond recall, has yet rocked the foundations of his interrogator's materialism. *Summer and Smoke* is not one of Williams's best plays, but, taking it in the round, it is a sound handling of a delicate theme.

In his other plays discussion of sex concerns itself all but exclusively with the physical element. Delicacy of treatment apart, this uniform [443/444] insistence on only one aspect of human love must impart a false impression. Serafina and Rosa and Alvaro and Stanley and Archie Meighan are types, single-minded in their approach to sex and marriage. Tennessee Williams would, again, more faithfully have mirrored actual life had he given us even a few more normal men and women: more normal in that they recognize the spiritual quality of marriage relations—and are happier for that recognition.

Finally, with regard to suggestive situations this may be said: it can be quite proper to convey that a man and woman are tempted to sin together, or have sinned; it is morally indefensible to depict their sin on the stage. In between these extremes lies the suggestive situation. A long drawn-out seduction scene, a woman disrobing or scantily clad, simulation of passionate embraces, can be highly inflammatory stage material. Whatever his own views on the matter and whatever his desire to show life as it is, the dramatist must respect the fact that he writes for a flesh-and-blood audience. He may not wantonly dangle morally dangerous material before them.

This is particularly true when the suggestive scene is a purple patch in the play. It is brilliantly depicted, drawn with a wealth of detail. It stands out. It resembles the similar passage in a book which tugs at the reader's imagination drawing him back to re-read it. Such a section, in play or novel, is also aesthetically unsound: it does not merge with the pattern; it distracts.

Some scenes there are, otherwise indictable, which are saved by a deliberate playing down of the situation, or by the presence of some other element which softens or relegates to a minor place the note of suggestiveness. (The opposite may also happen when the director or the performer betrays the dramatist by overplaying a scene.) In *The Rose Tattoo* there is about slovenly Serafina a curious dignity which tones down some of the suggestive nature of a number of her scenes with Alvaro. Rosa, on the other hand, lacks any such overriding quality. Her extreme youth and unhappiness win sympathy, but she is a wild child, to be restrained on a stage. As other examples, I would rule against Scene X of *A Streetcar Named Desire*, the Esmeralda-Kilroy scene in Block Twelve of *Camino Real* and a number of incidents in *Baby Doll*.

To write a play is difficult. It is harder to write a good play. The dramatist who chooses, as he may legitimately do, to treat of sexual matters shoulders a still heavier burden. His subject requires him to tread warily if he is to preserve the delicate balance between free artistic expression and his moral responsibility as a man. However sincere his intention, he may fail at times to do so. Whatever the cause—lack of ability, unsure artistic touch, cloudy judgment or momentary impatience at restraint—he fails. We should not pass too hard a sentence on him. It is an honest failure. **[444/445]**

Can this be said of Tennessee Williams? I do not think so. Repeatedly his work has met with wide disapproval. It may be conceded that many of those who criticize him are swayed by mere hearsay and have little first-hand knowledge of his plays. But most of them are well-informed. They are not cranks; they are men and women of sense and maturity and balance; they judge reasonably, with adult knowledge of human nature and of human responsibility. Their verdict does not impress Tennessee Williams. He writes what he wants to write—not what they want him to write. He goes his own way. Those who like may follow him. Those who do not care for his plays may seek their entertainment elsewhere, at the musicals or the comedies. To suspect his sincerity may be to do him an injustice. Because he believes in his own approach and his own methods, he too may be said to have failed honestly. But, objectively, it is his critics who are right and he who has often been wrong.

*   *   *

Here is a last quotation. It introduces a further impression, personal perhaps, left by the plays of Tennessee Williams.

ALMA: . . . Have you ever seen, or looked at a picture of, a Gothic Cathedral?

JOHN: Gothic Cathedrals? What about them?

ALMA: How everything reaches up, how everything seems to be straining for something out of the reach of stone—or human—fingers? . . . The immense stained
windows, the great arched doors that
are five or six times the height of the
tallest man—the vaulted ceiling and all
the delicate spires—all reaching up to
something beyond attainment! To me—
well, that is the secret, the principle back
of existence—the everlasting struggle
and aspiration for more than our human
limits have placed in our reach. . . . Who
was it that said—oh, so beautiful thing!
—'All of us are in the gutter, but some
of us are looking at the stars!'

JOHN: Mr. Oscar Wilde.

ALMA: (*somewhat taken aback*) Well, regardless
of who said it, it's still true. Some of us
are looking at the stars!¹

On looking back over the plays, back
over the sadness and sorrow that engulf
Tennessee Williams's characters I see
them as men and women without God.
Most of them allow Him little or no place
in their lives. They do not recognize that
their desperate grasping at fleeting human happiness reflects the hunger in every human heart for something above
[445/446] and beyond and infinitely greater than themselves. It is the desire for
ultimate happiness which is to be ours
after death with Almighty God. Like Alma's cathedrals, we are straining and
reaching up, but not to something beyond
attainment.

I wonder if this is more than a personal
impression, if it is a somewhat unexpect-
ed by-product of Tennessee Williams's
work. I wonder, too, if he is at all conscious of conveying that impression. He
is too informed a man to be unaware of
that human desire for God. And he is, I
judge, too sincere to ignore it should he
recognize the place it occupies in men's
lives. If or when that recognition comes,
he may well write one of the great plays of
the twentieth century.

[445] ¹*Summer and Smoke.* Part I, Scene VI.

Tennessee Williams' Early Heroines*

ROBERT EMMET JONES, Assistant Professor of French at the University of Georgia, is the author of critical articles on the French dramatists Lenormand and Camus and of a book, *The Alienated Hero in Modern French Drama* (1960).

Critics have generally agreed that the heroines of Tennessee Williams are his finest creations. They dominate the plays in which they are found, and to them, as representatives of certain Southern types, Williams has brought much insight. This insight, which is at once poetic and sociological, has, since 1945, provided the American theater with several characters who may well rank in future histories of American dramatic literature with Eugene O'Neill's Anna Christie and Nina Leeds as the most successful creations of dramatic heroines in the first half of the twentieth century.

There are basically two types of women in the plays of Williams: the women who are the relics of the moribund tradition of gentility in which Williams himself was reared, women who are unable to accept the twentieth century and who prefer living in the illusive and legendary world of something that never really was—the mythically cavalier Old South;[1] and the healthy, uncultured, basically sensual women, usually of Latin origin, by whom Williams has been attracted in his more recent plays, and who seem to have been conceived by their creator, if not as representatives of a sort of salvation, then at least as attractive earth goddesses whose salvation is their own sexuality. I propose in this paper to study the first type of heroine, for by studying her, I believe, some important facets of the dramatic art of Tennessee Williams may be revealed.

The Civil War was as destructive to the Southern landlords as the French Revolution had been to the French nobility. Where once had been a rigid social system based on slavery and ruled by many cultured, wealthy aristocrats, there was, after the Civil War complete anarchy and loss of values. When the economic system on which this society had been based was destroyed, the society itself fell with it.

When his plantation was broken up, the Southern aristocrat was faced with three alternatives. He could accept the changes the war had made and conform to the new society. He could migrate west and start again, or he could retire from active life in the new South, live in a world of false values, and become increasingly alienated from the society which he had sired unknowingly and which had rejected him. The proudest (and the weakest, perhaps) chose the last way. It was certainly the easiest. But, as the years rolled by, this group, still **[211/212]** retaining its pre-war viewpoint and ignoring all who were not acceptable by the old standards, steadily degenerated.

Tennessee Williams is the poet of this decline. His world is the world of the New South with, in his early plays, especial

[1]For a complete discussion of the myth of the cavalier Old South see W. J. Cash, *The Mind of the South*, Doubleday Anchor Books (Garden City, N. Y., 1954).

*Robert Emmet Jones, "Tennessee Williams' Early Heroines," *Modern Drama*, II (December, 1959), 211-219.

emphasis on the place of the aristocrat in it. This world is one of fragile beauty and unnatural horror, of lost dreams and poetic visions, of animal sex and refined deviations, of first-generation Americans and their blue-blooded wives, of failure and unhappiness, seldom of success. It is a world of yesterday and today, practically never of tomorrow. The characters of Williams always look to the past for their salvation. They cannot understand the present or, if they do, they are powerless to act within it because they will seldom compromise with it. They are damned the moment they come on stage.

It was during the years between 1944 and 1948, between the writing of *Battle of Angels* and *A Streetcar Named Desire*,[2] that Williams created the character for which he is most renowned—the neurotic Southern white woman of aristocratic origin. Be she Cassandra Whiteside of *Battle of Angels* living among the poor white trash of a town in the deep South, or Amanda Wingfield of *The Glass Menagerie* in the slums of Saint Louis, or Blanche DuBois in a near-slum section of New Orleans, or Alma Winemiller of *Summer and Smoke* in Glorious Hill, Mississippi, a sleepy town invaded by the crass commercialism of the twentieth century, the Williams heroine exists mainly in illusion, denying today and living an imaginary yesterday. These women, of whom Blanche and Amanda are the best realized, are haunted by the past and cannot or will not cast off its fetters. They live in a world of paper lanterns and moonlit lakes, a world of gentility where courtly men crown them the eternal belle of the ball, where everyone desires them and they save their favors for a phantom. They are pathetic because they are incapable of meeting and triumphing over the demands of their times, and the society in which they live will not and cannot accept them on their own terms.

These four women—Alma, Cassandra, Blanche, and Amanda—have much in common and, in fact, are really the same person at different stages of life. Alma Winemiller is in the process of revolting

against the limitations of her secluded life as a minister's daughter in Glorious Hill. Through an obvious metamorphosis, from a creature of repression to one of sexual license, she becomes a willing magnet to travelling salesmen. Cassandra Whiteside is the same character who has been having nocturnal "gentlemen" callers for many years. She is a decided nymphomaniac whose main interests are men, liquor, and "jooking." She is perverse and, unfortunately for her town and the few decent [212/213] people with whom she comes into contact, a law unto herself. Blanche DuBois has gone through the stages at which we have seen Alma and Cassandra; through her sexual and concomitant mental idiosyncracies, she has lost all contact with reality and is ripe for a mental institution. Amanda had married a telephone man who deserted her after siring their two children. Only because she was domesticated at an early age, Amanda does not become a nymphomaniac, but her origins and her reactions to life indicate her absolute kinship with Alma, Cassandra, and Blanche.

These aristocratic heroines of Tennessee Williams are, unfortunately, and this is their tragedy, the victims of a double standard observed in the society in which they were reared. To the Victorians—and the Old South in its later days was predominantly Victorian—woman was the pure pedestaled goddess worshipped from afar by the impure and animalistic man whose saviour she was supposed to be. W. J. Cash says:

. . . the Yankee must be answered by proclaiming from the housetops that Southern Virtue, so far from being inferior, was superior, not alone to the North's but to any on earth, and adducing Southern Womanhood in proof.

The upshot, in this land of spreading notions of chivalry, was downright gyneolatry.[3]

Good women were supposedly sexless; they were not supposed to think about,

---

[2] Although produced later, *Summer and Smoke* was written before *A Streetcar Named Desire*.

[3] W. J. Cash, *op. cit.*, p. 97. See also John Dollard, *Caste and Class in a Southern Town*, Doubleday Anchor Books (Garden City, N. Y., 1957), pp. 137-138, for further comment on this subject.

much less enjoy the act of procreation. Those who did were suspect, and female society, thus, consisted of good women (sexless) and fallen women.

The men, as the society degenerated, sold their plantations piece by piece to finance their epic fornications,[4] but the ideal of the virginal woman remained the same, if it did not actually become intensified.

Lastly, the increased centrality of woman, added up with the fact that miscegenation, though more terrifying than it had been even in the Old South, showed little tendency to fall off despite efforts to build up standards against it, served to intensify the old interest in gyneolatry, and to produce yet more florid notions about Southern Womanhood and Southern Virtue, and so to foster yet more precious notions of modesty and decorous behaviour for the Southern female to live up to.[5]

To the young ladies reared in the shadow of this antebellum standard, the twentieth century, whose modernizing influence was in many pernicious ways being felt in the South, was anathema. And yet it was impossible to live according to the old code. Formerly these girls would have been married by their families to wealthy planters and thus [213/214] would have been assured of respectability within the social structure if they lived up to the standards set for them. However, the young planters and other eligible men had changed, too, as their society had evolved. No longer fettered by their own conventions, they married, usually for money, more full-blooded girls of the lower classes, the daughters of wealthy men who formerly had been socially unacceptable, and often for sexual reasons women their grandmothers would have ignored. Many of the planters were effete and impotent, often they were homosexual—like Blanche's husband, Allan.[6] And, reared to be a lady, the girl who had no money and was terrified of becoming a spinster (the most pathetic and ill-treated being in the South) was faced with an impossible choice. Her pride forbade her marrying beneath her (although Blanche's sister, Stella, did just that) and demanded that she marry a gentleman even if he was

sexually deficient. She would not and could not remain single. In *Battle of Angels* there are two women, Cassandra and Myra, who have already faced this choice, as had Amanda in *The Glass Menagerie*, and both *Summer and Smoke* and *A Streetcar Named Desire* are concerned with women who face the same problem.

Now since this choice is an impossible one, certain aspects of the characters of these various heroines influence their final actions and decisions. Due, no doubt, to the double standard mentioned before, each of these women is emotionally immature. Yet each, with the exception of the older Amanda, has strong sexual desires, usually tending towards nymphomania. Each began life in an atmosphere of refinement in a closed society where she tantalized, and rather sadistically so, the many gentlemen callers she received. Unconsciously she desired to belong to these men physically, but, because of the code under which she lived, she turned her desires into coquettishness, affectation, and evasion. She refused to admit the existence of sex as such; the thought of it was degrading. And the men who could find more profitable and less mentally exhausting sexual outlets elsewhere turned from her. With the realization that her youth was passing, this typical Williams heroine, giving way to her own desires, became desperate and eventually began to do whatever men wanted. Through giving her body she could at least belong, if she could not belong in any other way.

Sex obsesses her as it obsesses all Puritans. She is ever conscious of it. Notice, for example, the constant reactions of Alma, Blanche, and Cassandra to the male body. The physical side of life, which socially and verbally these heroines find so repulsive, exerts a mysterious and [214/215] all-powerful fascination over them, and they finally submit to it and

[4]Cf. Tennessee Williams, *A Streetcar Named Desire*, New Directions (New York, 1947), p. 45.
[5]W. J. Cash, *op. cit.*, p. 137.
[6] The theme of the impotent, effete, or homosexual male in the New South has been portrayed by many Southern writers of our century, among them Faulkner, Capote, Lampkin, Williams, In fact, they tend to indicate that he is a major social type.

rationalize their reasons for doing so. Yet they are not wholly aware of what they are doing. Thus there is always something curiously virginal about them even though, technically, they are whores. Through sex, the great leveller of all society, however, they are degraded rather than exalted because they cannot give themselves over to it wholeheartedly. This is excellently indicated in *A Streetcar Named Desire* in a scene between Blanche and her sister, Stella. Stella has escaped the neuroticism to which her sister has fallen prey by completely accepting physical love with her husband, an animal-like Pole, Stanley Kowalski. Through her marriage she has become a Woman, much as Serafina of the later *The Rose Tattoo*. No matter how sordid her existence, no matter how degrading her compromise with life, Stella has security and a sense of fulfillment in her love for her husband. Blanche, who herself uses sex to cling to when all else is gone, cannot understand her sister's submission to what she believes is an animal-like existence.

BLANCHE: Yes, you are, your fix is worse than mine is! Only you are not being sensible about it. I'm going to do something. Get hold of myself and make myself a new life!
STELLA: Yes?
BLANCHE: But you've given in. And that isn't right, you're not old! You can get out.
STELLA: I'm not in anything I want to get out of.[7]

The importance of the sexual function is extremely pervasive in the plays of Tennessee Williams, and it becomes a liberating force in his later plays. In the earlier plays, however, it is a binding force because his heroines are ladies. The heroines are always conscious of the fact that they are ladies. They never forget it, nor will they allow others to do so. Their heritage is something no one can ever take from them, for they are all well-born; Blanche and Cassandra come from the oldest families in their section of the country. The early Williams heroine is, in her own mind, never anything but a lady, and a consciousness of the niceties of existence excuses her in her own eyes

for her transgressions. Blanche, amidst the squalor of her sister's home, still acts the lady, and she really believes she is one, even though Stanley attempts to break through her pride and convince her she is just a common whore. Amanda, Blanche, and Cassandra all remember the plantations on which they were born, or where it must be assumed that they were born. Like Alma in the rectory of her father, they were protected at home by the social code. That this code has long since disappeared is obvious from the name of Blanche's family estate—Belle Reve. The very name, with its grammatical inconsistency, is a symbol of the degeneracy of the family and of its flight from reality. [215/216]

The fact that the changing social conditions of the world have made it impossible for these heroines still to be protected by their past means that when these women are thrown into the world they must accept it and adjust to it or become outcasts from it. Cassandra will not adjust. She prefers finding solace in liquor and men. Amanda lives completely in the past, as if the present did not exist, and her family consequently goes to pieces. Alma cannot reconcile her nascent sexuality with her puritanical rearing and becomes a neurasthenic and later a whore. Blanche is forced to become a school teacher in order to preserve a shabby gentility. Her search for something to which she may belong finds roots only in casual affairs with men and boys. Eventually, because of her license, she is relieved of her teaching duties and has to go to her sister for protection.

But these heroines never find anything in the contemporary world to replace their former security. Their past, or rather their idealized past, cannot be recaptured. And yet they seek to recapture it by various means. Blanche tries to revive it through memory. She will not accept the fact that she must come to grips with reality and live according to its exigencies in order to retain some amount of sanity. She refuses reality.

[7]Williams, *A Streetcar Named Desire*, p. 74.

BLANCHE: I don't want realism.
MITCH: Naw, I guess not.
BLANCHE: I'll tell you what I want. Magic! (*Mitch laughs*) Yes, yes, magic! I try to give that to people. I misrepresent things to them. I don't tell the truth. I tell what ought to be the truth. And if that is sinful, then let me be damned for it!⁸

To Blanche reality is an electric light bulb which is too blinding to be endured; everything must be seen by candlelight which never shows the shabbiness and horrors of the present. She says, "I can't stand a naked light bulb any more than I can a rude remark or vulgar action."⁹ If a light bulb is a symbol of reality in the plays of Tennessee Williams, there are many symbols of escape from reality, the most obvious among them being the candle. The doppelgänger of Alma, the glass menagerie of Laura, and the automobiles of Cassandra are other symbols of that escape.

Death, desertion, and decline surround these women, and they have been ever present in the lives of Williams' heroines. The age of chivalry, which has been romanticized to them in their youth, has disappeared. Their homes have been sold, their families have died, sickness and mental breakdown have been everywhere. Blanche says:

. . . All of those deaths! The long parade to the graveyard! Father, mother! Margaret, that dreadful way! So big with it, it couldn't be put in a coffin! But had to be burned like rubbish! You just came [216/217] home in time for funerals, Stella. And funerals are pretty compared to deaths. Funerals are quiet, but deaths—not always.¹⁰

Along with a consciousness of general decay in her society, the early Williams heroine has undergone a far more violent experience, has known one particularly crucial bout with reality which has so terrified her that she refuses to see reality again. Blanche's husband committed suicide, a tragedy she had caused through a careless remark. Amanda's husband deserted her. Alma is jilted by young Doctor John. Cassandra watched her great-aunt die. And yet, paradoxically, these

heroines try to recapture the past which has been one of death. In the past they were comparatively secure; they had their families for support, even though the various members of these families were slowly dying.

Seeing the romanticized past die before their very eyes, these heroines cling all the more firmly to the romantic aspect of it. The past thus represents at the same time a way of life which has been idealized to them in their childhood and death which has destroyed this way of life. Therefore, incapable of meeting the responsibilities that death has put before them in their later formative years, they consciously ignore the horrible aspects of the past and seek to embrace its careless, pleasant aspects in order to retain "the glory and the dream," that world of imagination which is peculiar to childhood; this accounts for the aura of all-pervasive immaturity which tends to make them seem less responsible for their acts than they really are. Blanche says:

His Auntie knows that candles aren't safe, that candles burn out in little boys' and girls' eyes, or wind blows them out and after that happens, electric light bulbs go on and you see too plainly. . . .¹¹

In the few moments when these heroines are not self-deluded they recognize the past as representing death. But while the past symbolizes death to these women the present does not symbolize life, but rather desire. That death and desire are opposites in the vocabulary of Tennessee Williams may be seen in all his early plays. Desire is an escape from death, a means of forgetting it, and this seems to be a fixed idea in the author's mind.

We're all of us locked up tight inside our own bodies. Sentenced—you might say—to solitary confinement inside our own skins.¹²

Cassandra Whiteside says, and she might

⁸*Ibid.*, p. 139.
⁹*Ibid.*, p. 62.
¹⁰*Ibid.*, p. 25.
¹¹*Ibid.*, p. 129.
¹²Tennessee Williams, *Battle of Angels*, Pharos, nos. 1-2, Murray (Utah, Spring, 1945), p. 47.

be talking for all the heroines of the early plays of Williams:

I'm rotten. Neurotic. Our blood's gone bad from too much interbreeding. They've set up the guillotine, not in the Place de Concorde, but here, inside our bodies![13]

Desire and death, like love and hate and other opposites, are often [217/218] indistinguishable, because the boundaries which separate them are so vague; and while these heroines are trying to escape death, or their conception of death, they are unconsciously embracing it in the form of desire, for desire is the guillotine set up in their hearts.

These heroines believe that through physical desire and its consumation they will belong, that they will achieve Life and escape Death. They do not realize that desire fails unless it is accepted wholeheartedly, as by Stella Kowalski. Their responsiveness to and pleasure in the sexual function is merely the result of a desperation into which their anomalous social position has forced them. At times they realize this. Blanche says:

I was never hard or self-sufficient enough. When people are soft—soft people have got to court the favor of the hard ones, Stella. Have got to be seductive—put on soft colors, the colors of butterfly wings, and glow—make a little—temporary magic just in order to pay for one night's shelter! That's why I've been—not so awf'ly good lately. I've run for protection, Stella, from under one leaky roof to another leaky roof—because it was storm—all storm, and I was—caught in the centre . . . People don't see you—MEN don't—don't even admit your existence unless they are making love to you. And you've got to have your existence admitted by someone, if you're going to have someone's protection. And so the soft people have got to—shimmer and glow—put a—paper lantern over the light . . . .[14]

But moments of introspection like this are comparatively rare in Williams' plays. His women are more the passive pawns of social forces and their own emotions than active participants in what Williams seems to consider life's tragedy. No one of them battles her destiny, because no one of them seems to realize what it is. Blanche, representing a cultured yet corrupted tradition, has not the strength

of character even to triumph over the brutal Stanley Kowalski, for whom culture is just a dirty word. Cassandra and Alma have no sense of real dignity. Believing their birth and breeding to have given them innate dignity, they are still weak, neurotic, and ineffectual beings for whom self-indulgence is the line of least resistance. There is little that is healthy about them. They, more so than Blanche and Amanda, are case histories which might have been culled from a psychiatric textbook.

There is little that is tragic about the early Williams heroines. They are sometimes intentionally comic, and often pathetic and melodramatic, but they never are tragic. Blanche and Amanda cannot be tragic figures because they have been defeated before their appearance on stage. We watch them grovelling before their fate, their machinations with destiny, their defeated pride, their illusions about themselves [218/219] and their fellow man.

We watch their attempts at compromise: Amanda, in choosing a husband for her daughter; Blanche in coming to stay with Stella. Amanda and Blanche, like Cassandra and Alma, become of interest mainly from a sociological standpoint. The tragedy of these women is the tragedy of the civilization which bore them, nourished them, and then cast them out. They are social fossils in an age of commercialism and tawdriness. Their defeat is the defeat of a culture which is, as Williams demonstrates, destroying itself, and which cannot brook the encroachments upon it. If we pity Blanche and Amanda, it is because they are beautifully portrayed examples of defeated human beings. They are living characters whose reactions to life and actions in life are familiar in one way or another to all of us. We may understand and pity them, but it is difficult for us to admire them as noble in any sense of the word. They are too weak, passive, and neurotic to be tragic.

[13]Ibid., p. 42.
[14]Williams, A Streetcar Named Desire, p. 91.

The Profitable World of Tennessee Williams*

SIGNI FALK, Associate Professor of English at Coe College, has published several poems and critical articles.

Tennessee Williams has been called "an artist to the fingertips," "a master of sensitive characterization," a writer with "hypnotic qualities," of "exquisite tastes," and "the foremost new playwright to have appeared on the American scene in a decade." And yet, the fact that many critics, after having ridiculed a particular play unmercifully, have given the highest praise to the acting and the production, raises the question whether the quality of the playwright's work has not been obscured by brilliant productions. A partial list of performers is impressive: the late Laurette Taylor as Amanda in *The Glass Menagerie* and in the film version, the late Gertrude Lawrence; Kim Hunter, Marlon Brando, and Jessica Tandy in *A Streetcar Named Desire*; Margaret Phillips and Tod Andrews in *Summer and Smoke*; Maurine Stapleton in *The Rose Tattoo*; Barbara Bel Geddes and Burl Ives in *Cat on a Hot Tin Roof*. And above all, a dramatist, most of whose work has been interpreted by so distinguished a director as Elia Kazan, must indeed call himself fortunate.

Tennessee Williams is frequently credited with returning poetry to the theater. He has been compared with Eugene O'Neill whose work is significant for poetic overtones. Both dramatists are concerned with sensitive spirits trying to find their niche in a mammon-worshipping society. Both are interested in describing decadent aristocratic families as well as tramps from the fringe areas; in portray-

ing the corroding effect of empire-building; in deploring the homelessness in America of sensitive, creative souls; and in praising uninhibited expressions of physical love as superior to a socially imposed restraint upon passions. But the differences outnumber the similarities. O'Neill leaves the impression of a writer who has hacked away at the pseudo-religious crustations that dwarf men's lives and has attempted to find a more honest relationship between man and his God. O'Neill described the soul-destroying quality of New England puritanism, which does not make people happy though it makes them successful business men and pillars of society. It is the hypocritical pretense to goodness that O'Neill hates and against which his poet-heroes struggle. In so doing he may have resorted to all the stage tricks, played every chord for emotional effect, exaggerated his symbols to the point of the grotesque to make his point, but he was always a man of ideas. He was, in the parlance of recent criticism, a dramatist as thinker.

One of the most frequently repeated jibes thrust at Williams is that he feels but does not think, or "only thinks that he feels." He has [172/173] uttered a number of elaborate pronouncements about the significance of his own plays which have little to do with the plays themselves. In the preface to *The Rose Tattoo*, a lusty "comedy" about two sex-starved females portrayed against a chorus of "man-crazy women" keeping up a cacoph-

*Signi Falk, "The Profitable World of Tennessee Williams," *Modern Drama*, I (December, 1958), 172-180.

ony of urgency throughout the play, he says that he is interested in ideas about the "arrest of time," and "that special condition of a *world without time*," and the nobility of Greek tragedies. Since *The Rose Tattoo* is an amusing paean to sexual indulgence, his sententiousness makes him sound like a high school orator on a binge: "The great and only possible dignity of man lies in his power deliberately to choose certain moral values by which to live as steadfastly as if he, too, like a character in a play, were immured against the corrupting rush of time." He prefaces another play, *Camino Real*, with the lines from a Shaw character: "I believe in Michelangelo, Velasquez, and Rembrandt; in the might of design, the mystery of color," a rather conceited statement from the author of that confused "phantasmagoria of decadence." In the preface to *Cat on a Hot Tin Roof*, he says, "I thought of myself as having a highly personal, even intimate relationship with people who go to see plays. . . . I still don't want to talk only about the surface aspect of their lives, the sort of things that acquaintances laugh and chatter about on ordinary social occasions." The correlation between this noble statement and the conversation in the play is remote, to say the least. One dramatic critic wonders if even in the world of Tennessee Williams people really *do* ask one another, as they do in this play, "How good is he in bed?"

In actual playwriting Williams tends to give to a character a kind of punch line of philosophical comment which might, perhaps, be considered a thesis statment of the play. It usually sounds, however, like the concluding argument to a very different subject. Its relationship to the characters and the action is usually peripheral. For instance, the bedroom farce of Serafina and Alfaro of *The Rose Tattoo* is to be dignified, it seems, by the line, "Love and affection! in a world that is lonely and cold." And again, after more noisy pursuits than a class-B movie would allow, *Camino Real* closes with the line, "The violets in the mountains have broken the rocks." And still again, to the cynical and alcoholic Brick, who drinks his way through *Cat on a Hot Tin Roof*, his frustrated wife, Margaret, speaks the final lines: "Oh, you weak, beautiful people who give up with such grace. What you need is someone to take hold of you—gently, with love and hand back your life to you, like something gold you let go of."

After seeing the plays, one is left with the feeling that Williams is basically a sentimentalist who fluctuates like a thermometer in uncertain weather between bathos and poetic rhetoric, between the precious and the bawdy, and between adolescent admirations and histrionic [173/174] displays of violence. He sobs over failures, the aimless, weak, frustrated seekers; envies vicariously his own characters, male and female, radiantly happy in their physical love; idolizes those men who inherited the virility of a prize bull; and lacerates those human beings, mostly women, driven by an unsatisfied sexual hunger. Perhaps he *is* a dramatist who feels rather than thinks, because he seems to be more interested in emotional crises involving a few character types than in developing an idea, or character, or action, as is habitual with the Greeks he professes to admire. Like so many modern writers who are afraid that they will be uttering the obvious, he indulges in the kind of obvious symbolism that has been called "ladies' club mystifications," in fancy names and fancy settings, in mood music, in tableaus—affected Madonna poses and settings in della Robbia blues. There is so much posturing in the plays, so much of the same thing over and over again, one has the feeling that Williams writes like a man who has spent hours before the mirror, playing a limited number of roles in a variety of exotic costumes.

This Pulitzer prize-winning dramatist has confessed, "The more I go on, the more difficult it becomes not to repeat myself," perhaps one of the truest statements he has made to date about his work. If one considers the types that keep reappearing in his plays, and what they represent, he will find that the world of Tennessee Williams is a very limited one, where people are characters created by a writer who is sometimes perceptive and honest, sometimes sentimental and cruel, and sometimes merely vulgar. The fact that this dramatist has been able to provide for gifted actors and actresses a kind of shorthand script for characterization that has enabled them to add to their own prestige suggests that the *commedia dell' arte* technique has not been relegated to the history books. It is also obvious that Williams has been able to endow his few stock types with such an effective emotional coloring that he not only obscures their basic similarities but also what they really have to say for themselves.

The rebel-dreamer-failure type is a favorite with the dramatist. The Tom Wingfields almost seem like autobiographical figures who might have existed before their creator found the golden key to the box office. Tom, the unwilling breadwinner in *The Glass Menagerie,* trapped by his mediocre warehouse job and the "hawklike attentions" of his mother, writes poetry on the boss's time and escapes to the movies at night where he dreams of far-away places like his father, "a telephone man who fell in love with long distance" and left for good. Tom's situation is pitiable but his vague longings, his inarticulate hopes, and his shiftlessness are so much romanticized that it seems as if the writer were making virtues out of weaknesses.

A variation more sentimental than Tom is Kilroy of *Camino Real,* a [174/175] twenty-seven-year-old American boy with a heart in his body "as big as the head of a baby," one-time boxing champ now looking for a woman not "afraid of a big hard kiss." Like Tom he is vaguely rebelling against something in America that might be identified as the crass American dollar; since there is no escape from this grim valley of greenbacks, the unlucky boy can only indulge himself in self-pity and lovemaking. A third example, Brick in *Cat on a Hot Tin Roof,* an ex-football player with a sick conscience over his

friend's death—the relationship between these two men is left in murky doubt—holds the stage record for self-pitying drinkers. His big howl against American life is "mendacity" which includes his greedy brother, the church, the luncheon clubs, and his wife's craving to have a baby. A typical Williams blubberer, the inheritance he faces is a dreary prospect: "twenty-eight thousand acres of the richest land this side of the Valley Nile." It is just the kind of thing to drive a young American to drink.

Williams' most passionately lyrical tribute is bestowed on a type of male animal, a figure worthy of citation at an international stock show. Stan Kowalsky of *A Streetcar Named Desire* has not been spoiled by the American Way of Life: "Animal joy in his being is implicit in all his movements and attitudes. Since early childhood the center of his life has been pleasure with women, the giving and taking of it, not with weak indulgence, dependently, but with power and pride of a richly feathered male bird among hens. . . . He sizes up women with a glance, with sexual satisfactions, crude images flashing into his mind and determining the way he smiles at them." He belongs to Williams' concept of the Elysian Fields, the heaven of poker players, "men at the peak of their physical manhood, as coarse and direct and powerful as primary colors." When Stan, a drunken primitive with a single idea about women, takes the deranged Blanche DuBois, a sentimental prostitute, off to the bedroom and speaks the line, "We've had this date from the beginning!" Williams has arrived theatrically. It is reported that waves of titillated laughter swept over the audience. It was the effect, no doubt, that Williams sought. But it bears no resemblance to the Greek tragedy with which he identifies himself.

Williams' amusing eulogy of Stan is repeated in *The Rose Tattoo* about Serafina's second mate, the Italian truckdriver, Alvaro, Eat-a-Horse. Radiantly virile with "massively sculptured torso and bluish-black curls," but so inarticulate that "he frequently seems surprised at his own speeches and actions," he never leaves any doubt about his sexual prowess. A third representative appears as a young doctor in *Summer and Smoke*. John Buchanan, a clumsy dramatic symbol not only of the Body but also of the Soul, is supposed to retain his nobility in spite of dissipating his Promethean energy in liquor and sex. With considerable posturing and self-pity this virile American escapes a [175/176] stagnant society and "a doctor's life [that] is walled in by sickness and misery and death."

Williams' best virile male character to date is Big Daddy in *Cat on a Hot Tin Roof*, sixty-five and woman-hungry, a cancer-ridden plantation owner who built up an estate which he inherited from two homosexual bachelors. He is a contradiction to the Williams tradition because, although he seems to have made a lot of money, prosperity has not spoiled his character. Virile, lusty in speech, disappointed in, but still loving his alcoholic son, Brick, with whom he seeks a kind of communication and understanding, he is a considerable character when he is free to talk. But Williams was obviously stymied. It is a curious deviation from dramatic laws that the playwright would drop Big Daddy from the last act of the play only to bring him back at the request of his director, Elia Kazan, very briefly, and for an antiquated and a vulgar story that had to be deleted for the sake of public taste. If there ever was a truism made in the theater, it can be said of Big Daddy: he is a character in search of an author.

A third type of male character, the gentleman caller, seems to represent the average American who more or less conforms to the mores of contemporary society. Jim O'Connor of *The Glass Menagerie* is unimaginative and ambitious, but not slated for distinction. He is not a radiant male, only an ex-football player. His self-esteem is momentarily restored by the crippled Laura who has been secretly infatuated with him since high school days. Complacent in his renewed euphoria, unaware of the depth of her

love, this blunderbuss dances with her—the music "The Golondrina," one of Williams' favorite records—and clumsily breaks the unicorn as he breaks her heart. About to leave for his date, he moralizes: "The power of love is pretty tremendous! Love is something that—changes the world—Laura!" The author has assigned to this young extrovert some of his favorite philosophy but it sounds like words of lip service from a man studying how to get on in the world.

Another gentleman caller is Mitch, Blanche DuBois' last hope in *A Streetcar Named Desire*, a blundering, aging mama's boy. Shocked by his fiancée's past, he throws apron-string ideals out the window and makes a comically ineffective pass at his streetwalker sweetheart. A third example, Rosa's sailor in *The Rose Tattoo*, is another good boy, a shellback with three equator crossings to his credit but his mother's teachings still in his heart. He is one of Williams' more slightly developed characters, but one of his best, and proof that when he is willing to deliver straightforward, honest writing, rather than indulge in phony symbolism and posturing, he can write with power. A fourth example of the gentleman caller is Roger Doremus in *Summer and Smoke*, more securely mother-attached than either Tom Wingfield or Mitch, a [176/177] dull young man who drinks lemonade with Alma and waxes enthusiastic about the meeting of his mother and father: "returning from India with dysentery they met on the boat."

Among the women characters Laura of *The Glass Menagerie* epitomizes Williams' fragile, pathetic Southern women. "Like a piece of her own glass collection, too exquisitely fragile to move from the shelf," she has retreated into her world of "little glass ornaments and phonograph records." In the characterization there are almost too many tears. Not only shy but neurotic, and saddled with a clanking brace, she is also harrassed by a determined and unimaginative mother. She meets her dream lover under the most trying circumstances, lives a whole lifetime of romance in a few minutes, only to be sickened by his pity. He breaks her unicorn as he breaks her heart, but she forgives. So many cards are stacked against the girl that the writer seems to have grown maudlin over his portrait of failure and pathos.

An escapist like her daughter, Amanda also lives unhappily in her cocoon of dreams. A Southern belle grown middle-aged and garrulous, she "flounces girlishly" whenever there is a man around. In her pathetic refusal to be realistic, she clings to such delusions as a certainty that she could have married any of her now wealthy gentlemen callers if she had not fallen in love with the man in the soldier suit, or her conviction that her children are exceptional. Distressingly prim, she grows furious over her son's declaration that "Man is by instinct a lover, a hunter, a fighter," forbidding him to use the word, instinct, when speaking of "Christian adults." It is a caustic picture that Williams paints of an over-refined, silly, oldish belle, who gains "dignity and tragic beauty" only when her chatter cannot be heard. In spite of the playwright's insistence that his play is not realistic, the better scenes in *The Glass Menagerie* involve this shrill hysterical woman trying to keep her daughter from being one of those ["] barely tolerated spinsters . . . stuck away in some little mouse-trap of a room . . . little bird-like women without any nest."

Another escapist, Blanche DuBois, unable to face family deaths and the decay of the estate to a "mere twenty acres and a graveyard," turns prostitute in her efforts to find kindness. She is married at sixteen to a young poet, sentimentally described: "Something different about the boy, a nervousness, a softness and a tenderness which wasn't like a man's, although he wasn't effeminate looking." She is widowed shortly afterwards because she discovers this shy boy's relations with an older man. She later becomes an English teacher with rather unusual extracurricular activities: "After the death of Allan—intimacies with strangers was all I seemed able to fill my empty heart with. . . . I think it was panic, just panic that drove me from one to another, hunting for some protection—here and there, in the most unlikely places— even, at [177/178] last, in a seventeen-year-old boy." Strangely enough, she seems surprised that her superintendent should find her "morally unfit for her position." But this may be only Williams' idea of callow American society, too insensitive to understand the exotic and the delicate.

This glamorized neurotic is another of Williams' tragic heroines of the South. Homeless, she descends upon her sister and behaves like an injured grand duchess. She lies about her age, lies about taking liquor, although she has emptied Stan's bottle, lies about her strict ideas of purity though she has been run out of town, turns sexy and exhibitionist before Stan's poker-playing friends, and goes on an emotional drunk with saccharine love songs. She, like her author, insists that she doesn't want realism, but magic. Her condition is deplorable. But the question arises whether she isn't basically another self-centered, dishonest woman, perhaps a nymphomaniac, and whether the writer is not guilty of trying to bewitch his audience with a sentimental portrait of a fraud.

Another pathetic misfit, Alma in *Summer and Smoke,* is an intellectual and spinsterish snob who gilds the lily in her Southern parish. For this bluestocking the Gothic cathedral symbolizes "the secret, the principle back of existence—the everlasting struggle and aspiration for more than our human limits have placed within our reach." But, according to Williams, this sensitive girl, rejected by her man who finds her incapable of "intimate relations," takes up with a traveling salesman, the first, presumably, of a series of bedroom adventures. The plight of the single woman, hag-ridden by family or other responsibilities, is a common story, and a rich subject for the theater, but obviously stage prostitutes are more easily described, and much more attractive at the box office.

If one of Williams' theories is that a better than average IQ makes a woman prissy and either sexually incompetent or sexually insatiable, then the opposite theory naturally obtains: woman is a mating animal who can find happiness only in sex. Blanche's younger sister, Stella, symbolizes the idea of fulfillment. Not only that, she is a Madonna figure whose "eyes have that almost narcotized tranquility that is on the faces of Eastern idols." It is startling to have the girl, a Madonna symbol, mated with a representative of Capricorn the Goat. Stan Kowalsky's treatment of his pregnant wife ranges violently and rapidly from drunken beating, breaking the furniture, to maudlin crying, "I want my baby," whenever the girl runs for cover. Stella tells her sister that she is so much in love with Stan that their intimacies make up for all the violence of his drunken orgies. It almost seems as if the writer has a theory that American girls are fed up with civilized lovers and would give their all to be beaten black and blue by alcoholically [178/179] odoriferous Neanderthal men.

Williams plays with the great mother symbol in a minor character, Nellie, in *Summer and Smoke;* she is an adolescent with the enthusiasm of a bobby-soxer and the aggressiveness of an aging streetwalker. Another is the voluptuous, uncomfortably corseted, love-lonesome Seraphina who quite candidly asserts that "the big bed was beautiful like a religion," and brags to her less amorous friends that she *"knows* what lovemaking was." Her happiest memory, she says, was knowing that she "conceived on the very night of conception." Her daughter, overendowed with her mother's glandular talents, but a "sweet, refined" girl according to her creator, propositions her sailor boy friend: "You don't need to be very old to understand how it works out. One time, one time, only once, it could be! God! to remember." Helpless before such importunate pleas, the able seaman risks discovery and "a ten-year stretch in the brig." The great mother symbol takes a different slant with Margaret, the cat on the hot tin roof, roused to anger because her husband no longer wants to sleep with her. A mercenary wench, she is also terrified that Big Daddy will cut them out of his will. Like her sisters-in-the-flesh she waxes lyrical about her man's one-time love-making: "with absolute confidence and perfect calm, more like opening a door for a lady, or seating her at a table, than giving expression to any longing for her."

These are the character types which keep reappearing in the world of Tennessee Williams. Most of them, according to discriminating critics, have been more deeply affected by the theater than by life. It is generally recognized that this writer has a talent for penetrating human character, for describing frustrations and various forms of escapism, as well as for catching the spirit of joyous living. However, when he obscures this special insight by indulging in theatrical lies, and creates scenes dripping with sentiment or relying on shock and violence for effect, then he deserves the ridicule he has received.

It is obvious that Mr. Williams takes himself very seriously, but that fact need not be the cue for others. He has not the range nor wisdom of a Gorky, nor the mordant sense of humor of a Chekhov, Russians with whom he has been compared. The Greeks to whom he himself so glibly refers often concerned themselves with passion, incest, and adultery, rather than biology. They described the effect of irrational indulgence, of love and ambition, or anger and revenge, of the illusion of happiness, of man's great possibilities and his follies, factors conducive to a good life or a tragic one. Greek drama was a part of a generally accepted moral order in which man, because he was a rational being, was partly responsible for the pattern of his life.

Mary McCarthy's caustic comment about *Streetcar*, overstating the point that "his talent is rooted in pay dirt," carries an element of truth: "His work

reeks of literary ambition . . . it is impossible to witness one [179/180] of Mr. Williams' plays without being aware of the pervading smell of careerism. . . . Whatever happens to the characters, Mr. Williams will come out rich and famous, and the play merely another episode in Mr. Williams' 'career'."

Even though his plays leave much to be desired, the actors, directors, and the producers have been able to make of his scripts exciting evenings in the theater. It is a curious comment on the mid-twentieth century that the success of Tennessee Williams rests, to a large degree, on his repudiation of values and attitudes which most intelligent and genuinely sensitive Americans care about. It is, indeed, a very curious comment on the times that his tawdry success has been accompanied, in so many quarters, by so much respect.

American Blues . . .*

KENNETH TYNAN (1927-   ) established a brilliant reputation in England as a theatre critic very soon after his graduation from Oxford University, where he had been a prominent member of the Oxford University Dramatic Society. He has published two books on theatrical subjects, *He That Plays the King; a View of the Theatre* (1950), and *Alec Guiness* (1953). With the photographer and designer Cecil Beaton he wrote *Persona Grata* (1953), a volume of brief contemporary biographies. Drama critic for the London *Observer*, Mr. Tynan was guest critic for *The New Yorker* during the 1958-1959 theatre season.

I

"Since 1920," Arthur Miller has said, "American drama has been a steady year-by-year documentation of the frustration of man": and the record supports him. Between the wars most of the serious American playwrights—Odets, for instance, Elmer Rice, Maxwell Anderson, Irwin Shaw, and Lillian Hellman—did their best work in the conviction that modern civilisation was committing repeated acts of criminal injustice against the individual. Their heroes were victims, such as Mio in *Winterset,* and they devoted themselves to dramatising the protests of minorities; it was thus that they ploughed the land cleared for them by O'Neill, the solitary pioneer bulldozer. For his long-sightedness they substituted an absorption in immediate reality; where he was the admonitory lighthouse, they were the prying torches. During the war their batteries ran out: since 1945 none of them has written a first-rate play. The mission of martyrology has been taken up by the younger generation, by Arthur Miller and Tennessee Williams.

Miller and Williams seem, on the face of things, to have even less in common than Ibsen and Bjørnson. Miller, a man of action, belongs to the thirties' tradition of social drama, while Williams, a poet *manqué*, looks ahead to a lyrical, balletic *Gesamtkunstwerk* in which (though I doubt whether he fully recognizes the fact) words as such are likely to have less and less importance. Yet the two men share much. Both echo the boy in *Awake and Sing* who says: "We don't want life printed on dollar bills." Miller is a rebel against, Williams a refugee from the familiar ogre of commercialisation, the killer of values and the leveller of men. "You know, *knowledge—ZZZZ*pp! *Money—zzzz*pp! POWER! Wham! That's the cycle democracy is built on!" exults the Gentleman Caller in *The Glass Menagerie*. But this is not their only joint exploit. Both reserve their most impassioned utterance for one subject, into which they plunge headlong, sometimes floundering in self-pity, sometimes belly-diving into rhetoric, but often knifing straight and deep: the subject of frustration. Lady Mulligan, in Williams' latest play *Camino Real*, complains to Gutman, the proprietor of her hotel, that he has chosen to shelter some highly undesirable guests. Whereupon:

*Kenneth Tynan, "American Blues. The Plays of Arthur Miller and Tennessee Williams," *Encounter* (England), II, (May, 1954), 13-19.

124

GUTMAN: They pay the price of admission the same as you.
LADY M.: What price is that?
GUTMAN: Desperation!

Techniques change, but grand themes do not. Whether in a murder trial, a bull-fight, a farce like *Charley's Aunt* or a tragedy like *Lear,* the behaviour of a human being at the end of his tether is the common denominator of all drama. When a man (or woman) arrives at [13/14] self-knowledge through desperation, he (or she) has become the raw material for a great play. The stature of the work will depend on the dramatist's honesty and skill, but its cornerstone is already laid. Though they take the same theme, Miller and Williams build very differently. In European terms, Miller is the Scandinavian: he has in fact translated Ibsen, whose fierce lucidity, humourlessness, and "odour of spiritual paraffin" he shares. Williams, on the other hand, is the Mediterranean, the lover of Lorca, sensuous, funny, verbally luxuriant, prone to immersion in romantic tragedy. Miller's plays are hard, "patrist," athletic, concerned mostly with men. Williams' are soft, "matrist," sickly, concerned mostly with women. What links them is their love for the bruised individual soul, and its life of "quiet desperation." It takes courage, in a sophisticated age, to keep faith with this kind of love, and their refusal to compromise has led both Miller and Williams into some embarrassing pseudo-simplicities. Their reward is in characters like Joe Keller of *All My Sons*, Willy Loman of *Death of a Salesman*, John Proctor of *The Crucible*, Blanche DuBois of *A Streetcar Named Desire*, Laura of *The Glass Menagerie*, Kilroy of *Camino Real*, who live together in the great theatrical line of flawed, victimised innocents.

II

Arthur Miller, who was born in Brooklyn in 1915, achieved his first Broadway production at the age of twenty-nine. The play, *The Man Who Had All The Luck,*

had a frame-work which Miller (himself a second son) later elaborated in *All My Sons* and *Death of a Salesman:* the relationship of two sons with their father. The protagonist is David, the elder, an unskilled garage hand in a midwestern town. His brother Amos, forcibly trained by Pat, a jealous and protective father, to become a baseball pitcher, gets nowhere, while the ignored David thrives, financially as well as maritally. His inability to fail makes David neurotic, and to deaden his sense of unworthiness he falls into the habit of ascribing his success to luck. In the final scene he is made to understand that "luck" is merely a word used by men less diligent than himself to explain his triumphs. "You made it all yourself," cries his wife, "It was always you." His hired man, the immigrant Gus, puts the play's case: a man must believe, he says, "that on this earth he is the boss of his life, not the leafs in the teacups, not the stars. In Europe I seen already millions of Davids walking around, millions. They gave up already to know that they are the boss. They gave up to know that they deserve this world." The point of the *drame à thèse* is weakened because the principal characters are too obviously pawns in Miller's hands: what stays in the mind is the craggy candour of the dialogue. Miller, like Williams, is committed to prose drama, in which both men have uncovered riches which make the English "poetic revival" seem hollow, retrogressive and—to use Cyril Connolly's new coinage—præteritist.

Pat, David's father, is guilty only by implication: Joe Keller in *All My Sons*, staged by Elia Kazan in 1947, is a criminal in the legal sense. Shadily, he has been acquitted of manufacturing faulty aircraft parts during the war, and when the play opens his partner is in gaol, taking the rap for him. Of Joe's two sons, one has been killed in action, and the other, Chris, intends to marry his brother's ex-fiancée, the convicted partner's daughter. Chris is a militant idealist, ashamed of having survived the war; material possessions sicken him, unless they have been purely and honourably acquired—"Otherwise what you have is loot, and there's blood on it." Miller concentrates on two shifting relationships: between Chris and his girl, and between Chris and his father. Joe Keller (like Willy Loman) had to compromise in order to live; and Chris (like Biff in the later play) is overwhelmed by the revelation of paternal guilt. How can he marry the daughter of a man who was imprisoned because of his father's perjury? Miller solves this classic impasse with a smart stroke of melodrama: unconvincingly, Keller accepts the burden and shoots himself.

"I'm his father," says Keller at one point, "and he's my son, and if there's something bigger than that I'll put a bullet in my head." This message, more symphonically orchestrated, reappears in Miller's best play, *Death* [14/15] *of a Salesman*, which Kazan directed in 1948. *All Our Fathers*, as Daniel Schneider suggested, would be an appropriate alternative title. Willy Loman and his two sons, the sensualist Happy and the mysteriously retarded Biff, are ruined by their belief in "the wrong dream," the mystique of salesmanship. "What are you building?" says Ben, Willy's millionaire brother, "Lay your hand on it. Where is it?" Unlike most hero-victims, Willy is not cynical about the values which are corrupting him; he is pathetic because, brightly and unquestioningly, he reveres them. As the play begins Biff, the quondam college hero, has returned penniless to his Brooklyn home, where he finds his father going crazy with failure to sell. The ensuing action covers the next twenty-four hours: in a series of beautifully welded interlocking flashbacks, we pursue Willy's thoughts into the past, back to the germinal moment of calamity when he was surprised by Biff in a hotel room with a half-dressed tart. This encounter, with its implied destruction of the father-god, stunted Biff's career and left Willy with a load of remorse redoubled by the fact that he, too, was the unsuccessful one of two brothers. Memory explodes the

cocoon of illusions within which he preserves his self-respect, and (ostensibly for the insurance money) he commits suicide.

The play is Miller's triumph in the plain style; it rings with phrases which have entered into the contemporary subconscious. "He's liked, but he's not—well liked"; "The woods are burning, boys"; Ben's complacent "The jungle is dark but full of diamonds, Willy." More memorably, there is Mrs. Loman's anguished rebuke to her sons for having scorned their father:

"Willy Loman never made a lot of money. His name was never in the papers. He's not the finest character that ever lived. But he's a human being, and a terrible thing is happening to him. So attention must be paid. He's not to be allowed to fall into his grave like a dog. Attention, attention must be finally paid to such a person."

Charley, Willy's neighbour, speaks an epitaph over him which has the same groping, half-articulate power:

"And for a salesman, there is no rock bottom to the life. He don't put a bolt to a nut, he don't tell you the law, or give you medicine . . . Nobody dast blame this man. A salesman is got to dream, boy. It comes with the territory."

There is a fair amount of otiose breast-beating in the script, and Miller's prose sometimes slips into a sentimental rhythm of despair which could be convicted of glibness. But the theatre is an impure craft, and *Death of a Salesman* organises its impurities with an emotional effect unrivalled in post-war drama.

Willy Loman goes to his fate without knowing exactly why it has overtaken him. The heroes of Miller's last two plays are also defeated, but they know what forces have beaten them: the enemy in each case is identified. In 1950 he adapted *An Enemy of the People*, turning it into a racy contemporary pamphlet. His temperament chimed with what he describes as Ibsen's "terrible wrath," and the dilemma of Stockmann, the betrayed crusader, duplicated Miller's own, that of the lifelong democrat who learns, from the example of his own country, that majority rule is not infallible. Stockmann is vanquished by the pusillanimous stupidity of the mob, on which, in the original, he launches a furious attack. Miller softens it in translation, thereby forfeiting the objectivity which allowed even Ibsen's heroes their weaknesses. Anger is a great simplifier, and Miller is an angry writer. *An Enemy of the People* marks his decision to weight the scales in favour of the oppressed minority man.

"Before many can know something, *one* must know it": Stockmann's affirmation steers us towards *The Crucible,* Miller's most recent play, produced in New York last January. The bird's-eye compassion of *Salesman* has now been replaced by a worm's-eye sympathy which extends only to the "right-minded" characters. Though it draws plain contemporary parallels with its subject, the witch-hunt at Salem, it deals with not an overtly political play: it is the refusal of a stubborn intellect to enter into enforced allegiances. "I like not the smell of this 'authority'" says Proctor, the [15/16] hero. In Salem, as in Stockmann's township, nonconformity was allied with sin, an attitude which Miller detests so savagely that the play often resembles the trial scene from *Saint Joan* with the Inquisitor's speech deleted. The inquisitors in *The Crucible* are unmotivated fiends, and the atmosphere in which they flourished is never explored or accounted for.

The action stays close to historical fact. A group of flighty wantons, charged with engaging in mildly orgiastic rites in a wood near Salem, hit on the notion of exculpating themselves by accusing their neighbours of having sent the devil into them. The ringleader, Abigail, swears her sister-conspirators to silence in a speech which exemplifies the gnarled, sinewy, 17th century prose which Miller employs:

"Let either of you breathe a word, or the edge of a word . . . and I will come to you in the black of some terrible night and I will bring a

pointy reckoning that will shudder you. And you know I can do it. I saw Indians smash my dear parents' heads on the pillow next to mine, and I have seen some reddish work done at night, and I can make you wish you had never seen the sun go down!"

The girls' accusations are believed; a tribunal is set up; and the hangings begin. Proctor's wife is arrested, and his attempts to exonerate her lead to his own arrest: in a fine, clinching line he demands: "Is the accuser always holy now?" If he confesses, giving a list of those who infected him with diabolism, he will be freed; if not, he will be executed. At their last meeting his wife tells him how another of the condemned died:

"Great stones they lay upon his chest until he plead aye or nay. They say he give them but two words. 'More weight,' he says. And died."

Head high as the drums roll, Proctor sacrifices himself for his principles, a commonplace "Victorian" martyrdom worthy of a mind much less subtle than Miller's. *The Crucible* is disturbing because it suggests a sensibility blunted by the insistence of an outraged conscience: it has the over-simplifications of poster art.

In *The Devils of Loudun,* a much more searching analysis of witch-hunting, Aldous Huxley mentions the euphoria of the "adrenaline addict," a type to which Miller seems at present to belong. "There are many people," Huxley says, "for whom hate and rage pay a higher dividend of immediate satisfaction than love," this satisfaction being derived from "their psychically stimulated endocrines." Bad temper, which produces cramp in the creative muscles, is an enemy of art; and though *The Crucible* is on the right side morally, socially and politically, it is the artistic equivalent of a closed shop. "For the Poet," said Sidney, "he nothing affirmeth, and therefore never lyeth." *The Crucible,* full of affirmations, is also full of emotional half-truths: which will do for a leader-writer, but not for a playwright of Miller's giant stature.

III

Tennessee Williams' genius has no social commitments, but many æsthetic ones. His faults, like Miller's, are the defects of his virtues. The present cast of Miller's mind traps him in the present, the male preserve wherein history is shaped, and the universal preoccupation is with action and incident; Williams trades in nostalgia and hope, the past and the future, obsessions which we associate most strongly with the great female characters —Marguérite Gautier, Cleopatra, Hedda Gabler, and Tchekov's women, none of whom cares for today half as much as she cares for yesterday or tomorrow. His plays thus have the static quality of dream rather than the dynamic quality of fact: they bring the drama of mood to what may be its final hothouse flowering.

Williams is a Southerner, born forty years ago in Columbus, Mississippi, and his work first reached Broadway when his "memory play," *The Glass Menagerie*, was produced in 1945. It turns a burning-glass on to a storm-proof family unit, insulated against life by its careful preservation of gentility. A stage direction reads:

> The apartment faces an alley, and is entered by a fire-escape, a structure whose name is a touch of accidental poetry, for all of these huge buildings are always burning with the slow and implacable fires of human desperation. [16/17]

Here live Amanda, garrulous and suffocatingly maternal, her cynical son Tom, and her crippled daughter Laura. Retrospectively, Tom tells the story of how he invited a Gentleman Caller to dinner as a possible beau for Laura, and how the Caller, affable though he was, revealed that he was already spoken for. Laura's spinsterhood is confirmed; Amanda's hopes are dashed; but neither of these minor disasters is made to sound mawkish. Williams' wry wit acts as a caustic to the wounds. In Amanda, fussy and conversationally archaic, he shows the perfection of his ear for human speech, and also the extent of his tact: she never becomes a

grotesque. The play is not a major achievement, but its opacity is as precise and marvellous as a spider's web.

You Touched Me!, on which Williams collaborated with Donald Windham, is of interest only because it dealt (like *The Glass Menagerie*) with the impact of reality on illusions, in this case on two isolated, mutually infectious virgins; and because it was adapted from the short story of the same name by D. H. Lawrence, one of Williams' heroes. It was followed in 1947 by *A Streetcar Named Desire*, which was directed by Kazan, who seems to have an instinct for the best of both Miller and Williams. It is perhaps the most misunderstood of his plays: the English and French productions were both so blatantly sensationalised that Williams' underlying lyric fibre passed unnoticed. If Willy Loman is the desperate average man, Blanche DuBois is the desperate exceptional woman. Willy's collapse began when his son walked into a hotel apartment and found him with a whore; Blanche's when she entered "a room that I thought was empty," and found her young husband embracing an older man. In each instance the play builds up to a climax involving guilt and concomitant disgust. Blanche, nervously boastful, lives in the leisured past; her defence against actuality is a sort of aristocratic *Bovarysme*, at which her brutish brother-in-law Stanley repeatedly sneers. Characteristically, Williams keeps his detachment, and does not take sides: he never denies that Stanley's wife, in spite of her sexual enslavement, is happy and well-adjusted, nor does he exaggerate the cruelty with which Stanley reveals to Blanche's new suitor the secrets of her nymphomaniac past. The play's weakness lies in the fact that the leading role lends itself to grandiose overplaying by unintelligent actresses, who forget that when Blanche complains to her sister about Stanley's animalism, she is expressing, however faintly, an ideal:

> "Such things as art—as poetry and music— such kinds of new lights have come into the world since then! . . . That we have to make

grow! And *cling* to, and hold as our flag! In this dark march toward whatever it is we're approaching. . . . *Don't—don't* hang back with the brutes!"

When, finally, she is removed to the mental home, we should feel that a part of civilisation is going with her. Where ancient drama teaches us to reach nobility by contemplation of what is noble, modern American drama conjures us to contemplate what might have been noble, but is now humiliated, ignoble in the sight of all but the compassionate.

In 1948 Williams reworked an earlier play, *Summer and Smoke*. Its heroine, Alma, is Blanche ten years younger: a Southern virgin concealing beneath "literary" affectations a sense of inadequacy in the presence of men. Her next-door neighbour, a notorious rake, tries to seduce her and is boldly repulsed. He shows her an anatomy chart, and explains that the human body is a tree inhabited by three birds, the brain, the belly, and the genitals: where, he asks, is the soul of which she speaks and for which, in Spanish, her name stands? Ironically, he ends up reformed, whereas Alma, her sexual instincts newly awakened, moves to the other extreme: they exchange attitudes, passing almost without contact. *Summer and Smoke*, a needlessly symbolic morality play, is sentimental in that its characters are too slight to sustain the consuming emotions which are bestowed on them.

Nobody could say that *The Rose Tattoo* (1950) did not contain large characters. It is the most thoroughgoing star vehicle of the last ten years, the fullest expression of Williams' romanticism, written for his adored Anna **[17/18]** Magnani, whose shaky acquaintance with English unfortunately prevented her from playing the leading part. Here Williams pleads the cause of sexual love as its own justification. "So successfully," he says in his preface, "have we disguised from ourselves the intensity of our own feelings, the sensibility of our own hearts, that plays in the tragic tradition have begun to seem untrue." At a time when Miller's

plays were growing colder and more intellectualised, Williams' blazed hotter and more sensuous. His heroine is a poor Sicilian immigrant whose husband, a truck-driving smuggler with a fabulous capacity for sexual devotion, has been shot. She learns to her horror that her man has been faithless to her, but the realisation does not prevent her from joyously taking as her new lover a man who physically resembles the dead ideal. The play's complex structure—short scenes linked by evocative snatches of music—is too poetic for its theme, but the virtuosity of the writing, alternately ribald and pathetic, is tremendous. Does it alternate between tragedy and farce? That is because it was meant for a great actress, whose gift it is to switch emotional gear, change from a Siddonsesque pose to a bout of nosepicking without a moment's hesitation. Williams' fault, as in *Streetcar*, was to have overestimated English-speaking actresses. It would take a Magnani to play the scene in which Serafina, the heroine, entertains her new lover, out of whose pocket, as the poetic tension mounts, there falls a neatly packaged contraceptive. Sardou never asked as much of Bernhardt, nor D'Annunzio of Duse.

Kazan renewed his association with Williams in the spring of 1953, when he directed the violently controversial *Camino Real*. This is a phantasmagoria of decadence, as limpidly rebellious to modern civilisation as a Bix Beiderbecke trumpet solo is to a Paul Whiteman orchestration. The published text has a unity never achieved by the acting script. It carries to its conclusion Williams' dictum: "I say that symbols are nothing but the natural speech of drama." In a preface he adds: "I have read the works of 'thinking playwrights,' as distinguished from us who are permitted only to feel. . . ." The result is a tranced play of hypersensitivity, a weird drug-work of wit, terror, and inertia.

It is set in a mythical Central American coastal town. Stage left is the Seven Seas Hotel, where live Byron, Casanova, and Marguérite Gautier, ghosts of the aristocratic way of life; stage right are a pawn-broker's shop, a fortune-teller's tent, and a flophouse, where, among the outcasts, we encounter the Baron de Charlus. On the Camino Real love is forbidden and "hermano" is a dirty word. Upstage is an arch, giving on to a desert, where a hot wind blows and whither no one dares travel. Williams' hero is Kilroy, the new arrival at this fetid microcosm of modern life: the embodiment of youth and enter-prise, he was once a prizefighter but had to abandon his career because: "I've got a heart in my chest as big as the head of a baby." He is elected the town butt, and the police deck him out in a clown's costume, complete with electrically-spark-ing nose. How does this simpleton fit in with the filth of the Camino Real? Williams answers the question in writing which seems too often to have been com-posed in a state of *kief*. He indulges in vague, roseate aphorisms; nor can he re-sist theatrical shortcuts such as a noisy aeroplane crash and *two* chases down the aisles and into the boxes of the theatre, devices which assist the play about as tellingly as a consignment of marijuana would help an anti-narcotics campaign. Yet out of the strident blare of the action, Williams' faith in Kilroy's truth, in a child's mistrust of phoneyness, emerges with overwhelming clarity. For those anarchists who escape he has undisguised sympathy. Byron, for example, says of his later works: "They seem to improve as the wine in the bottle—dwindles. . . . *There is a passion for declivity in this world"*; but when, having roused him-self, he departs into the murderous desert, Williams gives him a splendid epitaph: *"Make voyages!—Attempt them!*—there's nothing else!"

Kilroy, too, attempts the voyage: but only after a serio-comic encounter with a character called the Gypsy, who organ-ises and advertises the local fiesta, at which her daughter, in a loony parody of a fertility ritual, annually **[18/19]** recov-ers her virginity. The Gypsy's garish cyn-icism ("File this crap under crap") struck the New York critics as the most recog-nisable thing in the play, along with Kil-roy's seduction of the Gypsy's daughter, a grossly comic scene in which the two young people repeat to each other eight times the talismanic words: "I am sin-cere." Surviving a brisk attempt to mur-der him, Kilroy journeys through the perilous arch, accompanied by Don Quixote, that other liegeman of the lost cause, who ends the play with a movingly symbolic cry: "The violets in the moun-tains have broken the rocks!"

Many charges can be brought against *Camino Real*. It has too many italics, too many exclamation marks; it depends too much on boozed writing and aureate dic-tion. Its virtue is in its affectionate cham-pioning of the flyblown, inarticulate stra-tum of humanity. Perhaps, when Quixote and Kilroy reach the snowy upper air of the unnamed mountains, they will become subjects for a play by Miller, whose artis-tic life is dedicated, like Shaw's, to a be-lief in progress towards an attainable summit. Williams' aspirations are imagi-native and hence unattainable; and therein lies the difference between them.

Complementary, yet irreconcilable, Miller and Williams have produced the most powerful body of dramatic prose in modern English. They write with equal virtuosity, Williams about the violets, Miller about the rocks. The vegetable re-inforces the mineral; and the animal, a dramatic element feared or ignored in the English theatre, triumphantly reinforces both.

Better than Europe?*

ERIC BENTLEY (1916-   ) has been European correspondent for *Theatre Arts* (1948-1949) and dramatic critic for the *New Republic* (1952-1956). He has held academic appointments at Black Mountain College (1942-1944), the University of Minnesota (1944-1948), and Columbia University (where he has been Brander Matthews Professor of Dramatic Literature since 1953), and has travelled widely in Europe observing and assisting in theatrical productions. His study of modern drama, *The Playwright as Thinker* (1946), his translations of the German playwright Bertold Brecht, and his series of anthologies (*The Modern Theatre*, 1955-1960, and *The Classic Theatre*, 1958-   ) have established his reputation as one of the ablest and most provocative contemporary critics. *In Search of Theater* (1953; reprinted by Vintage Books, Inc. 1955) is an account of the author's reactions to plays seen in theatres throughout Europe and America. The excerpt reprinted here was written in 1949.

News of *Death of a Salesman* reached me in Germany some months ago. Arthur Miller (I was told) had been kept off the boards up to this in the western zones and played only in the Russian zone—as anti-American propaganda. Now he had been greeted in New York as the important American playwright.

Salesman was the first play I went to see on coming ashore. It was an exciting evening. In the auditorium there was an infectious feeling—unusual in American theater—that the occasion was an important one. On the stage was a pretty savage attack upon what in Germany is being held up as an idyllic "American way of life." The New York audience seemed impressed, even if I didn't see "strong men weeping," as I had been told I would.

To my mind, *Salesman* is first and foremost an occasion, a signal event in New York theatrical life. In the second place, it is one man's performance, a rock of a performance, strong enough to hold·up any play. I mean Lee Cobb's rendering—or creation?—of Willy Loman.

If American actors give very poor renditions of Frenchmen and Englishmen, they often give a marvelously nuanced account of their own countrymen, and none more brilliantly—with more body and bounce—than those who worked with Clurman and Odets in the Group Theatre. This theater, it might be said, undertook the study of American life on its lower social levels to see what could be taken over into stage performance. Lee Cobb's work in *Salesman* is presumably the most triumphant application of this [84/85] patient research. He brings to it a knowledge of the salesman's character (as expressed in his limbs, the hunch of his shoulders, vocal intonation, facial expression) which is not provided in the script. Coming to this performance straight from Paris, I was struck with the completeness of its Americanism. What an idiom expresses in language, Lee Cobb can express in stance or movement or vocal color.

I suppose the performance is also a triumph of the Stanislavsky approach to a role. Cobb is deeply sunk in the role

*Eric Bentley, from "Better than Europe?" in *In Search of Theater* (New York: Alfred A. Knopf, Inc., 1953), pp. 84-88.

(though not so deeply that he can't place a witticism in the lap of the audience). Each small movement seems to come welling up from the weary, hurt soul. According to the pattern, Cobb strongly identifies himself with the role; and the audience identifies itself with Cobb. Thus the attempt is made at what Miller himself has called the tragedy of the common man. We all find that we are Willy, and Willy is us; we live and die together; but when Willy falls never to rise again, we go home feeling purged of (or by) pity and terror.

Meanwhile, what has become of the attack on "the American way"? Has it been successfully subsumed under the larger heading "the human way"? This is what Arthur Miller's admirers tell us. Are they right? The impression I had was not of the small purpose being included within the large, but of the two blurring each other. The "tragedy" destroys the social drama; the social drama keeps the "tragedy" from having a fully tragic stature. By this last remark I mean that the theme of this social drama, as of most others, is *the little man as victim.* Such a theme arouses pity, but no terror. Man is here too little and too passive to play the tragic hero.

More important even than this, the tragedy and the social drama actually conflict. The tragic catharsis reconciles us to, or persuades us to disregard, precisely those material conditions which the social drama calls our attention to and protests against. Political antagonists of Miller have suggested that he is a Marxist who, consciously or unconsciously, lacks the courage of his convictions—or is it that "Stalinism" today welcomes a sentimental haze? Certainly, had *Salesman* been written a dozen years earlier, it would have ended with a call to revolt, and would thus have had more coherence than the play Miller has written. Or is Miller a "tragic" artist who, without knowing it, has been confused by Marxism? **[85/86]** There is no need to make of any criticism of the play a special accusation against its author, for its confusions are

those of a whole class, a whole generation.

It is interesting that critics who have never showed any love for poetry praise *Salesman* as a great poetic drama. The poetry they like is bad poetry, the kind that sounds big and sad and soul-searing when heard for the first time and spoken very quickly within a situation that has already generated a good deal of emotion. I think it was Paul Muni who made the classic comment that in *Salesman* you can't tell where the prose leaves off and the poetry begins. You can tell, though, that the prose is often relatively satisfactory and that the poetry is ham. Mere rhetorical phrasing—as witness any of the longer speeches. What is relevant here is that this kind of poetry contributes very liberally to that blurring of outlines which enables Miller to write a social drama and a tragedy at the same time and thus please all.

Absolutely everything in the production contributes too; and thus Elia Kazan and Jo Mielziner please all. The great vice of Miller's style is a false rhetorical mode of speech heard only on Broadway and in political speeches. There is an equivalent of this rhetoric in Kazan's directing and Mielziner's designing and lighting. Things move fast in a Kazan show. So fast you can't see them. If anything is wrong, you don't notice. If a false note is struck, its sound is at once covered by others. One has no time to think. "Drama isn't time to think," the director seems to be saying, "it's action that sweeps you off your feet." The Mielziner staging reinforces the effect. It is above all murky. It reveals—or hints at—a half-world of shadows and missing walls and little spotlights that dimly illuminate the corridors of time. As to this last point, Mielziner is of course staying close to the form of the play Miller gave him, a play in which the chief formal device is the flashback. Now, there is no reason why time in a play shouldn't go backward instead of forward. The thing is that the device of going back has always up to the present been used to create one sort of emotional state: that of nostalgia, mystery, phantasmagoria. (I have in mind examples as different as *Double Indemnity* and *Red Gloves*.) In fact the flashback has become primarily a way of rendering these [86/87] moods, and there is usually something portentous and false about it. We never know where we are. "Light," the designer seems to be saying, "makes of the stage a magic carpet, carrying us wherever we wish." But where *do* we wish? Mielziner helps Miller to be vague.

If it is too much to ask that Miller know which of two feasible plays he wanted to write, one can ask that he clear aside rhetorical and directorial bric-a-brac and look more closely at his people. Has he given us a suitable language for his tarts (in the whoring sequence)? Are the sons of Willy *seen* with the eye or just constructed from the idea that the present generation is "lost"? Is the Alaskan uncle more than a sentimental motif? After all that Mildred Dunnock does for the wife's part, is Willy's marriage *there* for us to inspect and understand down to its depths? It would be unfair to push these questions as far as Willy himself, for he could not be a satisfactory character while the central contradiction of the play stands unresolved. Is his littleness the product of the capitalist system? Or is it Human Nature? What attitude are we to have to it? Pity? Anger? Or just a lovely mishmash?

Arthur Miller seems to be a serious writer. He is therefore, among playwrights, a man in a thousand. He knows what the other playwrights know: how to shape up a story for actors. But he wants to write truly. He knows that there is more drama in the actual facts than in the facts as modified by threadbare rhetoric and directorial legerdemain. If he can in the future act more resolutely on this knowledge, *Salesman* will *not* be the great American drama of the midcentury.

I went back to see *Streetcar Named Desire* this summer out of interest in Uta Hagen's acting. Her performance is good enough to compel a reconsideration of the play—her performance and that of An-

thony Quinn as Stanley Kowalski. Quinn's achievement is negative but substantial: he cuts down the number of laughs that his lines can register in order to be more loyal to the play's meaning. Stanley is brutal, and Marlon Brando was quite wrong for the part. Brando has muscular arms, but his eyes give them the lie. Not discouraged, perhaps, by Kazan, he gave us an Odets character: [87/88] Stanley Kowalski of Brooklyn whose tough talk is but the mask of a suffering sensitive soul.

In the original production a strange, unintelligible young woman from England walks into an American household where the husband (from Brooklyn, as mentioned) seems fated to be her victim. That she has victims we soon feel sure. (Critics have written of Blanche Dubois as a nymphomaniac.) Significant looks are exchanged. When Stanley seizes her and throws her onto the bed she is getting what she asked for.

In the present production an almost Southern American girl suffering from the decaying gentility of her family loses her balance entirely when she finds her boy friend is homosexual, and unintentionally drives him to suicide by a taunting comment. For a time she sleeps with all the boys she can find, losing her job and earning the reputation of a whore. Getting something of a grip on herself, she tries to make a new start. Her old attachment to gentility returns. She acquires a respectable boy friend. But the sister she is staying with has a husband who is a brute. He smokes out Blanche's history, tips off her boy friend, and rapes Blanche into the bargain.

The second story is the one Tennessee Williams wrote. Presumably Kazan must take some of the responsibility for the changes made when the play first went into production. Was he trying to make it more sensational? The early audiences, one recalls, fairly licked their chops over the sexiness of the play. Much that seems meant honestly enough in the script was delivered to the audience, especially by Brando, in that special Broadway intonation which says: "Get this—it's a crack."

Or is Kazan identifying himself with Kowalski, true to his memories of the Group Theatre rather than to his new acquaintance with Williams?[1]

Possibly the ending—Blanche's being led off to an asylum—is more convincing in the earlier version, though it is decidedly stagy in both. Jessica Tandy's Blanche was more or less mad from the start. Uta Hagen's is driven mad by Kowalski (on top of many antecedent causes). But she has been so sane up to this point that one cannot but ask: what is this? Can a sister just send someone to [88/89] an asylum without any medical advice? If so, which of us is safe? And even if Blanche is mad at this moment, will she remain so?[2]

Thus, Miss Tandy's interpretation fits the ending better but Uta Hagen's fits the main body of the play. Williams does not write with complete coherence. As with Blanche, so with Kowalski. On the whole Marlon Brando's performance was just a tour de force: a rather feminine actor overinterpreting a masculine role. Yet when Anthony Quinn portrays Kowalski as an illiterate we are surprised at some of the big words he uses.

But there is a deeper incoherence in *Streetcar,* one that recalls Arthur Miller as well as *Glass Menagerie.* Williams can write very well when he writes realistically, when, for example, he writes dialogue based on observation of character; in fact, all his dramatic talent lies in that direction. But he seems to imagine that his talent is lyrical; read his poems (in *Five Young American Poets 1944*) and you will see that it is not. The love of lyricism seems to affect Williams' work in the same way that vagueness of purpose affects Miller's. The outlines are blurred. So Kazan asks the musicians to play softly behind the scenes, and Mielziner turns the lights out. It takes all the hard, swift prose of Uta Hagen's acting to redeem *Streetcar* from the bad poetry of author, director, and designer.

The critic never knows exactly what the director's part in a production has been. But if some critics may permissibly praise Kazan, others may permissibly express some worries about him. Obviously he is a master of his craft and a great showman. And he adds to the efficiency of the Broadway showman a Group Theatre man's interest in social problems and in American life. I think too he is able (for what this is worth) to speak for the present phase of American history in sharing the confusions of Miller and Williams. Out of these confusions come the positive qualities of Kazan's productions: the nervous tension, the pace, the drive —above all, the chiaroscuro. *Life as phantasmagoria:* this may not be the formula Kazan has consciously adopted, but it is what he shows on the stage.

---

[1] In all fairness, I should admit that when I directed the play myself I could not stop the audience's laughing *with* Kowalski *against* Blanche (1952).

[2] Miss Hagen tells me that her Blanche was not meant to seem mad even at this moment, the point being precisely: which of us is safe? (1952).

"Modernism" in Modern Drama*

JOSEPH WOOD KRUTCH. For biographical information, see "The Tragic Fallacy," by Joseph Wood Krutch, reprinted on page 6.

Neither Miller's *Death of a Salesman* nor Tennessee Williams' *A Streetcar Named Desire* is a cheerful play. Both end with what looks less like a tragic affirmation than like a simple confession of defeat. Neither Willy Loman nor Blanche Dubois is likely to strike the spectator as a very dignified or very noble character, and both are completely [123/124] destroyed—as, say, Hamlet and Othello are not completely destroyed—when the story ends. Loman is a suicide and Blanche is being led away to a madhouse.

Obviously neither Miller nor Williams plainly commits himself as do Maxwell Anderson and O'Neill to either the form or the ethical content of classic tragedy. Moreover, neither exhibits, as plainly as it seems to me O'Neill exhibits, a determination to seek persistently for something in the universe outside man to which he can appeal and "belong." It is possible to interpret *Death of a Salesman* as brutal naturalism and *A Streetcar Named Desire* as a sort of semi-surrealist version of the Strindbergian submission to destructive obsessions.

If such is a proper summation, then Miller and Williams, the two most widely discussed American playwrights of the moment, follow O'Neill and Anderson only as Sean O'Casey followed Synge. They represent, that is to say, the collapse of a reaction and illustrate, as did O'Casey, an irresistible pull in the direction of nihilism and despair.

Perhaps, indeed, that is the proper interpretation to be put upon their work and their current popularity. I am unwilling, however, to leave the subject without suggesting the possibility that there may be something to be said on the other side, and at the risk of being accused of over-interpretation, I should like to say it.

So far as *Death of a Salesman* is concerned, it seems reasonable to suppose that it is intended as something a little more than merely detached "scientific" naturalism. Most spectators, I think, assume that it embodies some "social criticism," and most, I imagine, assume that the social criticism is of a sort by now very traditional. In this view, Willy [124/125] Loman is the victim of an unjust competitive society. He was first corrupted by its false ideals and then exploited by those shrewder and more ruthless than himself. Society made him what he was, and in a better society his fate would have been a happier one. In all this there is, of course, nothing incompatible with what I have been loosely calling "modernism." The doctrine and methods of the naturalists lend themselves very readily to such "social significance."

What makes it impossible to dismiss *Death of a Salesman* as merely left-wing naturalism is the curious fact that Miller himself seems to be some sort of pluralist and that his play could be interpreted, not as a demonstration of the workings of social determinism, but as a study of the effects of moral weakness and irresponsibility. Willy Loman is a victim

*Joseph Wood Krutch, from "Modernism" in Modern Drama (Ithaca, N. Y.: Cornell University Press, 1953), pp. 124-129.

of society, but he is also a victim of himself. He accepted an essentially vulgar and debased as well as a false system of values. He himself says, and the audience seems to be expected to believe him, that he might have led a happy life if he had followed his own bent and become, for example, a carpenter, instead of submitting to the prejudice which makes a salesman more respectable than a man who works with his hands. His tragic guilt—and it is his, not society's—was, in this view, a very old-fashioned one. He was not true to himself. Thus the moral of the play becomes a classical moral and must necessarily presume both the existence of the classical ego and the power to make a choice.

Seen in this light, Miller becomes a moralist, at least in the sense and in much the same fashion that Ibsen was still a moralist. He has found his way back along the road which leads to determinism and the disappearance of the ego at least to the point where the dramatic disciples of Ibsen first [125/126] entered upon it, and *Death of a Salesman* thus becomes a qualified reaffirmation of the individual's privilege of being, within certain limits, what he chooses to be.

The case of Tennessee Williams is different but equally dubious. As I have already suggested, the most obvious interpretations put him plainly among the despairing explorers of pathological states of mind just as the obvious interpretations put Arthur Miller among the sociological naturalists. In all his most striking plays, *The Glass Menagerie, Summer and Smoke,* and *A Streetcar Named Desire,* the chief character is obsessed, and in the last two the obsession takes a sexual form. Madness seems to interest the author more than anything else, and at least in the third and most successful of the plays a quasi-expressionist technique is used for the purpose of persuading the audience to see certain of the events from the standpoint of the heroine's abnormality rather than from its own presumably objective point of view.

In each of the three plays there is another recurrent theme. Each of the heroines numbers among her obsessions the fact that she is or was "a lady." In each the ideal of respectability, the sense that her parents and her remoter ancestors lived in accordance with some code to which she herself would like to be loyal but which no one with whom she comes in contact acknowledges, is so strong as to appear crucial. In *The Glass Menagerie* the mother sees her family disintegrating because it no longer finds her dream of respectability anything but annoying. In both *Summer and Smoke* and *A Streetcar Named Desire* the heroine seems to succumb to crude sexuality because she has so fanatically refused to accept a normal life among people who appear to her as hopelessly unrefined.

Tennessee Williams grew up in the South. Like so many [126/127] other Southern writers, the existence of a decayed aristocracy was one of the inescapable facts of the society with which he was most familiar. That representatives of such a decayed aristocracy should appear in his plays may mean no more than that they were part of his experience. Nevertheless it seems to me obvious that his persistent concern with them does have a greater significance. These helpless survivors from the past, feeble and pathetic clingers to a dead tradition, take on the importance of symbols. They are not accidental facts; they mean something.

Upon the answer to the question "What do they mean? Of what are they symbols?" depends the whole meaning of the plays so far as our own special theme is concerned. Let us consider it in connection with *A Streetcar Named Desire.*

Blanche DuBois, a decayed aristocrat and a fanatical lady, has already lost her position as a schoolteacher because she is also a nymphomaniac. As the curtain rises we see her arriving alone and seeking refuge in the squalid home of her sister Stella, who has married a crude and brutal young man of foreign extraction. This sister has made what the psychologists would call "a satisfactory adjustment." She has rejected and forgotten the traditions of her past. She has accepted the frank squalor of her surroundings and the ignorant brutality of her husband, chiefly because she is reveling delightedly in his abundant and animalistic sexuality. Blanche, the nymphomaniac, is horrified by what some would call her sister's "normality." She makes a feeble and ridiculous attempt to instruct both her sister and the husband in the genteel tradition, and she is violently repelled by their contented animality. But because she can neither lead their life nor the genteel life of which she dreams, her last defenses crumble and she is led away to an asylum, certifiably insane. [127/128]

Everything depends upon, as the phrase goes, which side the author is on. It appears that to many members of the audience this question presents no difficulty. They are, and they assume that the author is, on the the side of the sister. She is "healthy," "adjusted," "normal." She lives in the present; she accepts things as they are; and she will never be confined to a madhouse. Her husband is crude, even somewhat brutal, but he is also virile; he is the natural man and one of literature's many kinsmen of Lady Chatterley's lover. Virility, even orgiastic virility, is the proper answer to decadence. Stella, the representative of a decayed aristocracy, is rejuvenated by a union with a respresentative of "the people."

Even more conspicuously than in the case of Arthur Miller's play, an alternate reading of the situation is possible. In Miller one suspects a sort of pluralism. In Williams the question presents itself instead under the form of an ambiguity.

By this I meant that while one section of the audience takes the side of Stella almost as a matter of course another section understands and shares Blanche's revulsion. Her instincts are right. She is on the side of civilization and refinement. But the age has placed her in a tragic dilemma. She looks about for a tradition according to which she may live and a civilization to which she can be loyal. She finds none. Ours is a society which has lost its shape.

Behind her lies a past which, at least in retrospect, seems to have been civilized. The culture of the Old South is dead, and she has good reason to know that it is. It is, however, the only culture about which she knows anything. The world of Stella and of her husband is a barbarism,—perhaps, as its admirers would say, a vigorous barbarism—but a barbarism nonetheless. Blanche chooses the dead past and be-[128/129]comes the victim of that impossible choice. But she does choose it rather than the "adjustment" of her sister. At least she has not succumbed to barbarism.

As I have said, one's choice of sides will depend largely upon one's attitude toward Stella's "virile" husband. The real question is whether he is villain or hero. If we knew which he is to his creator, we should know whether Williams should be classified among that group of "moderns" who see in a return to the primitive the possible rejuvenation of mankind or whether he belongs rather with traditionalists, such as the esoteric T. S. Eliot on the one hand or the popular Maxwell Anderson on the other, who maintain that from the past itself we shall still have to learn if we are ever to learn at all what civilization means.

I cannot tell you what Williams thinks or says. I can, after due warning, report a very significant thing which he is said to have said. At third hand I have it that when queried in conversation about the meaning of *A Streetcar Named Desire*, or rather about the significance of its chief male character, he replied: "It means that if you do not watch out the apes will take over."

If this report is accurate, and I repeat that I have it only at third hand, the question is answered. Williams, despite all the violence of his plays, despite what sometimes looks very much like nihilism, is really on the side of what modernists would call the Past rather than the Future—which means, of course, on the side of those who believe that the future, if there is to be any civilized future, will be less new than most modern dramatists from Ibsen on have professed to believe.

Tennessee Williams and Arthur Miller*

W. DAVID SIEVERS teaches English at Long Beach State College.

Of all recent dramas, *A Streetcar Named Desire* is the quintes-[**376/377**] sence of Freudian sexual psychology. Anyone familiar with Williams' one-act plays has seen clearly foreshadowed the development of Blanche DuBois of *Streetcar*. *The Lady of Larkspur Lotion* shows what a Blanche might have become if she had not met her nemesis in Stanley Kowalski —a derelict prostitute living on delusions in the French Quarter; a writer across the hall gives what might be the rationale for all the Blanches: "Is she to be blamed because it is necessary for her to compensate for the cruel deficiencies of reality by the exercise of a little—what shall I say? —God-given imagination?" Williams' *Portrait of a Madonna*, is another one-act which shows an old and still virginal version of Mathilda or Blanche manufacturing illusions—fantasies of rape and pregnancy—until she is taken away by the same doctor and nurse who come for Blanche when the *Streetcar* reaches the end of its tragic line.

A Streetcar Named Desire (1947) depicts characters who are volatile, colorful, deeply real for our times. With a mastery no playwright has equalled in this century, Williams arranges in a compelling theatrical pattern the agonized sexual anxiety of a girl caught between *id* and *ego-ideal*. Blanche DuBois arrives at her sister's squalid, dilapidated home in the French Quarter of New Orleans unconsciously playing a role, that of the gracious, refined lady of the old South—the same ego-ideal which Amanda held for herself. It is a sincere role, for it is the only one a sheltered Southern belle was raised to know. Blanche finds her sister, Stella, married to the shirtless Stanley Kowalski, a superbly original character who would have delighted D. H. Lawrence. "Since earliest manhood the center of his life has been pleasure with women, the giving and taking of it, not with weak indulgence, dependently, but with the power and pride of a richly feathered male bird among hens." Stanley immediately finds himself challenged and baffled by Blanche, whose "airs" are a defiance to his manhood and unconsciously dare him to conquer her. Blanche is overcome by his sensuality and almost vomits. She has met her match, and the play becomes an unconscious sexual battle between the two—although the principal battlefield is within Blanche herself.

Her sister, Stella (for Star) is anything but a star. She is a healthy housewife, adjusted to reality, expecting a child, and serenely happy in her physical relationship with Stanley. With unconscious jealousy, Blanche tries to split them apart and convince Stella that Stanley is an ape, "something sub-human, thousands of years old, a stone age cave man." In spite of Stanley's explosive temper, however, their violent quarrels always end in passionate [**377/378**] reconciliation, and for Stella it is the "things that happen between a man and a woman in the dark" that make her life in the slums of New

*W. David Sievers, from "Tennessee Williams and Arthur Miller," in *Freud on Broadway: A History of Psychoanalysis and the American Drama* (New York: Hermitage House, 1955), pp. 376-380, 388, 391-396.

Orleans worthwhile.

It is this relationship that keeps Blanche in sexual anxiety, which she keeps in check with hot baths and shots of whiskey. Her almost hysterical drive is to find protection and security, which in the Southern chivalric code could only come from a gallant gentleman. She believes that she has found such a man in Mitch, a friend of Stanley's. With him Blanche is all coyness and charm, shielding a naked light bulb with a little colored lantern—which Williams makes the symbolic theme of the play: people who cannot face reality try to pretty it up with the colored shades of illusion. Her efforts to play the lady with Mitch irk Stanley until he spills to Stella the scandal which he has been motivated to dig up on "Dame Blanche": she had been a prostitute in Laurel and had been thrown out of the worst hotel in town. Stanley's ironic tale of her nymphomania, complete with soldiers from the nearby army camp and the loss of her position as a schoolteacher for seducing a 17-year-old boy, is told contrapuntally against the giddy singing of Blanche in the hot bath— "It's only a paper moon . . ." In fact, Williams throughout *Streetcar* has orchestrated the sounds of the French Quarter with a superb musical feeling—its sexual throbbing, its sensual "blue piano" playing, the voices of Mexican women, the violent fights of the couple upstairs, and the hallucinatory return of the Varsouvienne music to Blanche as she recalls the tragic story of her love for her husband. Only to Mitch is she able to reveal the details of her marriage to a sweet-faced, poetic boy who turned out to be a homosexual and who shot himself after she had found him with a man. Mitch in turn confides to her of his sick mother, and betrays himself as a boy with an Oedipus complex, wanting to escape his mother yet loyally worshipping her. In their mutual loneliness, Blanche and Mitch embrace passionately, and there is in this scene promise that marriage might be a salvation for them. But the tragedy for Blanche is that she has already whetted the appetite and sadism of Stanley, and now he becomes

her *Ate* who tells Mitch about her past and destroys his illusion of her. Instead Mitch comes, drunk and vindictive, to seduce Blanche. His mother-attachment blocks what might have been a solution for him—Blanche now "isn't clean enough to bring into the house with his mother." He tears the colored lamp shade off to hold the naked bulb up into Blanche's haggard face. Unable to seduce Blanche as he hoped, he leaves and Blanche packs in a state of shock, deluding herself that she is going for a moonlight swim with spectral gentleman callers. When Stella is rushed to the [378/379] hospital in labor, Blanche is left alone in the house with Stanley; if ever there were an *obligatory scene* in the drama, this is it. Although she tries to defend herself with a broken bottle, Stanley quickly disarms her and rapes her, saying, "We've had this date with each other from the beginning."

When Stella comes home from the hospital with her baby, Blanche is again having a hot bath, and has mentally withdrawn from reality. She believes that an old gentleman caller whom she wrote is coming to take her away. Stella and Stanley summon the doctor and nurse from the state mental asylum, although Stella feels guilt over commiting her sister and does not accept Blanche's story of Stan raping her. Though she does Blanche a technical injustice, it cannot alter her psychological destiny. Blanche is too psychotic now to be helped by the Kowalskis, and has transferred all her life-hope from Mitch to the illusionary gentleman caller whom she is sure will phone her. When the doctor arrives, she seems aware at first that he is not the gentleman caller, but when the doctor uses charm and gentleness instead of force, Blanche goes off with him at the end humbly grateful for his solicitous attention.

In *A Streetcar Named Desire*, Williams has depicted profoundly the origins and growth of schizophrenia. He has shown Blanche struggling to master her conflicting drives of sex and *super-ego*, to live up to an inner image of a belle of the old South while living in circumstances in which it is an anachronism. At first she is in rebellion against her own nature but in touch with reality. As the various doors of escape are closed to her and she finds Stanley across her one remaining path, her mind is unable to cope with this impossible conflict. She closes the door to reality and escapes to a psychotic world where gallant gentlemen will give her shelter.

There were some critics who considered Blanche as fit only for a hospital but not the tragic stage. Edward Chodorov, for example, questioned in his letter to the present author whether *Streetcar* met the requirements of tragedy. The director of the Broadway production, Elia Kazan, takes issue with Chodorov's position and in an astute analysis calls the play a poetic tragedy:

We are shown the final dissolution of a person of worth, who once had great potential, and who, even as she goes down, has worth exceeding that of the 'healthy', coarse-grained figures who kill her.

It is not merely an academic issue to test a play such as *Streetcar* by the classic, Aristotelian standards, for with it much of the modern drama may stand or fall. As Kazan points out, Blanche is a character **[379/380]** of some dignity who strives to rise above her circumstances. In the love scene with Mitch she lifts the play to universality, and Williams achieved the tragic irony of Sophocles in the discrepancy between reality and Blanche's distorted impression of it. Aristotelians balk, however, at the fact that Blanche achieves no insight, and to the contrary regresses until her final exit is made with no sublime tragic awareness of the forces that determined her destiny. But there is an escape from the dilemma— modern psychoanalytic psychology suggests a reinterpretation of Aristotle that restores *Streetcar* to the rank of tragic drama and at the same time confirms the universal insight of the observant Stagirite. It is simply that although Blanche closes her mind to any awareness as she

escapes to psychosis, the insight happens *to the audience.* Williams is able to depict with his raw power the growth of psychosis out of simple defense mechanism, to show the conflict in a sensitive spirit between ugly reality and the quest for beauty. Blanche's tragedy is that of the individual unable to integrate the sex drive, to reconcile the physical hunger with tender and spiritual yearnings. Because of her sheltered background she cannot find security by other means than sexual ones. Thus she has as little free will to choose her destiny as had Oedipus. By illuminating Blanche's sickness, by dramatizing the dark unconscious forces with which Blanche grapples and by which she is defeated, the dramatist, like the psychoanalist, makes it possible for others to be purged of guilt and fear, to say "There, but for the grace of whatever mental health I have been able to achieve, go I." To understand and participate in Blanche's fate is to escape it. Williams must be credited with a psychological masterpiece; *Streetcar* is powerful naturalism but also infinitely more —it affords a clear perception into the pressures that degrade, both the social forces which make for an environment of brutality and the individual's unconscious forces which make him a psychic cripple helpless to deal with his environment. Blanche is no less a tragic figure than Antigone or Medea—whether she is literally destroyed or whether it is only her mind seems but a technicality. It is a tragic experience in the theatre to participate in the disintegration of a personality. **[380/388]**

FATHERS AND SONS

Arthur Miller, the author of what many consider to be the most important drama yet written by an American, brings to a climax the psychological drama thus far in the twentieth century. By comparison with Tennessee Williams, Miller is more objective, more socio-political in his orientation, less poetic, better able to depict men than women, and more systematic than intuitive in his play construction. From his plays and the comments on his questionnaire it would seem that Miller, of all American playwrights, comes the closest thus far to illustrating Freud's prediction that ultimately writers will assimilate psychoanalysis ". . . at so deep a level of knowing that they will not be aware that they are employing it: it will have to them the character of self-evidence."

Although it was a Broadway failure, Miller's first play, *The Man Who Had All The Luck* (1944), is interesting for its foreshadowing of his major theme—that of the relationship of fathers and sons. In this connection Miller stated in his reply to the questionnaire on Freudian influence: "Have never identified any ruling idea of mine with Freud, although the struggle of father and sons (which of course antedates Freud) seems to be central to his theories." He did not, however, know which of Freud's theories were most influential on his work, and had never discussed his characters with a psychoanalyst. He said that he had "dipped into a few" books by psychoanalysts "but could never finish one." [388/391]

The father-son relationship is shorn of extraneous plot complications and brought superbly to realization in the Pulitzer-Prize-winning *Death of a Salesman* (1949). No son ever depicted a more epic father with all the characteristically American ambitions and frailties of fatherhood than did Miller with Willy Loman. Where the dramaturgy in *All My Sons* was realistic and retrogressive in Ibsen's tradition, in *Death of a Salesman* it is subjective, free-associational and deeply psychoanalytic. Enriching our theatre with a fresh use of the stream-of-unconscious technique which Miller must have mastered as a radio writer, his characters do not return to the past—rather the repressed past returns subtly to the present, gradually to take possession of the deteriorating mind of Willy. We first see Willy past the age of sixty, coming home exhausted, un-

able to complete his trip, carrying his two huge (and symbolic) salesman's cases which [391/392] weight him down. Willy's car had been going off the road as he day-dreamed "such strange thoughts," brought on by the return of Biff, his thirty-four year old son, who is still a wanderer and failure. Biff had come home the day before and the old hostility between father and son had flared immediately. Willy is volatile, impulsive, emotionally trigger-sensitive, and ambivalent toward Biff. He calls him a lazy bum one minute and "he's not lazy" the next. Willy is a quixotic dreamer, wanting greatness for his sons, Happy and Biff. Willy's tragedy is that his dreams for Biff are totally out of touch with the reality of Biff's deeply rooted feeling of inferiority. Happy, the younger son, suffers none of Biff's insecurity and is nearer to following in his father's footsteps, working in a store, keeping a car, an apartment and women who are like bowling—"I just keep knockin' them over and it doesn't mean anything." Both boys wish they could find a nice girl like Mom and get married, but neither makes any effort in that direction.

More and more, the past returns to Willy, his old red Chevy of 1928, his memory of the open horizon before apartment buildings hemmed in their home. As his hallucinatory free associations are visualized, the realistic lighting fades, a projected pattern of remembered sunlight through the leaves surrounds his skeletonized Brooklyn home, and flute music is heard (we learn later Willy's father was an itinerant maker of flutes). Willy's first regression is to Biff's young manhood when he simonized the car and was captain of the high school football team, for whom the cheering section goes wild yelling "Loman." Willy even found excuses for Biff's petty thievery in his headlong wish-fulfillment for him to be great.

Bernard, the son of his old friend, Charley, next door, would help Biff study, but Willy's ambitions for Biff do not run in that direction. Willy's motto is, "Be liked and you will never want." Willy's ideal is a salesman who at eighty-four could pick up a phone and make a living getting orders. He visualizes himself as a likeable, witty, high-powered huckster, a go-getter, a "man-with-contacts." But to his wife, Linda, he confesses that selling isn't as easy as he tells the boys, that it actually comes hard to him and that he has a perpetual fear—almost paranoid—that people are laughing at him. Even as he tells Linda how much he loves her, he remembers a woman in Boston who came up to his hotel room and brought him a brief respite from the pressures of mortgage, insurance and refrigerator payments, the life of bills which he shared with his wife. As Willy tries to concentrate on a card game with Charley, he is haunted by the memory of Ben, Willy's older brother, who had just died and **[392/393]** who symbolizes for Willy all the material success he never achieved. Willy barely remembers his father, "just Mamma's lap and a man with a big beard." So Ben has become a father-image to Willy, and has given Willy the same feelings of unsureness and inferiority that he has given Biff. Ben has made his fortune in Africa and Alaska, and perpetually chants the leitmotif,

"William, when I walked into the jungle I was seventeen. When I walked out I was twenty-one. And by God, I was rich!"

While Willy is engrossed in his inner world, the boys and the mother are shocked at his mental deterioration; but Linda loyally insists that the boys respect him. She gives the play its universal social pertinence when she cries out:

But he's a human being, and a terrible thing is happening to him. So attention must be paid. He's not to be allowed to fall into his grave like an old dog. Attention, attention must be finally paid to such a person.

Realizing that his father is suicidal and has been hiding a section of rubber hose near the gas pipes, Biff agrees to stay home and try to live up to Willy's expectations. He renews a contact with a former employer who might help him (even though he had once stolen some basketballs from his store).

The next day Biff goes to see the man, hoping for a big loan which would enable him to go in business with Happy. Meanwhile Willy is in high spirits—the house will be paid for in one more installment—and he goes to his boss, the son of the man who employed Willy for many years, to ask for a transfer to a job that won't require travelling. The young boss, depicted not as a villain but merely as disinterested in Willy and preoccupied with a wire recorder of his child's voice, not only does not transfer Willy but fires him altogether. Willy cries out to Ben in his daze—"How did you do it? What's the answer?" Still seeking an answer and a meaning for his misdirected life, Willy goes to Bernard, now a successful attorney, and learns a crucial fact: it was after Biff came to see Willy in Boston that his attitude changed, he gave up high school and entered on his path of failure. "What happened in Boston, Willy?" Bernard asks, "that made Biff lose his ambition?"

After the big interview, Biff and Happy plan to meet Willy and treat him to a meal. But Biff had been curtly brushed off by the employer and had compulsively stolen a fountain pen off his desk. Willy joins them and they order drinks, a magnificently ironic feast of the failures. With a trumpet note jarring Willy, he hardly hears Biff tell of stealing the fountain pen; he staggers to the washroom in **[393/394]** panic, reliving the moment in Boston when Biff, coming up to get Dad to "fix" his flunk in math, surprised Willy with the other woman in the hotel room, and suffered a traumatic, dizzy loss of illusion about his father. Shocked to learn his father is a sexual human and not a God, Biff's Oedipal disillusion centers around Willy's giving the woman stockings he should have given Linda. Willy is left yelling to Biff on the floor of the washroom as the boys desert him for two wenches they have picked up.

As Willy clarifies in his mind what he must do, he feels a need to leave his seed behind him in a worthier form than his sons, and is found out in the dark, planting in the garden. Even contemplating his own funeral his ideas are grandiose—buyers from all over New England will come and Biff will see how well liked his father was. Biff comes to say goodbye to Willy, planning to go away for good, convinced that he is doomed to failure. Willy still has a paranoiac conviction that Biff is doing this merely to spite Willy, and refuses to shake his hand. But now Biff has come to an awareness of himself, to insight into the forces that made him what he is. "We never told the truth for ten minutes in this house!" he realizes. He is able to confess that he has been in jail, a compulsive kleptomaniac who stole his way out of every job, unable to endure not being a big shot. The father and son are at each other's throat viciously, and then Biff sobs in Willy's arms. Willy is elated that Biff loves him and cries out to his imaginary Ben, "Oh, if I could kiss him, Ben!" Willy imagines how great Biff will be with the $20,000 he can leave him from his insurance policy, and staggers out to be run over and killed by an auto.

His funeral is a quiet little postscript, to which no buyers swarm, merely his sons, his wife, and old Charley, who knows the meaning of Willy's tragedy: "He had the wrong dreams. All, all, wrong . . . He never knew who he was."

Dr. Daniel Schneider, author of *The Psychoanalyst and the Artist,* has written a provocative psychonalytic interpretation of *Death of a Salesman.* Paying eloquent tribute to the deep level of insight into unconscious forces which this play, like *Hamlet,* achieves, Schneider points out that the full power of Miller's work can only be assessed by noting what the play would be if the hallucinations were deleted. Without them the play is a routine bourgeois "death of a Babbitt." But with the "inner logic of his erupting volcanic unconscious," the play becomes a lucid experience. "It is visualized psychoanalytic interpretation woven into reality."

Schneider points out the symbolic nature of the three men's meeting in the restaurant—the eons-old Freudian totem-feast in [394/395] which the sons make peace with their father over sexual rivalry. When the results don't turn out as Willy hoped, however, and he learns that Biff has stolen the employer's fountain pen (a psychoanalytic symbol for castration, as were the stolen basketballs), Willy is forced to rush into the washroom in a castration-panic. Willy is deserted in favor of the "babes" and is left babbling impotently at the sexual, competitive assertion of his sons. Willy, himself a younger son and "low-man on a totem-pole," has a deep, guilty hatred for Ben who made the grade; he could have gone to Alaska under Ben's patronage, but he had to stay and out-do Ben. He is finally overwhelmed with his own guilt, although he cannot admit even to himself that he destroyed Biff by disillusioning him in Boston. Schneider concludes that, "It is one of the most concentrated expressions of aggression and pity ever to be put on the stage. If Arthur Miller's *All My Sons* was aptly named, then this work is All Our Fathers."

In the questionnaire to Miller, he was asked if he agreed with Dr. Schneider's Freudian interpretation of the play. His comment was:

He made several extremely fascinating observations; I cannot vouch for some of the interpretations; some of them are anthropological—(the "Totemic" idea). Impossible to "agree" or "disagree," because I do not know my sub-conscious well enough.

Miller reflected throughout his questionnaire a great respect for Freud's ideas and a humility toward the unconscious sources of his own creative power. When asked if he had ever sought for techniques to dramatize for the audience the workings of the unconscious (an academic question to the author of *Death of a Salesman*) he replied, "Always. The externalization of conscious but repressed, and unconscious thoughts and motives is the basic problem of dramatic structure."

To the question of which play most reflected Freudian psychology, Miller replied, "*Salesman,* I suppose. But again, for good or ill, am not conscious of using Freudian ideas, but am told that is what I do!" His general comment on the value of Freudian attitudes for the playwright is succinctly expressed:

Whatever I have received from Freud has come "through the air." It is part of me; I could not therefore evaluate it separately. All I can say is that analysts and analyzed people find corroboration in my plays from time to time and so I assume I have been "influenced." If so, it is a good influence. **[395/396]** I know enough to say, however, that the schematic use of Freud in art is disastrous. The problem of art is not to dramatize Freud, to 'prove' him, but rather to go beyond and discover the total truth of the making of man—the interaction of his inherited nature with the Society in which he must struggle to mature—and to so symbolize the disparate as to create 'beauty,' which is the ultimate organization of reality.

Death of a Salesman may prove to be the finest American tragedy thus far in the twentieth century. Certainly it is the one which best succeeds in compressing deeply understood psychological relationships into a form that is vibrantly alive in the theatre. Its success must indicate that there are enough Willy Lomans and sons among our playgoers to give universality to the subject. Its blinding flashes of insight into modern American standards make it the most overwhelming playgoing experience of our times. Gass-

ner has called it "one of the triumphs of the mundane American stage," although he interprets it as *drame bourgeois* rather than genuine high tragedy. True, there is no *anagnorosis,* no recognition by the tragic hero of the reason for his downfall. Willy goes to his death sure that his way of raising Biff was right and that Biff would be great. But the *anagnorosis* is there, and is given instead to Biff, who is purged of his father-hostility when he comes to see his father for what he is. Naively bungling through the parent-child relationship, Willy never knew where Biff got his inferiority feelings—nor where he got his own. But he dedicated himself to a high ideal, that of raising his sons well, and his ambitions are those of every man for his children. The final dignity is given to Willy by his wife, by the majesty with which she endows him. Coupled with Miller's profound understanding of the emotions of sons and fathers is a sure social point of view which sees the falsity of the "hail-fellow-well-met," "don't get caught at it" standards which the Willy Lomans hold up for themselves and their children. Finding oneself for Miller implies both psychological insight and social integration. The glib, false-front salesman, " . . . way out there in the blue, riding on a smile and a shoeshine," cannot help but be a tragic figure when viewed through the eyes of all his sons.

Suggested Topics for Controlled Research

The material reprinted in this volume has been selected to provide training for the student in the use of secondary source material as an aid to the fuller understanding of dramatic literature and in the correct presentation of his research. The plays themselves are, of course, the primary sources; and it cannot be urged too strongly that familiarity with the texts of the plays is a prerequisite to any use of the book. Some of the suggestions are for long research papers, others for more limited work; but their main purpose is to indicate the scope of the critical problems that can be investigated and documented from the materials contained in this anthology.

General Scope of the Suggested Topics

Perhaps the most difficult task for you as a student-critic is to learn how to use secondary sources judiciously: to regard critical essays not as definitive and authoritative statements to be accepted without question, but as attempts like your own, though probably better informed, to elicit the meaning from a work of literature and perhaps to evaluate it in comparison with other works. You soon discover that not all readers find the same things in a play or poem or react to it in the same way; that besides this, all art involves communication between artist and audience and, therefore, that there is often a disparity between what the author hoped to communicate, his *conception* of the work, and what he has achieved in the *execution;* and that not always is there complete harmony between the form of the work and its content. Discussion of these matters forms a large part of the province of criticism. Five main topics for research arise from these general observations: conception and execution; the plays as tragedies; evaluation of the criticism; the plays on stage; and evaluative comparison of the plays.

1. The conception and execution of *Death of a Salesman* and *A Streetcar Named Desire.*

(a) *Death of a Salesman.*

ARTHUR MILLER is an unusually frank author, given to explaining in print what his dramatic aims are and what he has tried to express in individual plays. It is tempting for you to accept the unity of conception and execution in this case, but it is excellent training in critical perception, as well as in the proper use of secondary sources, to assess the extent to which you—and the critics and reviewers represented here—believe that he has achieved or fallen short of his stated aims. This research topic is best approached by a series of questions.

What are the major points that Miller makes about tragedy and "social drama" in general, and *Death of a Salesman* in particular? How far do his statements about his plays accord with what he seems to you, and to the critics, to have achieved? What measure of agreement is there among the critics about his achievements and his faults? In the symposium on *Death of a Salesman,* Miller makes direct statements about his play and answers questions put to him. Does there seem to be any divergence of view between (a) Miller and his interviewers and

(b) the members of the panel themselves, on this subject of the unity of conception and execution? *Death of a Salesman* has been conceived by Miller as both tragedy and social drama, as can be seen from his two essays, "Tragedy and the Common Man" and "On Social Plays." John Gassner points out, in "Tragic Perspectives," that these two dramatic forms have often been considered incompatible. In disagreeing, he suggests certain conditions that must be met by the playwright if this objection is to be overcome. What are these conditions? Do you consider that Miller has anticipated the objections in his two essays? Does your reading of the play convince you that Miller has met Gassner's conditions? Have other critics and reviewers raised these points, explicitly or implicitly? Do their opinions support yours?

(b) *A Streetcar Named Desire.*

TENNESSEE WILLIAMS makes no direct comment, in his essay "The Timeless World of a Play," about what he wanted to achieve in *A Streetcar Named Desire*. But he does discuss the ideal effect of a play, the creation of a world which exists outside time, in which "events are made to remain *events*, rather than being reduced . . . to mere *occurrences*." What does he mean by this? How does he relate this idea to the effect which, he believes, a tragedy must produce on its audience? Has he, in *A Streetcar Named Desire*, satisfied his own theoretical requirements? Do the reviewers and critics seem to be in agreement that Williams has created this "timeless world" in his play? You will probably not find any *direct* discussion of this point; your task, therefore, will be to discover whether or not they treat the incidents of the plot and the actions of the characters as "mere *occurrences*" or as significant *"events."* You will have to be guided here partly by the tone of the critic; if he regards the play as just another Broadway success he is hardly likely to see very much in it as worthy of the term "event," in Williams' sense of the word.

2. *Death of a Salesman* and *A Streetcar Named Desire* as tragedies.

Perhaps the most interesting project involves research into the question of whether or not these two plays, or either of them, can legitimately be called "tragedies." They are both loosely termed "tragedies," but some critics have strong reservations about this. Your research work in this area will divide into three separate investigations (each of which could, if a shorter paper were required, be undertaken as a self-contained project) .

(a) What is a tragedy?

You will have to decide for yourself what a tragedy is, taking into account first of all the material in Part One of this book. A number of crucial issues raised by these writers will have to be given consideration. For example, should we be bound by the so-called "rules" of tragedy set down by Aristotle in his *Poetics*? Should we try to interpret Aristotle's comments in the light of modern experience or should we reject them, wholly or partially, in favor of a new theory of tragedy? Should we, indeed, have any preconceived theory of tragedy at all; would it not be better to rely on the impact which any given play has on us for our decision on whether or not it ought to be called a tragedy? These questions are, of course, also asked by many of the reviewers and critics represented in Part Three.

(b) Can tragedies be written today?

A more complex problem, to which you might give some thought, is that discussed at length by Joseph Wood Krutch in "The Tragic Fallacy": Are our attempts to write tragedies today, or to appreciate fully those written in the past, doomed to failure because of the temper of modern society and the modern mind? What are the major reasons for this as given by Krutch? What answers are suggested by other writers represented in this book? Do the dramatists themselves seem to be aware of this problem? Is the problem a general one, or are there characteristics of American civilization that make it more acute here? The article by Orrin E. Klapp is especially relevant to this topic.

(c) Are these plays tragedies?

This topic can be discussed either as the second stage of a long research paper dealing with the two plays (or either of them) in the larger context of tragedy or as a separate, shorter paper. In either case, your procedure will be to make a survey of the views held by the critics and reviewers on the appropriateness of the term "tragedy" as a generic classification of *Death of a Salesman* and *A Streetcar Named Desire*. Which of the critics accept the plays as tragedies without reservations? Which of them have reservations? Are these reservations concerned with the conception of the works or with their execution; that is, do the critics think the plays are based on a faulty notion of what tragedy is or what kind of person the tragic hero ought to be, or do they consider that the dramatists have failed technically, in characterization or language, for instance? What reservations are held in common by several critics? Is there any difference of opinion in this matter between reviewers and academic critics? Do the comments made soon after the first presentation of the plays differ from those made at a later date?

Several more limited topics, involving a comparison of critical pronouncements, can also be suggested in this area. For instance, how does Miller's idea of tragedy differ from Williams'? How successful are Willy Loman and Blanche DuBois as tragic figures? To what extent is the background of the two plays (broadly speaking, the Southern and the Eastern settings) important in connection with the tragic theme of each play? Do the dramatists extend their tragic vision to mankind as a whole, or have they written specifically American tragedies? What similarities and differences are there, in tragic form and theme, between these plays and others by the same author?

3. An evaluation of the criticism of *Death of a Salesman* and *A Streetcar Named Desire*.

As you read this book you will undoubtedly learn a great deal about the plays being criticized; but you will also find that the evaluation of the criticism itself, something which you probably do almost instinctively as you read several analyses of the same play, is an instructive topic for research, requiring great discrimination. Some critics will seem more convincing than others, and more reliable as secondary sources of evidence about the plays. A good starting point is the classification of the reviews and criticism according to the bias exhibited by the writer. "Bias," incidentally, is not synonymous with "prejudice"; it may refer simply to a deliberate limitation by the critic of the scope of his discussion. For instance, W. D. Sievers is primarily interested in investigating the influence of Freudian psychology on the American drama. Does this affect his assessment of the plays as works of art, particularly as tragedies? What bias is exhibited by Desmond Reid or Harry Taylor? In pursuing this topic you should take note of any special interests (for example, political or religious affiliation) of the publication in which the writing in question first appeared. But don't jump to conclusions: this may not be relevant.

4. Death of a Salesman and A Streetcar Named Desire on stage.

Ideally, you should not merely read a play but also see it performed in the theatre. The next best thing is to read the play imaginatively and to take note of what the reviewers say about the sets, the acting, the costumes, and the direction. One research project, then, might be the reconstruction of an actual performance and the evaluation of the play in *theatrical* rather than literary terms. What did the sets look like? How well did they function in helping to convey the atmosphere and theme of the play? What was the quality of the acting? How appropriately was the play cast? Did the actors' interpretation of their parts correspond with what the reviewers and critics thought the interpretation should be? Is there any evidence that particular performances by actors, or skillful direction, rather than inherent dramatic qualities, were responsible for the success of the plays? How important was the director in the production? Since both of these plays, in their original productions, were directed by Elia Kazan, this question should stimulate some careful study of the extent to which a director can become a creative artist in his own right, perhaps even superimposing his interpretation of the meaning of the play on the author's. What are the opinions of the reviewers and critics on this point?

A more limited subject for research in this area is the extent to which these two plays rely on theatrical "tricks" (for example, lighting and contrived climaxes) for their effect. Does the "theatricality" that some critics comment on detract from the claims made for these plays as serious drama? Are they entirely free from the "cheapness" and "sensationalism," or the compromises with artistic honesty, that are often associated, in the minds of serious critics, with Broadway successes?

5. An evaluative comparison of Death of a Salesman and A Streetcar Named Desire.

This topic involves a direct comparison between the two works in an attempt to arrive at a conclusion about which is the better play. You might note that since this is largely a subjective matter the evidence you select for presentation, and the way in which you present it, will be more important than the actual conclusion you reach. An obvious beginning could be made here with those essays in which both plays are discussed or with the reviewers (for example, George Jean Nathan) who have reported at different times on both plays. In making this comparison you should be very careful how you use the available evidence; avoid errors of logic. For example, the statement that *Death of a Salesman* is a more correct or more traditionally conceived tragedy than *A Streetcar Named Desire* does not necessarily imply that it is a better play or even a better tragedy. This kind of precision in the use of evidence should, of course, be the rule in any of the research papers that you write.

Suggested Sources for Library Research

The material reprinted in this anthology is a representative selection from what is available for research in the topics suggested and in other topics of your own choosing. Should you become interested in pursuing a topic in greater depth there. are many more sources to be found in your library. They can be conveniently grouped as follows:

1. Reviews and critical articles

To read the reviews of opening night performances you do not need to consult each newspaper separately if your library subscribes to the weekly *New York Theatre Critics' Reviews,* which reprints the reviews appearing in *The New York Times, New York Journal-American, New York Daily News, New York Post, New York Mirror, New York World-Telegram and the Sun,* and *New York Herald Tribune.* The leading magazines, such as *Time, Newsweek,* and *The New Yorker,* also review the more important openings. To locate these reviews, as well as background articles on the plays and their authors, consult the *Reader's Guide to Periodical Literature.* Both plays discussed in this anthology were published soon after their first production, and these published versions were also reviewed in newspapers and magazines. Bibliographical references, and brief summaries of these reviews, can be found in the *Book Review Digest.*

Details of critical articles appear in a number of sources. The *Reader's Guide to Periodical Literature* will also be helpful here, but the most complete listing, since it covers comparatively obscure learned journals as well as the most obvious sources, is the annual bibliography published in the April or May issue of *PMLA* (Publications of the Modern Language Association of America). This in-

cludes both foreign and American critical books and articles. Two other useful aids are the *Annual Bibliography of English Language and Literature,* issued by the Modern Humanities Research Association, and *The Year's Work in English Studies.* Since January, 1958, *Abstracts of English Studies,* appearing monthly, has summarized critical articles from leading American, and some European, periodicals in literature, including drama. The editors of drama anthologies usually write brief biographical and critical introductions to the plays they reprint; for details of these anthologies see the list of "Available Texts" in this volume.

If your research topic concerns Tennessee Williams, you will be saved a great deal of trouble. The periodical *Modern Drama* published a selected bibliography of material by and about Williams (Nadine Dony, "Tennessee Williams: A Selected Bibliography," *Modern Drama,* I [December, 1958], 181-191) and a supplement to this (Charles A. Carpenter, Jr. and Elizabeth Cook, "Addenda to 'Tennessee Williams: A Selected Bibliography'," *Modern Drama,* II [December, 1959], 220-223) that contain references to all the most important writing on Williams and his plays. Unfortunately, no such bibliography exists to date for Miller.

2. Biographical information about the playwrights and critics

Both Williams and Miller are to a significant extent subjective writers whose own lives and experiences have afforded material for their plays (though this material has, of course, been reshaped in the artistic processes). You may find it interesting, then, and relevant to critical discussion, to supplement the biographical information presented in critical articles with the more complete data available in purely biographical writing. You may also wish to know more about the critics and reviewers, so that you are in a better position to judge their qualifications and possible biases.

A useful reference work here is the *Biography Index,* which is a cumulative index to biographical material in books and magazines from January, 1946 to date. *Current Biography,* published monthly and cumulated annually, prints brief articles on prominent people. Williams and Miller are included in the *First Supplement* to *Twentieth Century Authors;* information in this publication is provided mainly by the authors themselves. *Who's Who in America* gives dates and facts about the lives of eminent living Americans; *Who's Who* performs the same function for British notabilities. You should also consult *Who's Who in the Theatre,* though this is not brought up to date so frequently as the latter works.

The annual *New York Times Index* will furnish references to articles and news items published in the *Times;* consult this under the index heading "Theatre."

3. Theories of tragedy

The material in Part One of this anthology, on the problems of modern tragedy, is necessarily limited. If you select a research topic involving a discussion of theories of tragedy you may wish to read more widely on this subject. A useful book to begin with is Allardyce Nicoll's *The Theory of Drama* (1931). More advanced studies are Herbert J. Muller's *The Spirit of Tragedy* (1956), T. R. Henn's *The Harvest of Tragedy* (1956), William G. McCollum's *Tragedy* (1957), and Richard Benson Sewall's *The Vision of Tragedy* (1959). Most studies of tragedy contain discussion of Aristotle's *Poetics,* so you should read this carefully. A valuable anthology of dramatic criticism, including theories of tragedy from Aristotle to the present century, is Barrett H. Clark's *Eu-*

ropean Theories of the Drama (rev. ed., 1947). *Types of Domestic Tragedy,* ed. Robert Metcalf Smith (1928), is an anthology of plays that you might consult if you are interested in theatrical precedents for Arthur Miller's tragedy of the "common man." This list is inevitably far from complete; you should pay attention to the bibliographies or footnotes in the books mentioned for further studies.

4. Historical Background

You will find that you understand the plays better if you consider them not only as isolated works but also against the background of the history of modern drama. Such terms as "realism," "naturalism," and "expressionism," employed in some of the criticism reprinted here, will have more meaning for you if you can relate them to certain movements in the history of the European and American theatre. There are several standard works that will serve as introductions to this subject. Perhaps the best is John Gassner's *Masters of the Drama* (rev. ed., 1954); the same author's *The Theatre in Our Times* is a less basic book, but it contains provocative chapters on Miller and Williams. *A History of Modern Drama* (1947), by Barrett H. Clark and George Freedley, is a more pedestrian work, though an excellent primer. Two books by Joseph Wood Krutch, *"Modernism" in Modern Drama* (1953), and *The American Drama Since 1918* (rev. ed., 1957), are excellent studies. Alan S. Downer's *Fifty Years of American Drama, 1900-1950* (1951) is one of the best short surveys of the American stage. Finally, for the more advanced student, Eric Bentley's *The Playwright as Thinker* (1946) is a stimulating study of the major and the minor movements in modern drama. Although it was written before Miller and Williams had come to artistic maturity, Bentley's book has some highly interesting speculative comments on the future of the theatre in our time.

The texts of the plays are available in several editions, as follows:

1. First Editions.

Miller, Arthur, *Death of a Salesman*. New York: Viking Press, Inc., 1949.
Williams, Tennessee, *A Streetcar Named Desire*. New York: New Directions, 1947.

2. Inexpensive Paperbound Reprints.

Miller, Arthur, *Death of a Salesman*. New York: Compass Books, No. C32, 1958.
Williams, Tennessee, *A Streetcar Named Desire*. New York: New American Library, No. D1529, 1951.

3. Drama Anthologies containing both plays.

New Voices in the American Theatre. The Modern Library. New York: Random House, 1955.
Tucker, Marion S. and Downer, Alan S., eds. *Twenty-five Modern Plays*, 3rd. ed.. New York: Harper and Bros., 1953.

4. Drama Anthologies containing Death of a Salesman.

A *Paperbound*

Four Modern Plays. New York: Rinehart and Company, Inc., 1958.
Steinberg, M. W., ed. *Aspects of Modern Drama*. New York: Henry Holt and Co., Inc., 1960.
Watson, E. B. and Pressey, Benfield, eds. *Contemporary Drama: 11 Plays*. New York: Charles Scribner's Sons, 1956.

B *Hardbound*

Bentley, Eric, ed. *The Play*. Englewood Cliffs, N. J.: Prentice-Hall, Inc., 1951.
Bierman, Judah, Hart, James and Johnson, Stanley, eds. *The Dramatic Experience*. Englewood Cliffs, N. J.: Prentice-Hall, Inc., 1951.
Gassner, John, *A Treasury of the Theatre: Ibsen to Ionesco*. New York: Simon and Schuster, Inc., 1960.

5. Literature Anthologies containing Death of a Salesman.

Brown, Leonard and Perrin, Porter G., eds. *A Quarto of Modern Literature*. New York: Charles Scribner's Sons, 1957.
Steinmann, Martin, Jr. and Willen, Gerald, eds. *Literature for Writing*. San Francisco: Wadsworth Publishing Co., 1961.